Natural Gas Vehicles
System Integration and Service

Online Services

Delmar Online
To access a wide variety of Delmar products and services on the World Wide Web,
point your browser to:
>**http://www.delmar.com/delmar.html**
>or email: info@delmar.com

thomson.com
To access International Thomson Publishing's
home site for information on more than 34 publishers
and 20,000 products, point your browser to:
>**http://www.thomson.com**
>or email: findit@kiosk.thomson.com

A service of **I⊤P**®

Lethbridge Community College Library

Natural Gas Vehicles
System Integration and Service

National Alternative Fuels Training Program

West Virginia University

Delmar Publishers

an International Thomson Publishing company

Albany • Bonn • Boston • Cincinnati • Detroit • London • Madrid
Melbourne • Mexico City • New York • Pacific Grove • Paris • San Francisco
Singapore • Tokyo • Toronto • Washington

NOTICE TO THE READER

Publisher does not warrant or guarantee any of the products described herein or perform any independent analysis in connection with any of the product information contained herein. Publisher does not assume, and expressly disclaims, any obligation to obtain and include information other than that provided to it by the manufacturer.

The reader is expressly warned to consider and adopt all safety precautions that might be indicated by the activities described herein and to avoid all potential hazards. By following the instructions contained herein, the reader willingly assumes all risks in connection with such instructions.

The publisher makes no representations or warranties of any kind, including but not limited to, the warranties of fitness for particular purpose or merchantability, nor are any such representations implied with respect to the material set forth herein, and the publisher takes no responsibility with respect to such material. The publisher shall not be liable for any special, consequential, or exemplary damages resulting, in whole or in part, from the readers' use of, or reliance upon, this material.

Delmar Staff:
Publisher: Robert D. Lynch
Acquisitions Editor: Vernon Anthony
Editor: Jack Erjavec
Production Manager: Dianne Jensis
Publishing Coordinator: Betsy Hough
Marketing Manager: Nicole Benson

Copyright © 1997
By Delmar Publishers
a division of International Thomson Publishing Company

The ITP logo is a trademark under license.

Printed in the United States of America

For more information, contact:

Delmar Publishers
3 Columbia Circle, Box 15015
Albany, New York 12212-5015

International Thomson Publishing Europe
Berkshire House 168-173
High Holborn
London, WC1V 7AA
England

Thomas Nelson Australia
102 Dodds Street
South Melbourne, 3205
Victoria, Australia

Nelson Canada
1120 Birchmount Road
Scarborough, Ontario
Canada M1K 5G4

International Thomson Editors
Campos Eliseos 385, Piso 7
Col Polanco
11560 Mexico D F Mexico

International Thompson Publishing GmbH
Königswinterer Strasse 418
53227 Bonn
Germany

International Thomson Publishing Asia
221 Henderson Road
#05 - 10 Henderson Building
Singapore 0315

International Thomson Publishing Japan
Hirakawacho Kyowa Building, 3F
2-2-1 Hirakawacho
Chiyoda-ku, Tokyo 102
Japan

All rights reserved. No part of this work covered by copyright may be reproduced or used in any form or by any means—graphic, electronic, or mechanical, including photocopying, recording, taping or information storage and retrieval systems—without the written permission of the publisher.

1 2 3 4 5 6 7 8 9 10 XXX 01 00 99 98 97

Library of Congress Cataloging-in-Publication Data

Natural gas vehicles: system integration and service / by National Alternative Fuels Training Program at West Virginia University
    p.   cm.
Includes index.
ISBN 0-8273-7901-3
1. Natural gas vehicles. I. National Alternative Fuels Training Program at West Virginia University.
TL228.N38   1996
629.22'043—dc21

96-37453
CIP

Contents

CHAPTER 4 - SYSTEM SPECIFIC ELECTRONICS

CHAPTER 5 - EMISSIONS

CHAPTER 6 - NGV OPERATION AND FUELING STATIONS

CHAPTER 7 - DIAGNOSTIC METHODS AND TROUBLESHOOTING

APPENDIX

GLOSSARY

JOB AIDS

Foreword

It is rare to have an opportunity to work on a relevant and exciting project such as this. Contemporary energy, environmental, and technological literacy issues cut to the essence of a dynamic and mobile society.

The importance of this effort to address critical issues associated with the quality of our environment and fuel dependency has been at the forefront of our vision. But a slightly different, perhaps more profound spirit emerged as we began our work. We soon came to recognize a "movement," in the traditional sense, to make the world a better place. This movement comprised individuals and companies, loosely organized advocates, officials, gurus, and practitioners—each contributing a positive energy to help place alternative fuels higher on America's agenda. To all of those who contributed to this ideal, thank you for your efforts and we hope you will find the result a contribution to your good work.

Larry McLaughlin, Project Coordinator
National Research Center for Coal and Energy
West Virginia University
Morgantown, West Virginia
May 1996

Acknowledgments

Many automotive and training professionals have contributed to this book. The blending of experts in alternative fuels, vehicle conversion and system configuration, emissions testing, diagnostic methods, regulation policy, and training involved dozens of people. Small group meetings and work sessions were supplemented with countless telephone calls, faxes, and mailings. We wish to sincerely thank everyone who contributed to this effort.

The material presented in this book could not have been collected without the cooperation of numerous alternative fuel industry representatives, committees, and individuals. From these sources, technical details and graphic examples were always forthcoming. Time was freely given to review sections of text or to participate in prototype training sessions.

The research community also contributed information on system and fuel performance as well as enabled us to access information sources to pursue our more obtuse questions.

Government, regulatory, and policy groups responded to our efforts in a helpful manner, always trying to "get the word out," by providing background information and updates on issues.

The funding to develop this material came from a grant from the U.S. Environmental Protection Agency, Office of Mobile Sources. Additional support came from the American Gas Association.

The following units at West Virginia University developed this text and related instructor materials:
• Department of Technology Education
• Mechanical and Aerospace Engineering Department
• National Research Center for Coal and Energy
• Office of Extension Information and Educational Technology
• Office of Community and Continuing Professional Education
• Office of Human Resources Research

Introduction

Historically, there have been two approaches to alternative fuel training in the United States. The first was an attempt to train through the existing manufacturers' distribution networks, an approach without formal structure and dependent upon the initiative of the individual distributor. It was an approach based on immediate demand, with each training program differing accordingly.

The second approach evolved as conversions became more complex. The later "third generation" technologies required that each manufacturer develop more in-depth courses for not only their distributors but also dealers and individual technicians. Further, almost all of the manufacturers insisted that in order to install the more sophisticated systems, technicians had to attend the factory training. There have been minimal prerequisites, if any, and little documentation or competency verification of those being trained. The level of development and the quality of the training material have varied widely, and the numbers of graduates from this system have been relatively low since the training sites are often remote and the schedules inconsistent.

The early efforts succeeded to the point that the industry growth outstripped the training capabilities of the conversion system manufacturers. At the same time, there was increasing awareness of the need to formalize the training, provide a structure, and improve the quality of the various programs.

The AGA was first to recognize the need for a national effort, and the association did two things toward this end. It initiated a formal testing procedure for CNG technicians under the auspices of the National Association for Automobile Service Excellence. This established a new category for automotive certification specific to CNG conversions in November of 1992. The second initiative, also in November 1992, was establishing the Alternative Fuel Vehicle Training Program (now the National Alternative Fuels Training Program) at West Virginia University with funding from the EPA. This was done to develop a national model for alternative fuel training that would produce standardized materials and establish a nationwide network of training institutions.

The approach of the National Alternative Fuels Training Program has been to start with a well developed core curriculum concerned with natural gas conversions and emissions and then to duplicate that format with subsequent alternative fuel training modules; e.g., NGV diagnostics, advanced electronics, and heavy-duty applications for alternative fuels. Concomitantly, the program has developed a method for delivering these programs regionally through the traditional educational providers, viz. the community colleges and vocational and technical schools. Critical to the program's success regionally has been the support of local distribution companies who have often been the sponsors for local training programs.

This manual is published with the hope that it provides a fundamental understanding of the conversion process with a heavy emphasis on the safety characteristics of high pressure natural gas systems and the unique differences between natural gas and gasoline as an automotive fuel, particularly with regard to exhaust emissions. It stops short of dealing in depth with specific products based on the position that this is more in the purview of the manufacturer.

It is my strong belief that the success or failure of this burgeoning market will not depend on the first sale of an alternative fuel vehicle, but rather on the second sale. Whether or not a fleet manager purchases another AFV will depend largely on his or her ability to get that vehicle serviced. This, in turn, will depend on establishing a pool of trained technicians to meet the needs of the industry. Addressing this "bottleneck" problem in the industry will require cooperation between systems manufacturers and the traditional automotive training providers. It is for this reason that West Virginia University is offering this manual.

William H. "Bill" McGlinchey

10/21/96

Skill Level

This material will be most effective when used by students who possess the following minimum skills and experiences:

- one year of automotive training associated with engine performance and service
- one year of experience as an automotive technician working on engine performance and service
- skill using basic automotive diagnostic tools and meters
- basic understanding of fuel combustion theory
- basic understanding of electronic engine control

Safety

Automotive training can be dangerous. Safe training and work practices must be followed at all times. This is true when working with any vehicle and any liquid or gaseous fuel.

Special precautions must be taken with alternative fuels in an education and training environment due to the general lack of experience in working with these fuels. Most teachers and students have decades of experience with conventional liquid fuels such as gasoline or diesel. Therefore, commonly held safe work practices are more easily understood and engaged. However, an alternative fuel such as compressed natural gas is in a gaseous state and under pressure. These new variables must be fully understood and safe work practices implemented in accordance with this understanding before students actually work with the vehicles, fuels, or conversion systems.

Study all related safety rules and discuss them with your instructor or supervisor and other safety experts. Make sure to ask your instructor about anything you do not understand.

The safety precautions identified in this text and related instructor materials are intended as general safe work and study practices. For actual vehicle, fuel, or conversion system safety information, it is necessary to use the factory safety recommendations as well as local, state, and national safety guidelines. In addition, we recommend to instructors that additional training on specific conversion products should be obtained before a vehicle using those products is converted or students are taught. It is ultimately the responsibility of the instructors and students using this material to remain current in the field. This includes obtaining all necessary regulatory, safety, and technical information to perform the job safely and according to industry and government standards.

Every effort has been made to ensure that the safety information in this document is accurate and complete. However, the authors assume no liability for errors or for any damages that result from the use of this text and related instructor materials.

CHAPTER 1

Introduction to NGV Technology

OBJECTIVES

- Understand the need for alternative fuel vehicles.
- Name the five different alternative fuels currently being used in the United States.
- Describe the basic advantages and disadvantages of alternative fuels as they compare to gasoline.
- Explain the difference between a bi-fuel vehicle, flexible fuel vehicle, and a dedicated fuel vehicle.
- List the advantages and disadvantages of an NGV.
- Describe the federal policies and programs which mandate the use of alternative fuels.
- List the regulatory organizations and their basic purpose as they affect CNG use in transportation.
- Identify by name each basic component used in NGV systems.
- State the primary function of each basic component used in NGV systems.
- Describe the potential customer of an NGV.
- Explain the options available when selecting a conversion system.

KEY TERMS

Methanol

Ethanol

Liquefied petroleum gas (LPG)

Compressed natural gas (CNG)

Bi-fuel vehicle

Flexible fuel vehicle

Dedicated fuel vehicle

Alternative Motor Fuel Act (AMFA)

Clean Air Amendments Act (CAAA)

Federal Energy Policy Act (FEPA)

California Air Resource Board (CARB)

American Gas Association (AGA)

National Fire and Protection Agency (NFPA)

Canadian Gas Association (CGA)

Fuel mixer

Computer "fixes"

OVERVIEW OF ALTERNATIVE FUELS

THE NEED FOR ALTERNATIVE FUELS

Demands on the transportation sector to help alleviate the problems of rising fuel costs and pollution are increasing every year. Transportation fuel accounts for 30 percent of the energy consumed in the United States. This accounts for 18 percent of the gross national product (GNP). The United States spends $55 billion a year on oil imports, 60 percent of which is consumed by the transportation sector. Imported fuel is subject to restrictions and price controls by foreign countries. Inexpensive domestic fuel alternatives could help reduce costs considerably.

There also are indirect costs associated with using petroleum-based fuels. An estimated $45 billion is spent annually on health care in the United States as a result of air pollution. A large proportion of this outlay is for health problems resulting from pollutants produced by the transportation sector. Adopting clean fuel technologies is imperative, if we are to have a cleaner environment. In order to make informed decisions about appropriate alternative fuels, operators must know the differences among the various clean fuel technologies.

DIFFERENCES AMONG ALTERNATIVE FUELS

Several alternative fuels are available. At this time, five appear to be most prominent: (1) methanol, (2) ethanol, (3) liquefied petroleum gas (propane), (4) electricity, and (5) natural gas. These five fuels are discussed briefly and compared with gasoline.

Methanol

Methanol has been used worldwide as a transportation fuel for several decades. The United States has a large domestic supply. Methanol is a noncarcinogenic, corrosive, toxic, and water-soluble fuel; it is produced from natural gas, coal, residual oil, or biomass. It is less flammable than gasoline and burns cleanly in an engine, resulting in lower emission levels. Methanol vehicles can be purchased from some automotive manufacturers. Methanol conversions are possible, but very expensive. Methanol vehicles require a special engine oil to perform properly. These vehicles accumulate more iron and lead in the oil, which decreases its lubricating ability. Engine wear, repair, maintenance, and overall life cycle costs are comparable to gasoline-powered vehicles. Engines tend to run cooler on methanol. Operators can expect a 10 percent increase in horsepower. More fuel storage capacity is needed for the vehicle to obtain the same range as it would have on gasoline. The methanol-to-gasoline storage ratio is generally 1.7 to 1. The basic components of a methanol-fueled vehicle are illustrated in Figure 1.1.

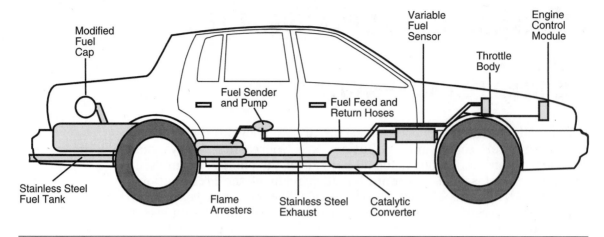

Figure 1.1 Methanol car

Ethanol

Ethanol also has been used throughout the world for several decades as a transportation fuel. Currently, an estimated 2.5 million ethanol vehicles are operated worldwide. The United States has a large domestic supply of ethanol harvested from energy crops (primarily corn and sugar cane) and municipal solid waste. Ethanol is less corrosive than methanol. It burns cleanly in an engine, resulting in lower emission levels than gasoline. Ethanol conversions are possible, but very expensive. Ethanol vehicles also must use a special engine oil. Engine wear, repair, maintenance, and overall life cycle costs are comparable to gasoline-powered vehicles. More fuel storage capacity is needed for the vehicle to obtain the same range it would on gasoline. The ethanol-to-gasoline storage ratio is generally 1.4 to 1. The basic components of an ethanol-fueled vehicle are illustrated in Figure 1.2.

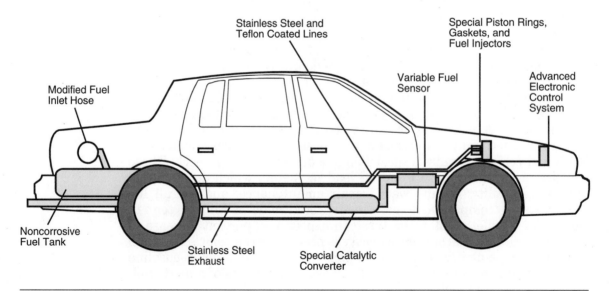

Figure 1.2 Ethanol car

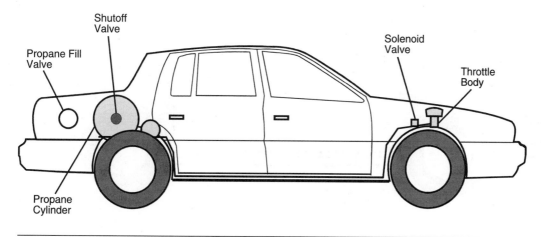

Figure 1.3 Propane car

Liquefied petroleum gas (propane) has been used as a transportation fuel for more than 60 years. The United States has about 350,000 of the estimated 3.5 million propane vehicles currently in use worldwide. Liquefied petroleum gas is a by-product of natural gas processing and crude oil refining. It is an odorless and colorless gas composed of propane and butane. In the United States, liquefied petroleum gas is primarily composed of propane; thus, it is usually referred to as propane gas. The distribution infrastructure necessary for supporting a major propane vehicle market is well developed. Propane burns cleanly, resulting in lower emission levels than gasoline, lower maintenance costs, and prolonged engine life. The cost of converting a vehicle to propane is typically $2,000 to $3,000. Propane has a higher octane rating than gasoline and can operate under a higher compression ratio, but power loss is about five percent due to lower volumetric efficiency. Vehicle range decreases by 10 to 20 percent. Propane-powered vehicles exhibit good cold weather starting capabilities and are generally safer than vehicles operating on gasoline. The basic components of a propane-fueled vehicle are illustrated in Figure 1.3.

Liquefied Petroleum Gas

Hundreds of electric vehicles (EVs) are operating in the United States today. EVs are powered by electricity stored in batteries. Recharging batteries usually takes eight to ten hours. The primary advantages of EVs are drastic reductions in noise and emission levels. However, these vehicles do not perform as well as gasoline vehicles. The driving range of an EV averages between 50 and 70 miles before the battery must be recharged. This range is affected by cold temperatures, vehicle load, and terrain traveled. Fuel cost for electricity is estimated to be between 60 cents and 80 cents compared to an equivalent gallon of gasoline. Acceleration and payload capacity are lower in vehicles powered by electricity. It is estimated that EVs require 50 percent less maintenance than gasoline-powered vehicles because their propulsion system has fewer mechanical parts. The basic components of an electric-powered vehicle are illustrated in Figure 1.4.

Electricity

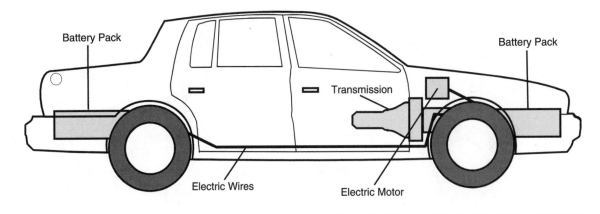

Figure 1.4 Electric car

Compressed Natural Gas

Natural gas has been used as a transportation fuel for more than 50 years. The United States has an abundant domestic supply of natural gas and an extensive distribution system to commercial, industrial, and residential sites (see Figure 6.5). To obtain greater volumetric storage capacity, natural gas is compressed. Natural gas burns much cleaner than gasoline, resulting in reduced emission levels, less contamination of engine oil, and longer engine life. Additional advantages of natural gas vehicles (NGVs) include the low cost of the fuel, low levels of emissions, and the relatively small investment needed to convert vehicles. Also, the bi-fuel vehicles can operate on either gasoline or natural gas. Natural gas appears to be one of the more promising alternative fuels because of its vast domestic supply, potentially improved emissions performance, and its excellent safety characteristics. The basic components of an NGV are illustrated in Figure 1.5.

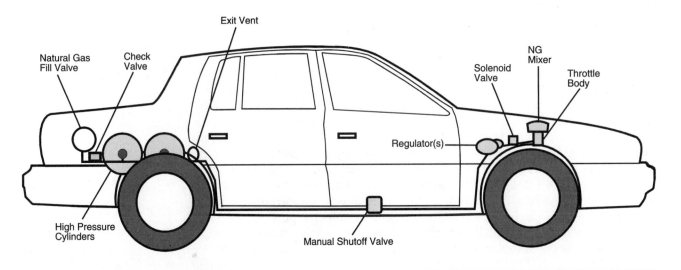

Figure 1.5 Natural gas vehicle

NATURAL GAS AS A FUEL

COMPRESSED NATURAL GAS

Natural gas is a fossil fuel extracted from underground reservoirs. The gas is composed primarily of methane (85 to 95 percent). It also contains other hydrocarbons, such as ethane, propane, and butane, and other gases, such as carbon dioxide, nitrogen, and helium. Methane is a greenhouse gas capable of trapping heat even though it has a low reactivity in ozone formation. Other than being compressed for storage, natural gas is used by motor vehicles exactly as it comes from the gas delivery systems. Because natural gas does not undergo sophisticated refining, as gasoline does, its composition and quality are inconsistent across the country. This means that the Btu/gal ratios (or energy content) vary and affect vehicle performance.

When natural gas is cooled to -260 degrees Fahrenheit at atmospheric pressure, the methane in natural gas condenses into a liquid, or LNG. LNG is clear (similar to water) but weighs less than 40 percent of the same volume of water. It is easily and safely transported and stored and can be vaporized and used later. LNG vapor is relatively difficult to ignite from exposure to or contact with a spark or high temperature surface. In the event of an LNG spill or leak, the LNG quickly vaporizes and leaves no lasting or residual contamination in soil or water. Like CNG, LNG can reduce emissions significantly. LNG is easily obtained in the United States at more than 65 locations. More than a trillion gallons are traded annually worldwide. LNG's unique cryogenic nature requires that it be stored in highly insulated containers to minimize the possibility of ambient heat entering the container and causing the LNG to vaporize. However, because LNG is a liquid, more volume can be stored in a smaller space. LNG is stored in tanks with integral rupture-resistance (include both an inner and an outer tank).

Natural gas transportation fuel is available today in every major community in the United States. It is the same natural gas that is supplied to American homes and industries. An extensive pipeline system is already in place to transport the fuel after it is cleaned and an odorant is added. Gas companies providing services for natural gas are well established nationwide.

The United States is one of the world's largest producers and consumers of natural gas. Natural gas accounts for approximately one-fourth of all the energy consumed by the United States. However, the transportation sector accounts for only about 3 percent of the natural gas consumed in the United States. Current reserves are sufficient to meet expected demand for more than 100 years. Although the future looks promising for NGV technology, it should be considered as only one of many alternatives to gasoline.

NATURAL GAS VEHICLES

Although NGVs are an emerging transportation technology in the United States, their use in the transportation sector is not new. Natural gas has been used to fuel vehicles since 1866. An estimated 30,000 NGVs operate today in the United States, most of which are light-duty trucks in fleet service. However, almost a million NGVs operate worldwide in such countries as Argentina, Canada, Italy, Russia, and New Zealand.

Most gasoline-powered vehicles can be converted to operate on natural gas. A vehicle can be converted to operate on either gasoline or compressed natural gas, or converted to operate exclusively on compressed natural gas. A vehicle that operates on either of the two fuels is referred to as a *bi-fuel* vehicle. A vehicle that operates on only one fuel is called a *dedicated fuel* vehicle. The fuel delivery system and carburetion system on a gasoline-powered vehicle must be modified in order to operate on natural gas.

Four primary components are necessary for a vehicle to operate on natural gas. Figure 1.6 shows the general location of each of those components. The first is a **high pressure fuel cylinder** to store the gas at a pressure of 2,400 to 3,600 pounds per square inch (psi). The second component is the **fuel line** which transports the fuel from the fuel cylinder(s) to the engine compartment. From there, it enters the third component, a **regulator(s)**. The regulator(s) functions as a pressure reducer. The fuel cylinder pressure must be reduced to a suitable working pressure to obtain the appropriate air/fuel mixture for combustion. The air and fuel are mixed in the fourth component, the **mixer**. Gaseous injectors replace the mixer component on late model fuel injected engines. Other supporting components may be necessary, depending on the type of vehicle and its desired capabilities.

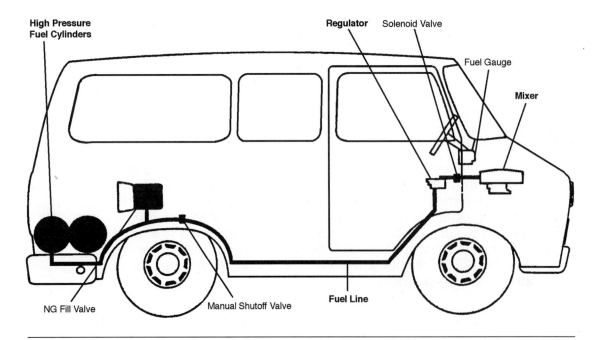

Figure 1.6 Bi-fuel van

Not all vehicles are recommended for NGV conversions. The cost of the conversion and ultimate efficiency are directly affected by the type of vehicle being converted. Consider the following suggestions when you plan NGV conversions:

1. Light-duty trucks and vans are better suited for conversion because of their cargo carrying capacity.

2. Automobiles are least desirable for NGV conversions when driving range is lengthy or unpredictable.

3. Carbureted vehicles, which are generally 1985 models or older, are not as efficient as fuel injected engines for NGV conversions. Carbureted vehicles generally utilize manifold heating, which reduces power.

4. Newer vehicles with computer diagnostic systems are better choices for NGV conversion because they have better potential for reducing toxic emissions.

5. Dedicated NGVs are more efficient and generally perform better than bi-fuel vehicles because their components are custom-tuned for a single fuel.

ADVANTAGES AND DISADVANTAGES OF NGVs

As with any fuel, natural gas has both advantages and disadvantages. Although NGV conversion is not appropriate for every vehicle in every transportation niche, it can satisfy the needs of many organizations. Therefore, it is important to understand the attributes of NGVs so that they can be weighed against consumer needs. The following advantages and disadvantages are made in comparison with gasoline vehicles.

Advantages of NGVs

- NGVs offer the potential for reducing exhaust emissions.

- Levels of reactive hydrocarbons (HC) may be reduced as much as 80 percent.

- Carbon monoxide (CO) levels may be reduced as much as 50 percent.

- Nitrogen oxide (NO_x) levels may be slightly reduced.

- Toxic pollutants are almost eliminated.

- Greenhouse emissions are approximately 15 percent less than those of gasoline.

- The United States has large natural gas resources which would help reduce dependence on foreign oil.

- An extensive pipeline system is in place.

- Gas companies are well established.

- No underground storage is required, eliminating the threat of polluting soil and underground water supplies.

- Higher octane ratings of between 120 and 130 enable higher compression ratios to be obtained.

- Natural gas requires no fuel enrichment. Because it is introduced into the engine as a vapor, its cold weather starting capabilities are generally good.

- Idling is smoother and engine operation is quieter.

- It is cleaner burning and the vehicles require less maintenance. NGVs have fewer deposits and less oil degradation, a longer period between oil and spark plug changes, and have an estimated 25 percent longer engine life.

- Natural gas is in a ready-to-use state, eliminating the added costs of refining.

- Cost per gasoline gallon equivalent is typically 30 to 60 percent less.

- A converted vehicle can retain its capability to operate on gasoline, thus extending its range and flexibility.

- NGVs are extremely safe to operate and maintain.

- NGVs can be easily reconverted to operate on gasoline; also, used NGV conversion systems can be reinstalled on other vehicles.

Disadvantages of NGVs

- Added weight from the fuel cylinder(s), ranging between 75 pounds and 275 pounds per cylinder, may reduce efficiency and load carrying capacity.

- Size and location of the fuel cylinder(s) may reduce cargo space.

- Some regions of the United States have few fueling stations.

- Conversion costs are generally between $2,000 and $3,500; the major cost is the high pressure fuel cylinder.

- Light-duty vehicles generally do not have the space needed for NGV fuel cylinder(s) to obtain ranges equivalent to a gasoline tank.

- On a bi-fuel vehicle, the engine cannot be optimized for both fuels, so one fuel may result in reduced performance.

- Power loss resulting from the displacement of engine air is around 10 percent. However, if the engine uses a heated intake manifold, 20 percent of the power may be lost. (The average driver may not be aware of this power loss under normal driving conditions.)

- NGVs can have problems due to "hot-start enleanment." After engine shutdown, the coolant continues to absorb heat from the engine, raising its temperature. If the vehicle is started soon after shutdown, the coolant's elevated temperature will heat the gas more than normal, resulting in a lower volumetric heating value and density.

- Because energy density of compressed natural gas is less than that of gasoline, more space for fuel is required to equal the range of the same vehicle operating on gasoline.

NGVs IN FLEET APPLICATIONS

Urban fleet vehicles are the best candidates for natural gas conversions for several reasons:

- Most fleets have centrally located fueling facilities. This is important because public natural gas fueling infrastructure is still under development.

- Fleet vehicles normally have short driving ranges.

- Because driving patterns usually are predictable, a fueling schedule can be maintained.

- Fleets usually contain trucks and vans having the space and suspension weight capacity for onboard fuel storage.

- Fleet vehicles generally travel more miles than private vehicles, allowing the investment to be recovered sooner.

- Most of the original equipment manufacturers (OEMs) are developing NGVs in sizes appropriate for fleet use.

Some estimates indicate that a fleet should have between 25 and 50 vehicles to recover investment over an acceptable period. Depending on the number of miles a vehicle travels, one to four years are needed to recover the costs of converting a vehicle to natural gas.

General Motors, Ford, and Chrysler all produce NGVs that meet the needs of many fleets. Currently, OEMs manufacture NGVs at a modest rate. It may be several years before OEM production meets market demand. Because of the small number of NGVs produced by OEMs, they cost $3,000 to $5,000 more than an equivalent gasoline vehicle. Conversions will remain an attractive alternative until purchasing OEMs becomes economical. In-house mechanics can convert and maintain vehicles to assure vehicle reliability, longevity, and reduced costs.

There are many reasons for fleets to convert their vehicles to NGVs. Substantial savings can be realized from the use of less expensive fuel and reduced maintenance. Reducing pollutants in the environment is an important long-term benefit. Energy security is important to the United States' economic competitiveness. Conversion also may improve a fleet's public image. Considering the many existing and proposed federal mandates for fleets to convert to clean fuel technologies, converting now will give fleet managers time to evaluate NGV technology before being required to use alternative fuels.

LEGISLATIVE AND REGULATORY POLICIES

LEGISLATIVE POLICIES

In recent years legislation has been passed in an effort to help combat air pollution emanating from the transportation sector. These policies mandate phasing in clean-burning fuel vehicles to reduce toxic and polluting emissions. In many cases these policies provide incentives and financial support to ease the transition to alternative fuels. The most influential federal policies and programs affecting vehicle transportation fleets are summarized below.

Alternative Motor Fuels Act (AMFA-1988)

The goal of the Alternative Motor Fuels Act (AMFA) is to encourage the development and use of alternative transportation fuels. The act directs the Department of Energy (DOE) to work with other agencies such as the General Services Administration (GSA), the Department of Transportation (DOT), the Environmental Protection Agency (EPA), state and local governments, and industry to help encourage and develop the use of alternative transportation fuels.

Three programs have been established to fulfill this goal: (1) the Alternative Fuel—Light Duty Vehicle Program, (2) the Truck Commercial Application Program, and (3) the Alternative Fuels Bus Testing Program. The objective of the Alternative Fuel—Light Duty Vehicle Program is to ensure that the majority of automobiles and light-duty vehicles purchased by the federal government are alternative fuel vehicles. The Truck Commercial Application Program is conducting commercial application projects for alternative fuel vehicles in real-world operating environments. The Alternative Fuels Bus Testing Program assists state and local government agencies in testing natural gas vehicles in urban areas.

Another directive implemented by the AMFA is the establishment of the Alternative Fuels Data Center (AFDC). The AFDC (1-800-423-1DOE) is operated and managed by the National Renewable Energy Laboratory in Golden, Colorado. It gathers and analyzes information on the composition, emissions, operation, and feasibility of alternative vehicle fuels.

Clean Air Act Amendments

The Clean Air Act was passed in 1963. It has been amended several times. The most recent amendments in 1990 initiate regulations to begin cleaning the air in cities considered air-quality nonattainment areas (Figure 1.7). Initially, the amendments required federal agencies and "fuel providers" (the utilities) to convert portions of their fleets as early as 1994. Private fleets of ten or more vehicles in these regions will be required to purchase alternative fuel vehicles beginning in 1998. Fleets operating light-duty vehicles will have to have 30 percent of their new vehicles purchased in 1998 operating on alternative fuels, 50 percent in 1999, and 70 percent thereafter. Fleets operating medium-duty vehicles will have to ensure that 50 percent of their new vehicles operate on alternative fuels.

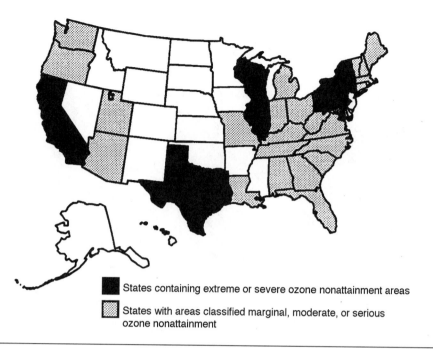

States containing extreme or severe ozone nonattainment areas

States with areas classified marginal, moderate, or serious ozone nonattainment

Figure 1.7 National ozone nonattainment areas

The Federal Energy Policy Act is designed to initiate the development and implementation of alternative fuel technologies. Under the law, $25 million per year will be appropriated for transit and school bus fleets to develop a clean-fuels urban bus program. Another $30 million will be allocated for providing low interest loans. Income tax incentives available through this act include deductions from $2,000 to $50,000 for clean-fuel vehicles and $100,000 for clean-fuel refueling stations. The Department of Defense and other research and development institutions will receive other financial support.

The law requires federal agencies and fuel providers to convert portions of their fleets as early as 1994. The law also encourages the purchase of more alternative fuel vehicles for federal fleets (Figure 1.8). It aims to have purchased 5,000 during 1993; 7,500 in 1994; and 10,000 in 1995. Federal fleet vehicles that operate on alternative fuels should reach 25 percent by 1996, 33 percent by 1997, 50 percent by 1998, and 75 percent by 1999. Ultimately, the law intends that 90 percent of all new vehicles purchased by 1999 and thereafter will operate on clean-burning fuels. This increased use of alternative fuels by federal fleets will help accelerate the development of an OEM market.

Note: Executive Order #12844 (November 1993) increased by 50 percent the number of alternative fuel vehicles mandated by the 1992 Federal Energy Policy Act for the years 1993 to 1995.

California is the most proactive state in the United States for establishing stringent vehicle emission standards. The air quality in many regions in California is so poor that CARB decided not to wait until federal mandates take effect. The standards being developed by CARB are higher than those called for by the CAAA. Many states have adopted or

Federal Energy Policy Act (FEPA-92)

California Air Resource Board (CARB)

Figure 1.8 States with mandated fleet conversions and/or conversion incentives

are adopting legislation similar to California's. If emissions standards have not been established by federal agencies pertaining to NGV conversions, following the standards adopted by the CARB is recommended (Figure 1.9).

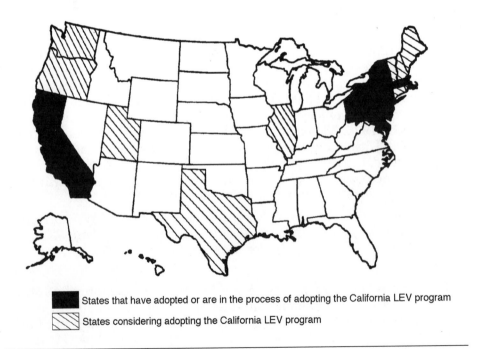

Figure 1.9 California Low Emission Vehicle (LEV) Program

Many state and local government agencies have their own policies, incentives, and legislation to implement alternative fuel vehicles. More than 30 states have alternative fuel transportation programs. Many of these states mandate the use of alternative fuels in some applications. Others provide incentive programs, such as tax credits, exemptions, rebates, and low-interest loans for owners of alternative fuel vehicles. A complete summary of state-by-state laws and incentive programs can be found by contacting the office of your state attorney general or your state department of transportation.

REGULATORY AGENCIES AND ORGANIZATIONS

A number of government agencies and private organizations identify, propose, and influence the laws, codes, and regulations pertaining to the natural gas vehicle industry. The Natural Gas Vehicle Coalition is researching the marketability of compressed natural gas vehicles. The United States Department of Transportation has developed strict standards for the certification, application, and maintenance of NGV fuel cylinders. The National Fire Protection Association (NFPA) has developed strict safety standards applying to all areas of the NGV fuel system. The American Gas Association (AGA) has rules and regulations on NGV equipment standards. Updated information on NGV regulations may be obtained by contacting the following:

American Gas Association
1515 Wilson Boulevard
Arlington, VA 22209

California Air Resource Board
9528 Telstar Avenue
El Monte, CA 91731-2900

Department of Transportation
400 7th Street, S.W.
Washington, DC 20590

National Fire Protection Assoc.
Batterymarch Park
Quincy, MA 02269

Local Regulations

Your shop safety policy should reflect the appropriate local and state laws that apply. For vehicle fueling and fueling appliances, refer to National Fire Protection Association 52 as a guide.

American Gas Association (AGA)

The AGA acts as the testing agency for the specifications set forth in NFPA 52. In addition, the AGA in conjunction with the NGV Coalition and the Canadian Gas Association (CGA) is working to establish a harmonized North American standard under the auspices of a new agency, the International Approval Services (IAS). The IAS will verify that the components being produced by manufacturers meet minimum safety standards and that conversion systems include an assembly of components that can be safely and adequately matched. Currently, the AGA 1-85 is the standard for the United States. The new IAS standard will be available soon.

PREVIEW OF NGV CONVERSION COMPONENTS

FUNDAMENTAL CONVERSION COMPONENTS

Before moving too deeply into the discussion of conversion, let's preview the components needed to convert a vehicle. While conversion is specific to each vehicle and to each conversion system, the components are essentially the same. The greatest variety in system components is in the electronic feedback systems and the mixing devices.

Starting from the fuel cylinder and working forward (Figure 1.10), these are components that every NGV will have:

- Fuel cylinder(s)

- Fuel lines

- Fuel lockoff device

- Manual shutoff valve

- Fuel receptacle with check valve

- Pressure regulator(s)

- Mixing system (device that mixes fuel with air)

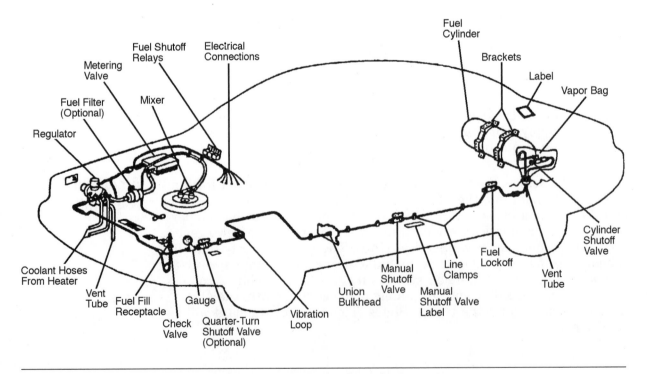

Figure 1.10 NGV system components *(Courtesy GFI Control Systems, Inc.)*

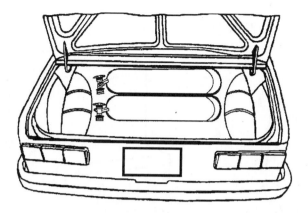

Figure 1.11 Fuel storage cylinders located in car trunk

The fuel cylinder is shaped similar to an oxygen bottle (Figure 1.11). Fuel cylinders are available in a variety of materials and sizes. The cylinder will store natural gas at pressures of 2,400 to 3,600 psi. Because of these high pressures, there are special safety considerations (see pp. 66–69 and pp. 199–203).

Fuel Cylinder

The NGV fuel lines connect the fill receptacle to the fuel cylinders and the fuel cylinders to the pressure regulator. The fuel lines and all other high pressure components should be able to withstand a hydrostatic test of four times their service pressures; given a service pressure of 3,000 psi, the high pressure components must be able to withstand pressures up to 12,000 psi. In addition, the fuel lines must be resistant to corrosion and vibration.

Fuel Lines

The manual shutoff valve (Figure 1.12) is a quarter-turn valve usually placed under the driver's door. It must be clearly marked so that in an emergency this valve can be used to stop the flow of natural gas to the engine compartment.

Manual Shutoff Valve

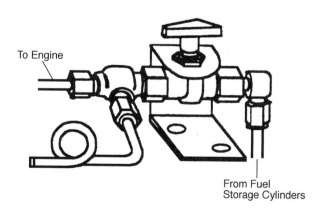

To Engine

From Fuel
Storage Cylinders

Figure 1.12 Manual shutoff valve

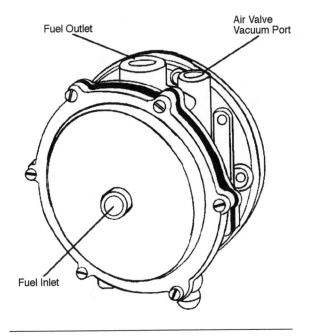

Fuel Outlet

Air Valve Vacuum Port

Fuel Inlet

Figure 1.13 Mechanical fuel lockoff device

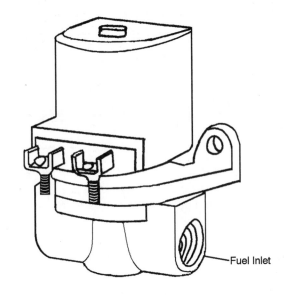

Fuel Inlet

Figure 1.14 Electrical fuel lockoff device

Fuel Lockoff Device

The fuel lockoff is a device that will stop the flow of gas when either the ignition is turned off or the engine stops running (Figures 1.13 and 1.14).

Fuel Receptacle with Check Valve

Each vehicle must have a receptacle (Figure 1.15) where it can be filled with natural gas. There are several standard locations for the fuel receptacle. Each fuel receptacle assembly must have a check valve to prevent the gas from escaping after refueling (Figure 1.16). An optional quarter-turn valve may be included in this assembly.

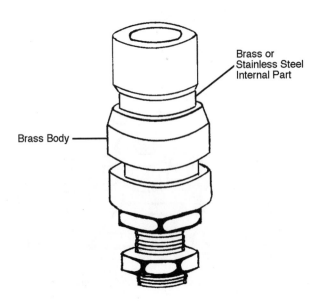

Brass or Stainless Steel Internal Part

Brass Body

Figure 1.15 NGV-1 fill receptacle

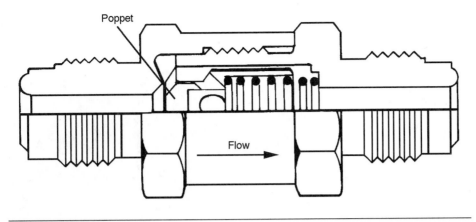

Poppet

Flow

Figure 1.16 Check valve cross section

Because the pressure in the fuel cylinder decreases as the fuel is used, and because the mixer depends upon a constant pressure for efficient operation, a regulator is installed. The primary (first stage) regulator (Figure 1.17) has an output pressure range of 80 psi to 200 psi. Some conversion systems have a secondary regulator. The secondary regulator reduces the pressure to near atmospheric. Another option is a multistage regulator (Figure 1.18) which combines one or more pressure reductions in a single unit.

Regulator(s)

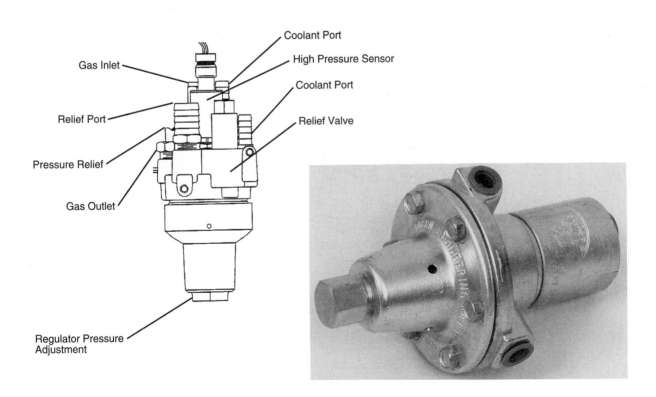

Gas Inlet

Coolant Port

High Pressure Sensor

Coolant Port

Relief Port

Relief Valve

Pressure Relief

Gas Outlet

Regulator Pressure Adjustment

Figure 1.17 Primary regulator. *Photo:* MECO primary regulator

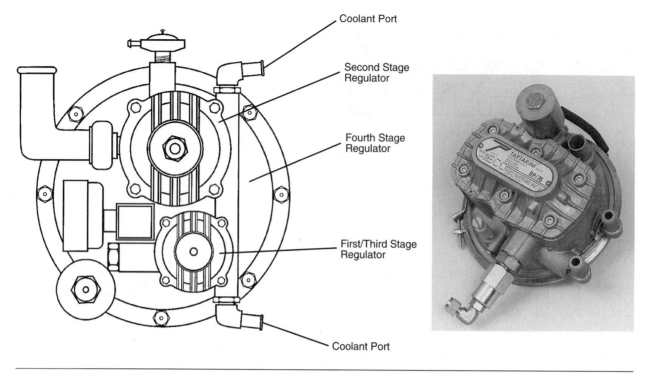

Figure 1.18 Multistage regulator cross section. *Photo:* Multistage regulator

Mixing System

In order to use natural gas in an internal combustion engine, a mixture in the range of 16.5:1 to 17.2:1 of natural gas to air (by weight) is needed. There are a variety of devices that achieve the goal of mixing natural gas and air in this range of ratios. Two of these are shown in Figures 1.19 and 1.20.

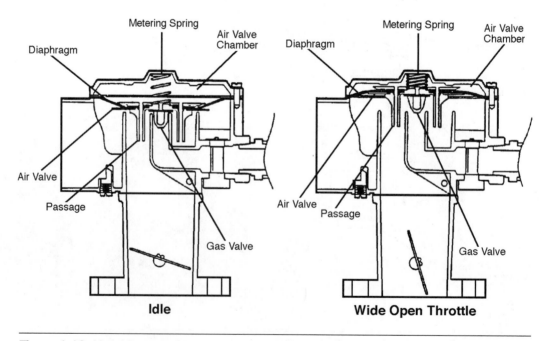

Figure 1.19 Variable venturi mixer

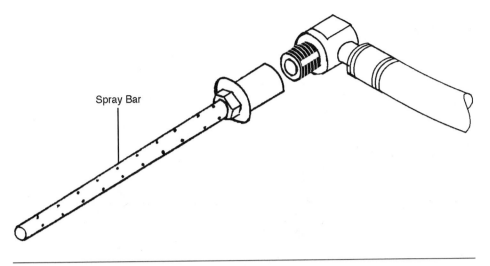

Spray Bar

Figure 1.20 Spray bar assembly

If the vehicles being converted are designed to operate as bi-fuel vehicles, the timing, in many cases, can be advanced for the natural gas operation to allow the fuel to burn more completely. Natural gas has a higher octane rating or slower flame speed. This property of natural gas is why the timing may be advanced from the setting for gasoline. If the vehicle being converted is a bi-fuel vehicle (operating on both natural gas and gasoline), then the timing adaptation system should be capable of advancing/retarding the timing according to the fuel being used. Some EFI (electronic fuel injection) systems with knock sensors are capable of regulating the timing without the need for additional electronics.

Feedback systems (Figure 1.21) provide an interface with the onboard computer of the vehicle being converted to maximize the vehicle's performance. There is a great deal of variety in the complexity of these systems. Typically, the more interactive the system is with engine sensors, the greater the level of performance the vehicle achieves.

Fuel monitoring systems function through the use of pressure transducers which provide a signal to a special NGV fuel gauge or the vehicle's original fuel gauge.

In bi-fuel vehicles, fuel selection systems switch the fuel type from natural gas to gasoline or vice versa. Fuel selection systems can be manual, automatic, or a combination of both (Figure 1.22).

Timing Adaptation System

Feedback Systems

Fuel Monitoring and Selection

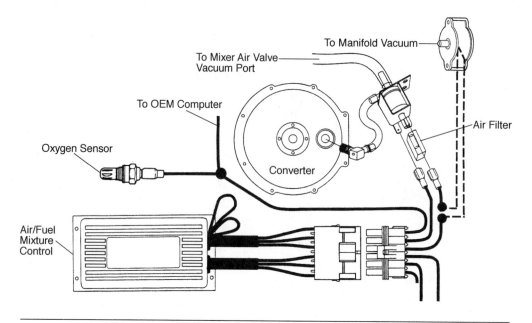

Figure 1.21 Aftermarket feedback system *(Courtesy Autotronic Controls Corp.)*

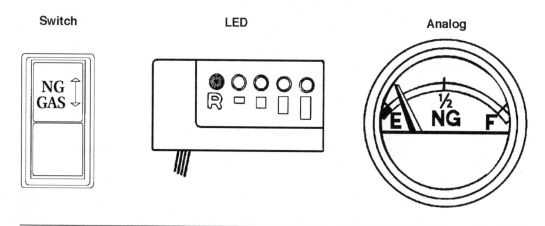

Figure 1.22 NGV fuel switch and gauges

VEHICLE COMPATIBILITY ANALYSIS AND SYSTEM SELECTION

SELECTING A VEHICLE

An obvious starting point for converting a vehicle to natural gas is selecting the conversion system. Before ordering a system, it is necessary to gather some information about the vehicle you are considering for conversion.

While nearly any vehicle can be converted to use natural gas, not all vehicles are good choices for conversion. A measure of common sense is needed in selecting a vehicle for conversion. Keeping in mind that a significant investment of both parts and labor will be necessary, inspect the vehicle selected for conversion as if you were buying a used car. Is it a mechanically sound vehicle? Will the vehicle be able to handle the extra weight of fuel cylinders? Is there adequate space for the fuel cylinders and other system components? Changing fuel systems will not correct any existing mechanical problems the vehicle had before conversion!

Decide if the vehicle type will make a good NGV conversion. Compacts and subcompacts are least desirable for conversions when long driving ranges are expected because they lack room for fuel cylinders. In addition, any added weight from the NGV fuel cylinders may change the handling characteristics and can affect mileage.

The age of the vehicle also should be considered. Newer vehicles with onboard computer diagnostic systems are much more efficient at controlling the fuel delivery system and reducing toxic emissions. Likewise, newer vehicles using injected fuel delivery systems have less power loss after conversion than do carbureted vehicles using manifold heating.

Although diesel-fueled vehicles can be converted, they generally are not regarded as acceptable conversion candidates due to high emissions of carbon monoxide and nitrogen oxides resulting from the engine design.

It is extremely important to analyze a potential conversion to ensure proper condition of the vehicle before proceeding. Generally, an acceptance test is applied to a vehicle that is a few years old or has a high odometer reading. This test will aid in evaluating the status of the vehicle's engine, compression ratio, fuel system, and ignition system. The results of this test will indicate if the vehicle is a good candidate for an NGV conversion. Acceptance measures commonly involve:

- Inspecting areas where cylinders are to be mounted for possible weakening due to rust and corrosion.

- Analyzing suspension potential for carrying increased loads resulting from onboard fuel cylinder(s).

- Performing a compression test to indicate if piston rings and valves are in proper condition.

- Checking the ignition system, the starting circuit, and the charging circuit to ensure proper operating condition.

- Analyzing engine, horsepower, carburetion, and emissions according to the manufacturer's vehicle performance standards.

It is very important to record the vehicle's power output over its speed range before making a conversion. This measure will be used as a baseline to indicate proper system installation and tuning. Improper installation or tuning may result in a significant loss of power and even an increase in exhaust emissions. Quality installation is imperative in ensuring operating efficiency and safety. Poor installation of NGV components is the principal cause of problems involving NGVs.

The Vehicle Manufacturer's Warranty

It is important to find out if the vehicle's manufacturer's warranty will remain in effect after conversion. If a conversion damages an OEM component, the warranty may be invalidated. Contacting the manufacturer before a conversion may help confirm what components and policies can be affected if failure is caused by the NGV conversion. Generally, the OEMs will honor warranties if the conversion does not affect the integrity of the gasoline operation.

GATHER VEHICLE INFORMATION

Once a vehicle has been targeted for conversion, gather the following information: vehicle identification number (VIN), year, make, model, engine size and model, and carburetion. Some conversion system manufacturers may need highly specific information such as the carburetor manufacturer and model, throat diameter of the carburetor, or specifics of the fuel injection system (e.g., multiport or throttle body).

Desired fill options must also be determined. The connector should be an NGV-1 standard, although there may be other types of connectors used in your region. The maximum pressures will likely be determined by the capabilities of the available compressors and, in some cases, by state or local laws.

It is also a good idea to test drive the vehicle before the conversion and see how it runs so that after the conversion is completed you will know what to expect. Take notes on performance, idle, acceleration, or any other noteworthy attributes of the vehicle's operation before conversion.

DRIVING NEEDS

What are the driving demands, environments, and regional realities placed on the vehicle targeted for conversion? Specifically, what range will the vehicle need? What is the service loop (how many miles a day)? Are there NGV fueling facilities on the vehicle's route? What is the payload requirement? What is the current fuel consumption of the vehicle?

After you answer these questions, it is possible to roughly estimate the fuel cylinder capacity required for the vehicle. It is ideal to have as much natural gas fuel storage capacity as the vehicle will carry (and you can afford), but the constraints of reality dictate that storage capacity is limited by such things as the design of the vehicle and the payload needs of the vehicle.

BI-FUEL OR DEDICATED FUEL

There are two major AFV options: dedicated and bi-fuel. A dedicated NGV uses natural gas as the *only* fuel in the vehicle. A bi-fuel vehicle carries both natural gas and gasoline (or possibly diesel) and is capable of running on either gasoline *or* natural gas.

Note: A flexible fuel vehicle can operate on one fuel or a mixture of two fuels (such as 85 percent methanol and 15 percent gasoline). This handbook discusses the dedicated and bi-fuel vehicle systems. Currently, there is no flexible fuel NGV-gasoline combination, but there is an NGV-diesel combination.

Several factors will help determine if the conversion should be a bi-fuel or a dedicated fuel system: (1) driving range and availability of refueling points, (2) fuel cylinder capacity, and (3) economics—costs and payback.

The range requirements of the vehicle may determine if a bi-fuel system is required. If the vehicle will be traveling long distances where NGV filling stations may not be available, then it may be necessary to install a bi-fuel system. Or if the vehicle will be used in environments that demand exceptional performance (e.g., law enforcement agencies, ambulance services, fire departments), then a bi-fuel vehicle would be the wise choice.

An estimate of minimum fuel cylinder(s) capacity can be calculated using the Fuel Cylinder to Mileage Matrix. Estimate the required mileage between refuelings (increase the estimate for safety's sake) and consider the fuel cylinder sizes that can meet the required mileage. Compare the possible fuel cylinder sizes required with the space available for mounting natural gas cylinders. If there is not adequate space for mounting the required fuel cylinders, then a bi-fuel conversion is necessary.

CONVERSION SYSTEMS AND MANUFACTURERS

There are many conversion system manufacturers, and the options available with the systems vary. Investigate what your needs are (regarding emissions, for example) before ordering the system because the manufacturer may not offer the specific options you need.

The simplest type of system is based on the natural aspiration of the engine. This type of system consists of a mixer mounted before (or on top of) the existing carburetor or intake. These systems were historically supplied by the same manufacturers who produced propane components. The more effective, comprehensive, and complex systems employ a wide range of electronic controls and feature varied levels of interaction with the vehicle's onboard processor. The performance, power, and emissions of a converted vehicle improve as interaction of the NGV conversion system and the vehicle's onboard processor increases and is maximized on a dedicated NGV.

The AGA (American Gas Association) has recognized and approved some system manufacturers as safe and reliable. The AGA serves as an overseer's group testing products to meet the NFPA 52 recommendations.

FUEL RECEPTACLES OR CONNECTORS

Before ordering a system, it is necessary to identify the type or types of fueling connectors to be used. It is highly recommended that you select an NGV-1 fuel receptacle because it is the established industry standard. Past fueling connectors have been proprietary to particular manufacturers, which caused difficulties when fueling in different areas of the country. The factors influencing the type of connector that will be used include the type of fuel receptacles in use in your region, the pressures used and, in some cases, state or local laws. If it is likely that the converted vehicle will refuel off-site, then the connectors used at the prospective refueling sites must be identified. Where there is a variety of fueling receptacles used at different refueling sites, plan to have several adapters in the vehicle.

The fuel receptacles you may encounter include: (1) NGV-1 standard (Figure 1.23), (2) quick connector (Figure 1.24), and (3) probe connector

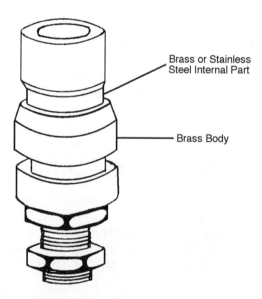

Brass or Stainless Steel Internal Part

Brass Body

Figure 1.23 NGV-1 fuel receptacle

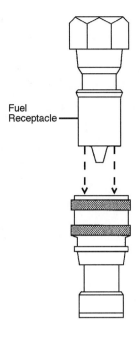

Fuel
Receptacle

Figure 1.24 Quick connector (replaced by NGV-1)

(Figure 1.25). Both the quick connector and the probe connector are obsolete and are mentioned only because some are still in use. Users of these connectors are encouraged to switch to the NGV-1. Ignition interrupts can be added to the fuel receptacle's assembly. An ignition interrupt is a device that does not allow the vehicle to run while being fueled. There is controversy regarding the usefulness of this component.

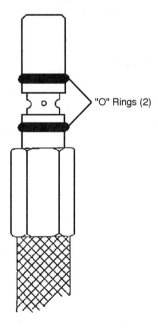

"O" Rings (2)

Figure 1.25 Fuel probe connector (replaced by NGV-1)

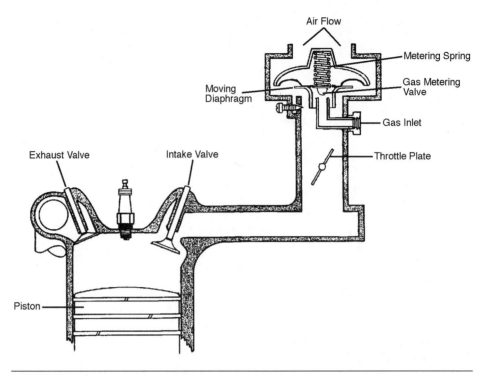

Figure 1.26 Variable venturi system *(Courtesy IMPCO Technologies, Inc.)*

CONVERSION OPTIONS: FUEL DELIVERY SYSTEMS

There are several basic types of fuel delivery systems: (1) variable venturi mixer (positive pressure), (2) fixed venturi mixer (zero or negative pressure), (3) fumigation, and (4) direct injection. Both the variable venturi mixer (positive pressure) and the fixed venturi mixer (zero or negative pressure) are similar in function to a conventional carburetor because they introduce the fuel into the intake air by the differential pressure from the engine.

The variable venturi mixer uses a moving diaphragm that allows the fuel to be released into the intake manifold proportionally to the vacuum created by the draw of the engine. Figure 1.26 illustrates the function of the vacuum activated mixer.

The fixed venturi mixer does not have a moving diaphragm but relies on a fixed, precision-machined venturi placed before the throttle plate to introduce the fuel mix (Figure 1.27).

Fumigation systems operate similarly to gasoline throttle body fuel injection systems. A series of injectors mounted remotely inject a specific amount of fuel determined by the electric pulses received by the injectors (Figure 1.28). A spray bar or nozzle placed at the throat of the intake manifold allows fuel into the intake based on the demand of the operator. The fuel is released from one or more injectors by a pulse from the fuel injection controller which varies the pulse time based on the demand. The injection system's electronics interface with the vehicle's onboard processors either directly or indirectly to determine the precise air/fuel mixture.

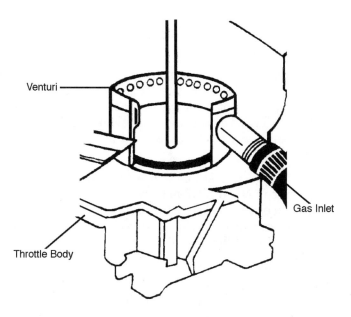

Figure 1.27 Fixed venturi mixer system

Direct injection systems are relatively new to NGVs. Operation is similar to that of a throttle body injector or port fuel gasoline injector. One or more high pressure gaseous injector(s) inject a specific amount of fuel into the intake based on the driving demand. These injectors can be placed at the throat of the intake manifold (throttle body) or individual intake runners (port or multiport). The fuel is released by a pulse from the fuel injection controller which varies the pulse time according to the demand. The electronics that control the direct injection systems can be independently controlled or controlled by the vehicle's onboard processors.

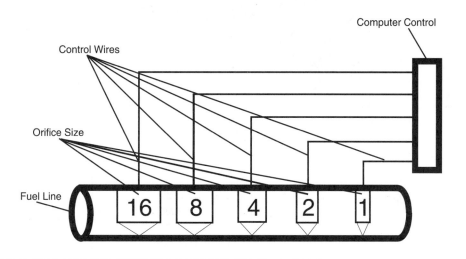

Figure 1.28 Conceptual diagram of a gas fumigation system

CONVERSION OPTIONS: ELECTRONIC

There are several different electronics systems to be considered in selecting a conversion system: (1) the emissions feedback system (open or closed), (2) a timing adaptation system, (3) fuel control systems, and (4) "computer fixes." These electronic options may only be available with particular systems and *may not* be capable of being randomly mixed with other components.

The emissions feedback systems are either open or closed loop. An open loop system receives no feedback from the emissions sensors (e.g., O_2 sensor) and, hence, the fuel mixture is not modified by the information that these sensors collect. A closed loop exhaust system obtains data from the exhaust and modifies the fuel mixture accordingly.

The options available (all intended for a bi-fuel vehicle) for the timing adaptation include: (1) early timing adaptation systems and (2) original equipment manufacturer timing adaptation systems. Early timing adaptation systems require advancing the distributor for natural gas and electronically retarding the timing for gasoline. Systems with distributorless ignitions allow the gasoline timing curve to remain the same while electronically advancing the timing for natural gas. These systems use an aftermarket electronic processor if the existing onboard computer is not capable of modifying the timing for natural gas (Figure 1.29).

Fuel switching systems and the fuel monitoring systems are available options for conversions which make the vehicle operation more pleasant or encourage the use of natural gas. If a manual switch is not desirable,

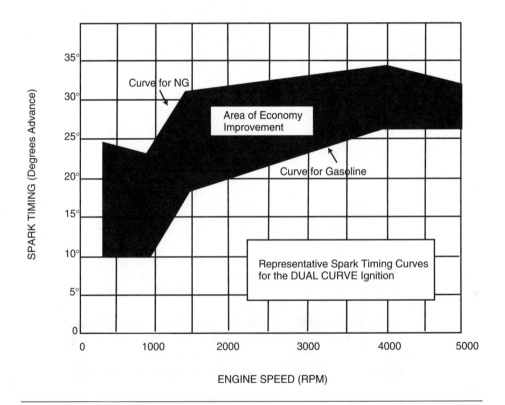

Figure 1.29 Timing chart *(Courtesy Autotronic Controls Corporation)*

select an electronic fuel switching system that is automatic (out of the operator's control). Such a system consists of a sensor and a simple logic circuit that switches the fuel from natural gas to gasoline only when the natural gas pressure drops below a preset level. Both automatic and manual fuel selection switches can be installed. The fuel monitoring system is a fuel cylinder gauge that uses either the vehicle's original fuel gauge or an additional gauge such as an LED bar, an analog gauge, or a low fuel indicator (see Figure 1.22).

Computer fix is a general term for electronic devices that modify the signal to the onboard computer when running on natural gas. These devices are included as needed, and decisions regarding computer fixes are made by the provider. The intent of such components is to avoid sending false trouble codes to the onboard processor due to the different operating characteristics of the fuels. The most common example is the oxygen sensor; if the signal from the O_2 sensor is left unmodified, a lean code when running on natural gas may be sent, prompting the onboard processor to attempt to correct the problem by modifying the fuel mix even though the mixture is correct for natural gas. Other examples include knock sensors, EGR sensors, and fuel injector codes.

CONVERSION OPTIONS: FUEL CYLINDERS AND FUEL LINES

There are several factors to consider in fuel cylinder selection. Previously we considered the storage capacity needed and the space required to mount the fuel cylinder(s). Other considerations in selecting cylinder size are:

- Physical placement of the fuel cylinder(s).

- Mounting arrangement and orientation (stacked, single, vertical, or horizontal).

- Strength of the selected mounting surfaces and reinforcement techniques.

- Space for the mounting brackets.

- Ground clearance (if applicable).

- Fuel line route.

- Route for venting gases (if mounted in enclosed compartment).

Failure to consider any of these factors may mean that you will order the wrong fuel cylinder(s) and end up with an unworkable installation. NFPA 52, Section 3-3, specifies safe mounting practices and should be consulted before making any final decisions on the fuel cylinders to be ordered.

Having selected an area on the vehicle for installing the fuel cylinder(s), you should be able to make a rough estimate of the amount of fuel

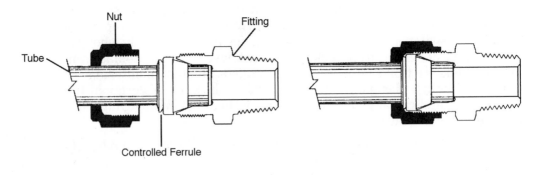

Figure 1.30 Cross section of a high pressure fuel line connector

line required. The fuel lines are composed of a corrosion-resistant, high-strength material, typically seamless stainless steel. Stainless steel tubing requires special tools and skills for bending (to be discussed later). The fuel lines also require special connectors (Figures 1.30 and 1.31).

Most system suppliers will provide these connectors. Appropriate high pressure gas sealants, bending mandrels, tubing cutters, and reamers are also required. Specially hardened cutting wheels are required for stainless steel because stainless steel tends to quickly wear out standard cutting wheels.

Conversion System Labels

All fuel-carrying components of the system must be labeled (NFPA 52, Section 3-2.4), including the fuel line from the final stage regulator to the mixer. The manual shutoff valve must be labeled. Labeling the pressure

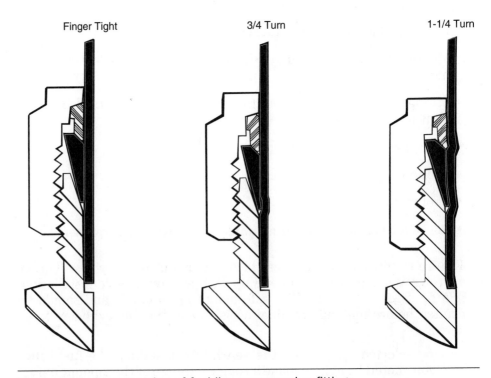

Figure 1.31 Cross section of fuel line compression fittings

CNG FUELED VEHICLE

MODEL #
SERIAL #
VIN #
INSTALLED BY
SYSTEM WORKING PRESSURE

TOTAL CYLINDER WATER VOLUME

CU. IN.:   LITERS:
CYLINDER RETEST DATE:

MANUAL SHUTOFF VALVE

HIGH PRESSURE, NO WELDING OR CUTTING

CAUTION: HIGH PRESSURE

WARNING: DO NOT WORK ON OPEN GAS LINES OR FITTINGS WITHOUT MAKING CERTAIN ALL TANKS ARE COMPLETELY SHUT OFF.

ALL CNG COMPONENTS MUST BE SERVICED BY AUTHORIZED MECHANICS ONLY.

Figure 1.32 NGV labels *(Courtesy IMPCO Technologies, Inc.)*

capacity of the system near the filling connector is required (NFPA 52, Section 3-11). State or local laws may require certain labels not normally shipped with the system (e.g., haz. mat.). While these labels should be available from the system manufacturer, you may need to order them separately (Figure 1.32).

CONVERSION SYSTEM SPECIFICATIONS, COST, AVAILABILITY, AND WARRANTY

Much like other purchases, shopping around for NGV conversion systems can pay off. Be aware that the conversion time is a major factor in calculating the total cost of an NGV conversion. Certain systems may be less expensive, but the increased installation time may offset these savings. Experience is the best guide in selecting a system. Contact a reputable conversion specialist for specific answers to questions you have. Availability of a system for the specific vehicle and the parts, if replacement is ever needed, should be a consideration. Warranty coverage is changing; it has traditionally been one year parts and/or labor with optional extended warranties of three to five years. New EPA regulations specify that the conversion emission warranty must be comparable to existing gasoline OEM warranties. Ultimately, these warranty options will be reflected in the prices of conversion systems.

Some manufacturers require you to attend their specialized training programs before they will sell you a conversion system. The intricacies of some systems justifies the extra training needed to be a proficient technician.

SUMMARY

- The transportation sector of the United States can dramatically reduce the negative effects of primarily using petroleum based fuels.

- The five alternative fuels currently in use in the United States are: methanol, ethanol, electricity, liquefied petroleum gas (LPG), and compressed natural gas (CNG).

- Alternative fuel vehicles are typically less expensive to operate and produce fewer harmful emissions.

- The disadvantages normally associated with alternative fuel vehicles are: cost of conversion, reduced operating range, reduced engine performance, certain safety characteristics, and lack of infrastructure needed to refill the vehicles.

- CNG is the most promising of the alternative fuels based on: safety, operating costs, conversion costs compared to other AFVs, domestic fuel supply, and available refilling infrastructure.

- Natural gas is a fossil fuel that is extracted from underground reservoirs in which current reserves should meet demand for over 100 years.

- Natural gas is composed primarily of 85–95 percent methane.

- A bi-fuel vehicle can operate on one of two different fuels; a flexible fuel vehicle can operate on one fuel or a mixture of two fuels; while a dedicated fuel vehicle can operate on only one fuel source.

- Natural gas is stored under high pressure (2,400 to 3,600 pounds per square inch) in order to increase the energy content and reduce the required storage space.

- The ideal vehicle for use as a bi-fuel vehicle will have the following characteristics: sufficient cargo carrying capacity, operated within a relatively short and predictable range, and be equipped with a computerized fuel injection system.

- The 10 percent power loss normally associated with operating on natural gas can be offset by taking advantage of higher compression ratios resulting from its 120–130 octane rating.

- Natural gas vehicles and their refilling facilities are more environmentally friendly than their gasoline counterparts due to reducing both air pollution and the possibility of soil pollution.

- A few of the government policies and programs designed to help the transportation sector ease into the increased use of clean burning domestic alternative fuels are: the Alternative Motor Fuels Act, the Clean Air Act Amendments, the Federal Energy Policy Act, and the California Resource Board.

- The major organizations used to maintain and control NGV's excellent safety standards are: the American Gas Association, the NGV Coalition, the International Approval Services, the Department of Transportation, and the National Fire Protection Association.

- NGVs have components designed specifically to ease driver operation and the refilling process.

- Various components are needed to reduce natural gas from its high storage pressure to a pressure which can be accurately mixed with the incoming air to provide for clean, efficient engine operation.

- The major components found on most NGVs are: high pressure fuel storage cylinder(s), high and low pressure fuel lines, manual shutoff valve, fuel lockoff device, fuel fill receptacle, pressure regulator(s), fuel mixer (fixed or variable venturi), electronic feedback system, and a fuel monitoring and selection system.

- A conversion system must be selected based on a number of options and installation restrictions.

- Fuel delivery options include: variable venturi mixer, fixed venturi mixer, fumigation system, or a direct injection system.

- Electronic system options include: emissions feedback type, timing adaptation system, fuel selection system, fuel monitoring system, and the use of computer "fixes."

- Fuel storage cylinder options include: type, size, number, and location.

- Installation requirements and restrictions include: cylinder location, type of fuel lines, routing of fuel lines, fuel line connectors, and numerous labels.

REVIEW QUESTIONS

1. Explain the effects of using alternative fuels in the transportation sector in the United States.

2. What alternative fuels are currently being used in the United States?

3. List three advantages and three disadvantages for each of the alternative fuels currently in use.

4. Describe the difference between a bi-fuel vehicle, flexible fuel vehicle, and a dedicated fuel vehicle.

5. Name the federal polices which affect the use of alternative fuels and describe their impact.

6. Name the regulatory agencies and explain their responsibilities in governing the use of CNG.

7. Identify the basic components that will be found on every CNG system.

8. Briefly describe the purpose of each basic conversion system component.

9. What factors are involved when considering a vehicle for CNG conversion and why are they important?

10. Define the various options which may be available from conversion system manufacturers.

CHAPTER **2**

NGV Conversion Components and Procedures

OBJECTIVES

- Determine a safe and practical location for all of the necessary conversion components.
- Understand what options are available for fuel cylinder selection and proper placement.
- Determine the type and routing of the fuel lines.
- Understand the safe use and service of high pressure fuel lines and connectors.
- Determine the purpose and location of the manual shutoff valve.
- Determine the purpose and location of the primary regulator.
- Determine the purpose, location, and type of fuel lockoff device to be used.
- Determine the purpose and location of the secondary fuel pressure regulator.
- Determine the purpose, location, and type of the fuel mixer to be used.
- Determine the location of the necessary wiring and electronic components.
- Understand some of the options available when selecting a conversion system.
- Understand what special equipment is needed for handling CNG and why.
- Understand the safety procedures involved in operating an NGV.
- Understand the safety procedures and equipment involved when refilling an NGV.
- Understand the safety precautions necessary for servicing an NGV.
- Know the NFPA guidelines governing the location and installation of conversion components where applicable.
- Know the proper procedure for correct installation of conversion components.
- Describe the engine and system testing procedure.

KEY TERMS

Fill valve
Pressure relief device (PRD)
Lockoff device
High pressure regulator
Second-stage regulator
Fixed venturi mixer
Variable venturi mixer
Closed loop

Open loop
Fumigation
Speed-density
Pulsewidth modulated
Acoustic emissions
Safety factor
Adaptive learning

DESIGN AND LAYOUT OF CONVERSION SYSTEM COMPONENTS

The design and layout section is where you mentally assemble all of the components of the conversion system. It is highly recommended that you make notes and sketches that will help you visualize how the system will be assembled and installed. In hopes of minimizing the costly effects of "Murphy's Law," it is wise to be thorough in designing and laying out the system. Before beginning the conversion, it will be necessary to have on hand such equipment as: various compression fittings, pressure gauges, leak detectors, tube benders, tube cutters, a four- or five-gas analyzer, good shop lighting, and, if possible, a chassis dynamometer.

LOCATION AND LAYOUT OF FUEL CYLINDER(S)

Discussed earlier were some of the options available for fuel cylinders and some of the considerations for mounting the fuel cylinder(s). Bearing those factors in mind, double-check to make sure the fuel cylinder(s) will fit, and that the place and position selected are appropriate.

When designing the fuel cylinder fit, try to imagine the most extreme situation the vehicle may experience, such as a high speed collision. Section 3-3 of NFPA 52 suggests a complete list of safety considerations including details on recommended practices. If you are not yet familiar with them, read all of them. Remember that during a collision the most vulnerable element of the fuel cylinder mount is the cylinder valve.

For design and layout purposes, consider the following factors:

- Is the fuel cylinder valve protected; i.e., with a PRD (pressure relief device) and associated fittings?

- If the fuel cylinder is going to be mounted in the vehicle compartment, is there a plan for all connectors to be vented?

- Is the fuel cylinder(s) placed in a manner that will provide for minimal damage during collision? The recommended placement is behind the front axle and in front of the rear bumper.

- Is there adequate road clearance if the fuel cylinder is mounted under the vehicle? NFPA 52, Section 3-3.12, states that there must be at least seven inches of clearance for a vehicle with a wheelbase of less than 127 inches (most passenger cars, pickup trucks, and vans fit this category) and nine inches of clearance for a vehicle that has a wheelbase greater than 127 inches.

- Consider the angle from the tire print to the front and rear bumpers.

- Is there clear access to the other side of the mounting surface and/or is there anything of importance that could be damaged there? In some cases the mounting brackets require reinforcement plates to

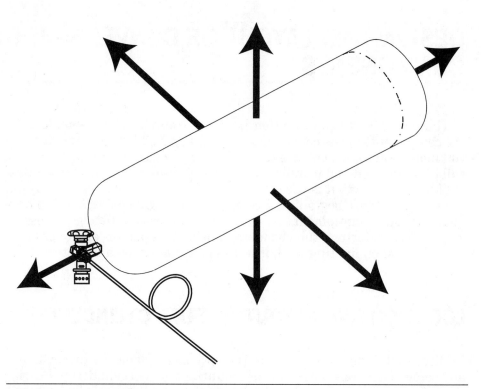

Figure 2.1 Six directions for stress test

be placed on both sides of the selected frame areas. In no case is single-wall sheet metal sufficient.

- Are the fuel cylinder(s) easy to guard, shield, and vent (if necessary)? The fuel cylinder(s) mounting location(s) must include suitable surfaces and room for mounting the shields, guards, and vents.

- Is there a good route for the fuel line, connections, stress loops, or valves to reach the fuel cylinder(s)?

- Is the intended mounting surface sturdy enough for the fuel cylinder(s)?

- Is the entire fuel cylinder(s) mounting apparatus sturdy enough to stay in place with a force of eight times the fully pressurized weight of the cylinder(s) in all six directions (Figure 2.1) with a maximum displacement of 1/2 inch?

- Is there space to install the venting system? Where will the system vent? Is the vent tube route clear of obstructions?

- Is there enough space for the mounting brackets? The brackets are larger than the fuel cylinder(s) and require extra room for the flanges that must be bolted together.

- Will the shape of the brackets allow the fuel cylinder(s) to be installed once the brackets are bolted down? The orientation of the installed brackets may be such that the brackets will interfere with placing the fuel cylinder(s) into the brackets (Figures 2.2 and 2.3).

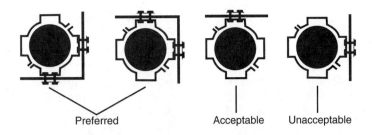

Preferred   Acceptable   Unacceptable

Figure 2.2 Proper and improper cylinder mounting procedures *(Courtesy CNG Cylinder Company)*

- As specified in NFPA 52 (1995), Section 3-3.1, containers shall be protected with a shield to prevent damage that can occur due to road hazards, loading, unloading, direct sunlight, and use of the vehicle. The shield shall be installed to prevent contact of the shield with the container and entrapment of materials that could damage the container or its coating.

- As specified in NFPA 52 (1995), Section 3-12.6, where a CNG container is removed from a vehicle in order to be installed within a different vehicle, it shall be inspected or retested in accordance with the inspection or requalification procedures of the standard under which it was originally manufactured before it is reinstalled.

FMVS 303, passed by NHTSA, applies to new vehicles manufactured by original equipment manufacturers or to converted vehicles. The standard applies to passenger cars, multipurpose passenger vehicles, trucks, and buses that have a gross vehicle weight rating of 10,000 pounds or less and use CNG as a motor fuel. Converters and upfitters must ensure that they have not rendered any of the converted vehicle's safety equipment inoperable. According to NHTSA, the converter of vehicles manufactured after September 1, 1995 must attest that the NGV fuel system they install does not leak more than federal standards allow. If NHTSA determines any of the equipment is defective, it has the authority to require manufacturers or converters to replace the equipment.

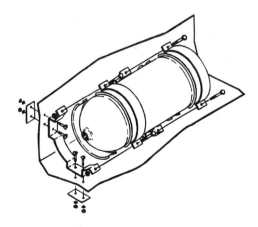

Figure 2.3 Cylinder bracket assembly *(Courtesy CNG Cylinder Company)*

Types of Fuel Cylinders

There are three types of fuel cylinders available: (1) steel, (2) aluminum/steel composites, and (3) full composite. The steel cylinders are the original fuel containers. The test date is traditionally stamped on the top of the steel cylinders; however, it is located on the wrapped area of a composite cylinder. To achieve higher pressures, the steel or aluminum cylinders are wrapped in a composite material, commonly fiberglass. Cylinders wrapped in a fiberglass composite material can accommodate a greater range of pressures, typically 3,000 psi to 3,600 psi. The higher pressure cylinders may be partly or entirely wrapped in a composite material. The main advantage of aluminum cylinders is the decrease in weight. The full composite cylinders contain no metal and are made from a combination of layered materials. Full composite cylinders are also some of the lightest and most expensive cylinders available.

While there may be a nominal 12-inch diameter cylinder available in each of the material types, it is important to note that not all 12-inch diameter cylinders will have the same outside diameter. This is especially important when choosing mounting brackets. Different cylinder sizes require specific mounting brackets. Use the cylinder manufacturer's recommendations for the correct cylinder/bracket fit. One future possibility is to have the cylinders become part of the vehicle superstructure. This technology is being researched by various manufacturers.

Storage Space Versus Fuel Cylinder Placement

Before settling on the placement of the fuel cylinder(s), consider that the space the fuel cylinder(s) will occupy may also be needed for storage or cargo. Remember to consider more than just the physical space the cylinder occupies; consider ground clearance, shields, and heat shields. Cylinders require eight inches of distance from any heat source. The expense of the fuel cylinder(s) is the other logical limitation of what size(s) of fuel cylinder(s) you will need.

If the minimum fuel cylinder requirement interferes with cargo capacity, then a certain amount of creativity may be needed. Fuel cylinders can be mounted in many different configurations. They can be mounted horizontally, vertically, or in bundles. Figures 2.4, 2.5, 2.6, 2.7, 2.8, and 2.9 illustrate several possible mountings.

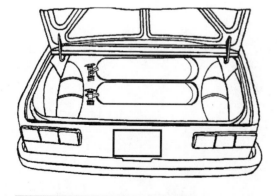

Figure 2.4 Cylinders installed in car trunk

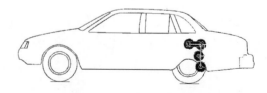

Figure 2.5 Cylinders in stack formation in rear of car

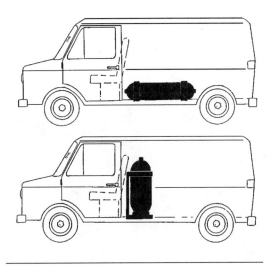

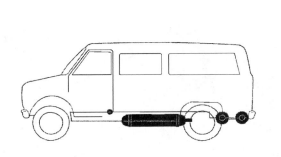

Figure 2.6 Cylinders mounted underneath van

Figure 2.7 Cylinders mounted inside vans

ROUTE AND LAYOUT OF THE FUEL LINE(S)

Having found a suitable placement for the fuel cylinders, the next thing to consider is the layout of the fuel lines. The fuel line serves as the path to fill the fuel cylinder(s) when refueling and to supply fuel to the engine. It is difficult to plan the route of the fuel line to the regulators, filling connections, bulkheads, and other connections when you have not yet determined where these components will be placed. Likewise, it would be difficult to lay out the components without planning the route of the fuel line first. These considerations emphasize why careful planning and layout are critical to the conversion procedure.

The fuel lines are typically welded or seamless stainless steel. Fuel line route planning has considerations similar to fuel cylinder layout. Where possible, route fuel lines along the inside of the frame rails or body components where they will be protected. Plan on placing fuel line clamps at least every two feet (Figure 2.10). Suitable mounting surfaces should be free of rust, have adequate access to the other side of the mounting surface (which should be free of other essential parts), have adequate

Components and Line Fit

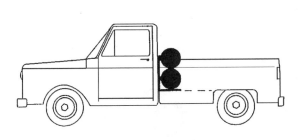

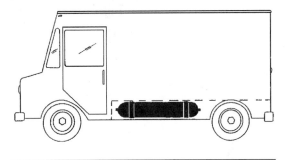

Figure 2.8 Cylinders mounted in bed of pickup truck

Figure 2.9 Cylinder loaded inside cargo truck

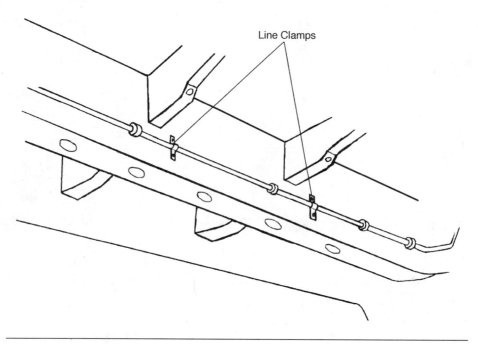

Figure 2.10 Fuel line installed along frame with line clamps

ground clearance, and be easy to guard and shield, if applicable. (See NFPA 52, Section 3-5, for specific fuel line shielding practices.)

The fuel line should be routed in a position where the flexing, bending, or twisting motions of the vehicle body will not shear off or otherwise eventually damage the fuel line. The location of safety valves, the manual shutoff valve, and the fuel receptacle must also take into consideration how the body of the vehicle may twist and flex. The fuel receptacle can typically be found in the engine compartment on bi-fuel vehicles and in the gasoline fuel receptacle on dedicated NGVs. However, there are many options regarding where to place the fuel receptacle (Figure 2.11).

There are also tricks and tips to consider when laying out the fuel line. The use of a bulkhead connector can save pulling a bent line through a small awkward hole. Remember to use a bulkhead connector or grommet wherever the fuel line passes through a frame member or body component (Figure 2.12). Remember that the frames of vehicles are carefully designed, so take extra time to *think* about where you are planning to drill a hole. Specifically, will it weaken the frame?

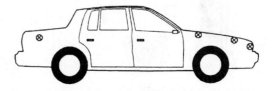

Figure 2.11 Possible fuel receptacle locations

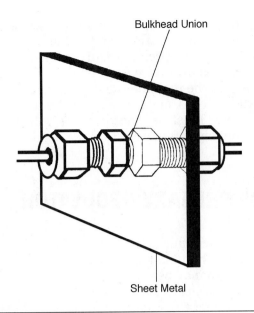

Figure 2.12 Bulkhead connector through sheet metal

LOCATION OF MANUAL SHUTOFF VALVE

The manual shutoff valve is a safety device consisting of a quarter-turn valve that is typically placed outside of the vehicle under the driver's door (see NFPA, Section 3-6) for easy access outside of the vehicle (Figure 2.13). The rationale for this valve is to have a readily accessible shutoff valve in times of an emergency or equipment failure.

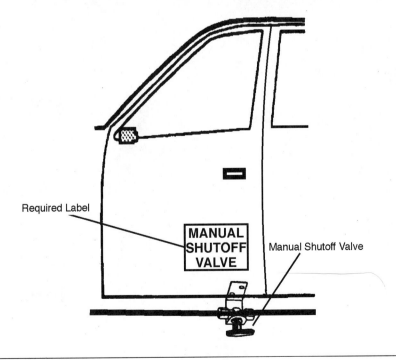

Figure 2.13 Typical location of manual shutoff valve

Fit of Manual Shutoff Valve

When planning the layout, check for availability of suitable mounting surfaces (use the same considerations as for the fuel cylinders and fuel lines). There may also be specific requirements, such as the DOT requirements for vehicles in service for school carriers. Check with your state DOT. Be sure that the fuel line route accommodates the placement of the manual shutoff valve. Consider putting a guard or shield over it, if applicable. Also, a decal must be placed on the vehicle to point out the location of the manual shutoff valve.

LOCATION OF PRIMARY REGULATOR

The primary regulator reduces the fuel line pressure to approximately 100 psi. The primary regulator also features multiple inlets and outlets, of which one or two may be unused and plugged prior to mounting. The primary regulator typically has National Pipe Threads (NPT). Also, consider the orientation of the regulator for proper access to the adjustments and the placement of the fuel lines. It is not recommended to use the primary regulator as a route from the filling connector to the storage cylinder.

Most NGV regulators (Figure 2.14) incorporate a diaphragm design that uses the atmosphere as a reference for the pressure drop (do not obstruct the hole for atmospheric reference). Because the pressure is dropping when the natural gas is expanding, the expanding of the gas absorbs heat. The gas expanding in the regulator takes heat from the

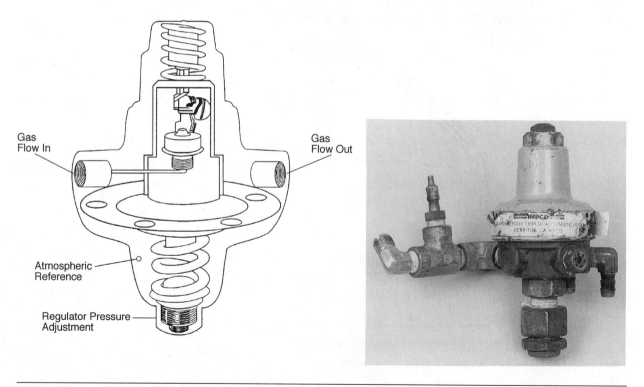

Gas Flow In

Gas Flow Out

Atmospheric Reference

Regulator Pressure Adjustment

Figure 2.14 Primary regulator cross section *(Courtesy Thermadyne, Inc.)*. *Photo:* High pressure regulator

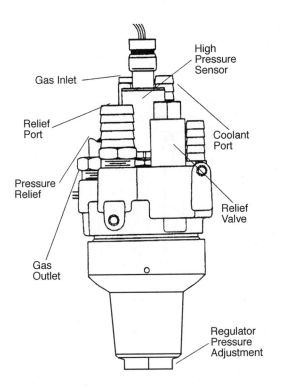

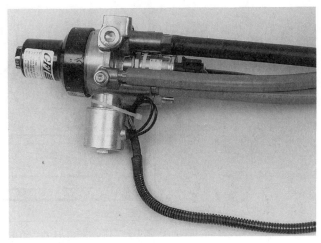

Figure 2.15 Primary regulator components. *Photo:* Primary regulator

surrounding materials and the regulator cools. To prevent frosting or freezing of the regulator, engine coolant is circulated through the primary regulator (Figure 2.15). This engine coolant circuit is typically spliced into the heater core lines and is usually routed through the housing of the primary regulator. Section 3-8 of NFPA 52 suggests regulator guidelines. Please read them.

When you plan the layout (Figure 2.16), several factors must be considered in selecting suitable mounting surfaces, including: (1) the primary regulator and associated brackets (consider what is on the other side of the chosen surface prior to mounting), (2) the fuel line in/out, and (3) the coolant lines with associated mounting brackets and points of origin (usually spliced into the heater core lines). Some systems incorporate "Y" splices instead of "T" splices. "Y" splices are directional.

Fit of Regulators

LOCATION OF FUEL LOCKOFF

The fuel lockoff is an important component designed for leak prevention and fire control in accidents. The fuel lockoff is an automatic means of stopping the flow of natural gas from reaching the engine when it is not running. This is accomplished by either (1) a vacuum sensing lockoff valve (see Figure 1.13) or (2) an electrical solenoid lockoff valve (see Figure 1.14). A complete system consisting of a primary regulator, fuel lockoff, and secondary regulator is shown in Figure 2.17. A vacuum sensing fuel

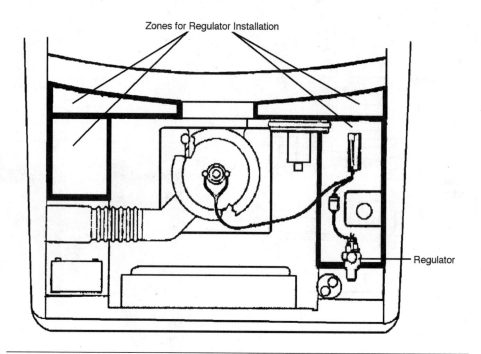

Figure 2.16 Zones for regulator installation

lockoff valve is a diaphragm that is opened by the vacuum formed in the intake manifold; hence the key can be in the ON or OFF position and natural gas will not flow into the engine compartment.

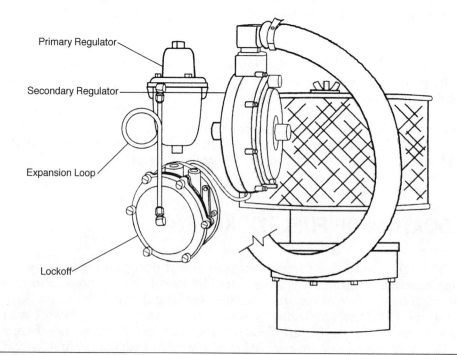

Figure 2.17 Regulators and lockoff assembly

The electrical valve is a solenoid that is normally closed. It is only opened by the ignition circuit. This lockoff can be placed in the high or low pressure fuel lines or, possibly, in the primary regulator. The Canadian Gas Association (CGA) specifies a similar system, although theirs must be placed in the high pressure fuel line near the fuel cylinders. The CGA version is likely to be the standard that will be adopted as the new "North American" IAS certification standard.

LOCATION OF SECONDARY REGULATOR

The secondary regulator drops the fuel line pressure from roughly 100 psi to approximately three ounces to five ounces of pressure per square inch in a variable venturi mixer system or close to zero in a fixed venturi mixer system. The secondary regulator has adjustments that may need to be accessed (Figures 2.18 and 2.19). The regulator is a diaphragm regulator and uses the atmosphere as a reference for the pressure drop (do not obstruct the hole for the reference). Section 3-8 of NFPA 52 suggests regulator installation guidelines.

Note: The secondary regulator is not needed with fuel injection systems and is included as a package with the primary regulator in other systems.

It is important to follow the manufacturer's recommendations for orientation or stalling may result from deceleration or sudden acceleration. Also, the secondary mixer may have an oil drain outlet that should face

Fit of Secondary Regulator

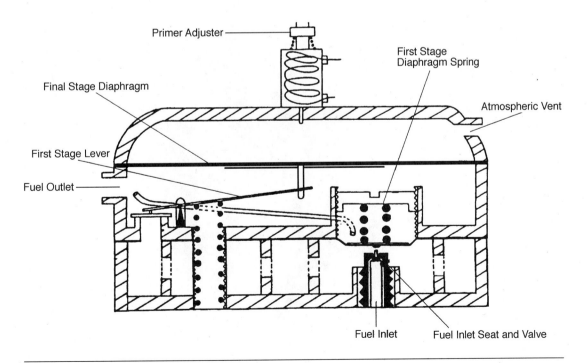

Figure 2.18 Secondary regulator *(Courtesy IMPCO Technologies, Inc.)*

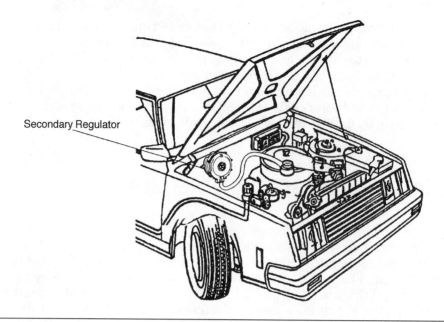

Figure 2.19 Secondary regulator installed *(Courtesy IMPCO Technologies, Inc.)*

downward to drain any condensation that accumulates. Other designs may recommend that the vapor hose be placed at the six o'clock position to drain the accumulated condensation and oil.

An additional consideration with multistage regulators may be the orientation with respect to vehicle movement. It is recommended by the manufacturer that the regulator package in Figure 2.20 be positioned perpendicular to the line of travel.

Figure 2.20 Inertial forces affecting regulator performance must be considered

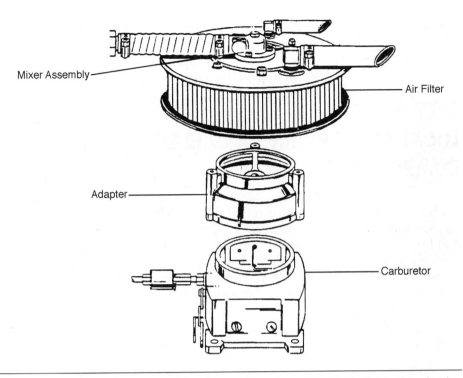

Figure 2.21 Mixer assembly with adapter *(Courtesy IMPCO Technologies, Inc.)*

LOCATION OF MIXER/FUEL INJECTION SYSTEM

The layout for the mixer, spray bar, and nozzle or injectors is primarily concerned with two factors: Is there room and where will the fuel line be routed? The layout must consider where the electrical wiring is routed and where to splice into the control circuit. Mixers, spray bars, nozzles, or fixed venturis are mounted above (before) the carburetor in a bi-fuel system. Adapters may already be available (Figure 2.21). If not, the installer may have to perform some fabrication. Often, the amount of clearance between the air cleaner cover and the mixer prohibits easy, straightforward mounts. Because of tight above-engine spaces, routing the fuel line may also be tricky.

Check for availability of suitable mounting surfaces, usually in/on the air cleaner. EPA rules will not permit any modification of emission control equipment. This applies to specially made air cleaners designed for easier mounting. Be careful to retain any existing preheat tubes, etc., on the original equipment. In some cases the mixer will require that the throat of the intake be shifted with special intake castings. Layout planning should include a means of securely attaching the mixer. The vapor hose route should be in the open. Do not route the vapor hose against the exhaust manifold, fan, or belts, or on top of anything that may pinch the vapor hose when closing the hood. According to NFPA 52, Section 3-2.4, the vapor hose must be labeled.

Check Fit of Mixer/Fuel Injection System

Note: Derive a plan for a PCV (positive crankcase ventilation) intake that is filtered and not downstream from the mixer/injector(s). Remember that there is now a fuel mixture in the air cleaner, and this should not be routed into the crankcase.

LOCATION OF WIRING AND ELECTRONIC COMPONENTS

Many systems require electronic modifications. These modifications include closed feedback systems for improved emissions performance and power, timing changes, and false code protection. Because most new vehicles feature digital electronic systems, the tolerance of the electrical signals must be tighter. Most electrical problems encountered probably will be due to poor connections (which increase resistance and drop the voltage enough to alter the signal).

Check Fit of Wiring and Electronic Components

When designing the layout for the electrical connections, look for spaces that: (1) are suitable mounting surfaces for electrical components, (2) are easy to guard and shield from moisture and vibration, (3) offer enough room to work where splices must be made, (4) allow for neat wire routing (use OEM layouts as a guide), (5) allow for accessibility to the timing apparatus, (6) allow for placement of the dashboard meters in clear view of the driver (and that they can actually be mounted where you want to put them), and (7) allow for placement of the switches where they can be reached, but not accidentally tripped or damaged.

Note: Watch out for magnetic fields and induction problems from secondary wiring.

SELECTING AN NGV CONVERSION SYSTEM

The market for natural gas vehicles is growing rapidly. The technologies that support natural gas vehicles are diverse and changing. Tighter emissions expectations have brought about improvements in the performance of NGVs and are, consequently, introducing entirely new design concepts to the natural gas vehicle industry.

ORDERING THE PROPER EQUIPMENT

Many NGV system manufacturers and suppliers have developed retrofit systems but few have produced custom-designed systems. If possible, install a system specifically designed for the vehicle being converted. Installation convenience and operating efficiency improve when you use a custom-designed NGV conversion system. Most companies request vehicle parameters with an order so they can provide a system that comes closest to meeting the vehicle's standards.

The term *kit* can be misleading. Although the major NGV components and accessories are purchased and delivered in a single package, it is not uncommon to discover unneeded parts or to have to purchase additional hardware. Because the structure and design of vehicles vary, the requirements for vehicle conversion also vary. The NGV conversion specialist must be a good designer, craftsman, and problem solver.

RECORD KEEPING BEGINS BEFORE INSTALLATION

One of the advantages of an NGV conversion is that the vehicle can be reconverted to operate exclusively on gasoline. A fleet can reuse the same NGV components on a succession of vehicles as old vehicles are replaced. The original investment in NGV conversion systems may transcend the lifetimes of many vehicles.

It is important to keep up-to-date and accurate records throughout the life of a conversion system. Any parts removed from the vehicle being converted should be labeled, packaged, and stored in a safe location for possible reinstallation later. Record the following information before beginning the conversion:

- date of the conversion

- make and model of the vehicle being converted

- serial number (VIN) of the vehicle

- name of the vehicle owner

- company and date of purchase of conversion system

- list of the conversion system components

- model and serial numbers of the conversion system components (e.g., fuel cylinder(s) test date stamp)

Alternative fuel conversions will now have to meet the same emissions and warranty standards as the OEM systems. Manufacturers are thus tailoring systems for specific engine families, and the systems are only warranted under that engine family or system combination.

REVIEW OF BASIC COMPONENTS REQUIRED FOR AN NGV CONVERSION

Relatively few additional components are needed for a vehicle to operate on compressed natural gas. As discussed in the previous chapter, the basic components include:

- NGV fuel cylinders

- high pressure fuel lines

- pressure reducers, referred to as *regulators* or *converters*

- gas/air mixer or fuel injectors

- safety valves

- fuel gauge

- wiring and electronic components

The vehicle's spark timing may be modified. Bi-fuel vehicles require a few more components, such as a timing modification device and a fuel selector switch. Other components may be necessary depending on vehicle type and performance demands.

NGV CONVERSION SYSTEM FUNCTION

Understanding the functional characteristics of an NGV with a carbureted engine versus one with a fuel injected engine is important in the selection of a proper NGV conversion system.

Figure 2.22 illustrates the location of various NGV components on an NGV with a carbureted engine. Natural gas enters the vehicle through the **fill valve**. The gas then enters the NGV **fuel cylinders**, where it is stored at approximately 2,400 psi to 3,600 psi. When fuel is needed, natural gas flows out of the cylinders past a **pressure relief device (PRD)**. The PRD is a safety device that releases gas harmlessly into the atmosphere if the pressure and/or temperature exceeds a safety standard.

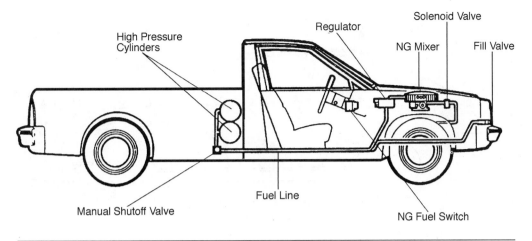

Figure 2.22 NGV components—carbureted engine

After the gas passes the PRD and the cylinder valve, it enters a stainless steel high pressure **fuel line**. Depending on the **lockoff device** contained in the conversion system, a fuel lockoff solenoid may be the next device the gas passes through. The compressed natural gas is then channeled through a **master shutoff valve**, from which the gas then flows into the fuel line in the engine compartment. As the compressed gas enters the engine compartment, it flows through a **high pressure regulator**. The high pressure regulator reduces the fuel pressure to approximately 100 psi.

The fuel then flows through the natural gas **shutoff solenoid**, which stops the flow of natural gas when the engine is either off or operating on gasoline. If the system is a mechanical-mixer style, the fuel then enters a **second-stage regulator**, which further reduces the fuel from 100 psi to near atmospheric pressure. The fuel must now enter the **gas/air mixer**, where the vacuum of the engine determines how much air to mix with the natural gas. If it is a fumigation system, there may not be any further need to drop the pressure. A manifold with natural gas fuel injectors mounted in it will release the appropriate amount of fuel based on information collected from the engine's sensors. The fuel is introduced into the engine generally at the throat of the intake manifold. The fuel finally enters the engine and is combusted.

In addition to the fuel delivery system, a few electrical components must be installed. A **fuel selector switch** (located on the dashboard) is necessary for the driver to select which fuel source to use. When gasoline is selected, the natural gas system automatically shuts off and the conventional gasoline system begins operating. A **timing modification device** is sometimes used to advance the spark timing when the vehicle is operating on natural gas and to return it to normal when gasoline is used. An additional **fuel gauge** is needed to monitor natural gas fuel availability. In closed loop systems, the vehicle's electronic control module and a variety of sensors are usually wired in to the NGV conversion.

Figure 2.23 illustrates the location of NGV components on an NGV with a fuel injected engine. The gas delivery system for the fuel injected engine is similar to that of the carbureted engine until the gas passes

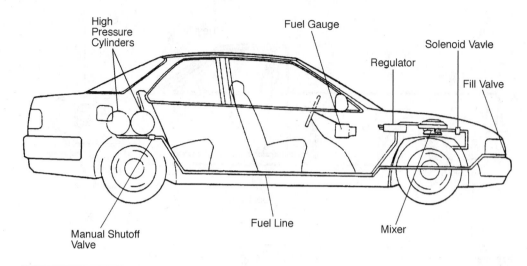

High
Pressure
Cylinders

Fuel Gauge

Solenoid Vavle

Regulator

Fill Valve

Manual Shutoff
Valve

Fuel Line

Mixer

Figure 2.23 NGV components—fuel injected engine

through the first-stage regulator. The second-stage regulator, the gas/air mixer, and sometimes the timing modification device are eliminated and replaced by a series of **fuel injectors** and an **NGV system control unit**. Fuel exits the regulator at a constant pressure, ranging from approximately 40 psi to 70 psi. The NGV system control unit determines the engine's instantaneous fuel requirements, activates the appropriate combination of fuel injectors, and automatically adjusts the ignition timing. The fuel enters into the engine's intake air stream. The fuel finally enters the engine's combustion chamber where it is ignited.

CONVERSION SYSTEM OPTIONS

Open Loop NGV Systems

The open loop systems developed for early NGV operation provided an acceptable level of performance for vehicles that did not have computer controls. These systems generally worked well, but had a major drawback: Conversion systems could be adjusted so that vehicle emissions were in violation of mandated emissions levels. These NGV conversion systems are often referred to as *first generation* or *core technology* systems. Much of the credit for development of these early systems goes to other countries, particularly Italy and New Zealand, which have a long history of natural gas vehicle use. The most common types of open loop systems are the *fixed venturi mixer* and *variable venturi mixer*.

Fixed Venturi Mixer

The fixed venturi mixer system depends on a vacuum signal to initiate the flow of natural gas to the engine. Flow does not start until the engine is cranked. When the engine is running, the air passing the fixed venturi mixer (which is mounted on top of the intake manifold) forms a vacuum and activates the regulator diaphragms. The vacuum from the engine regulates the flow of gas depending on the position of the throttle. Additional gas flow may be supplied by a power valve solenoid to provide for situations requiring full power. This type of system may also be referred to as a *zero* or *negative pressure system.*

Variable Venturi Mixer

The variable venturi system permits the flow of natural gas from the regulator as soon as the ignition is switched on. The gas flows to a mixer that is located at the carburetor throttle plate. When the engine is running, the gas flow is regulated by a difference in pressure between the engine's intake manifold and the atmosphere. The regulator and mixer diaphragms will move according to changes in atmospheric pressure. Change in the intake manifold pressure will open or close a valve, which maintains the fuel flow. Typically, there is a spring adjustment setting for rich/lean mix on this type of system. This type of system may also be referred to as a *positive pressure system.*

Closed Loop NGV Systems

While performance was acceptable in open loop systems, the driveability and emissions levels were not as acceptable as with the closed loop NGV systems. Closed loop NGV systems, similar to recent gasoline systems, incorporate a method of monitoring the O_2 sensor and adjusting fuel flow according to exhaust gas oxygen readings. This allows a more precise control of both emissions and performance. Many manufacturers use a computer during installation to customize the system to a particular engine/vehicle classification. This helps make the systems tamper-proof.

The majority of the closed loop systems are fumigation (fuel injection) based. The fumigation systems all share some common "under-the-hood" components. They all have some form of remote injector or injector manifold. The injectors are controlled by an NGV system control unit (provided with the system). The control unit is wired into the OEM electronic control unit and sensors. The information collected from the OEM electronic control unit and sensors determines the exact amount of fuel the injector(s) will release. The gas that is released from the injectors typically enters the intake manifold through the throat of the carburetor (similar to a throttle body) or through a venturi ring mounted on top of the intake manifold. Often, the venturi ring is referred to as a *mixer* because it is where the natural gas and air mix.

The following are examples of closed loop systems that may be available in your region. While they are all of the same class, they vary in components and function. Consider your vehicle requirements when selecting an NGV conversion system. (A discussion of specific commercial NGV closed loop systems is included in Chapter 3 in the section, "Electronic Control Systems.") As might be expected, conversion system manufacturers have their own marketing jargon. The jargon is not necessarily the same throughout the industry. Some of the more popular terms are presented.

Example #1

This is a computer-controlled (NGV system control unit), closed loop, adaptive learn (automatically adjusts to fuel energy content and driving styles) conversion system. Utilizing the speed-density principle (a means of determining how much natural gas is entering the intake manifold by measuring the differences in pressure and temperature for a given rpm),

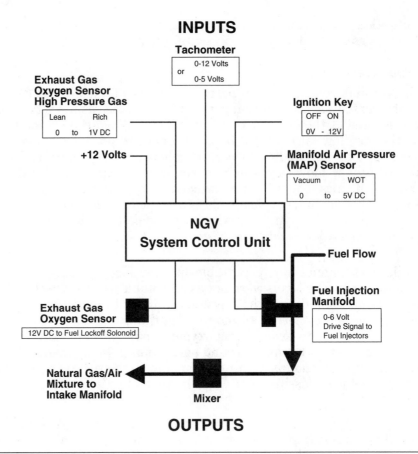

INPUTS

Tachometer

0-12 Volts
or
0-5 Volts

**Exhaust Gas
Oxygen Sensor
High Pressure Gas**

Lean	Rich
0 to	1V DC

Ignition Key

OFF	ON
0V - 12V	

+12 Volts

**Manifold Air Pressure
(MAP) Sensor**

Vacuum	WOT
0 to	5V DC

**NGV
System Control Unit**

Fuel Flow

**Fuel Injection
Manifold**

| 0-6 Volt
Drive Signal to
Fuel Injectors |
|---|

**Exhaust Gas
Oxygen Sensor**

12V DC to Fuel Lockoff Solonoid

**Natural Gas/Air
Mixture to
Intake Manifold**

Mixer

OUTPUTS

Figure 2.24 Schematic of Example #1 *(Courtesy Automotive Natural Gas, Inc.)*

software adjusts a fuel metering valve position in the gas flow to preset oxygen sensor switch points for different engine speeds and loads. It incorporates an automatic fuel selector (automatically switches between natural gas and gasoline) using the existing dash gauge for bi-fuel applications. This system uses a standard D-type regulator package that includes a first stage and a second stage with a fixed venturi mixer ring or nozzle combination.

Components:

- regulator package

- electronic control module (ECM)

- fuel metering valve

- mixer (just a ring on top of the manifold where the natural gas enters the engine)

- automatic fuel selector (automatically switches between natural gas and gasoline)

Figure 2.24 provides a schematic of Example #1.

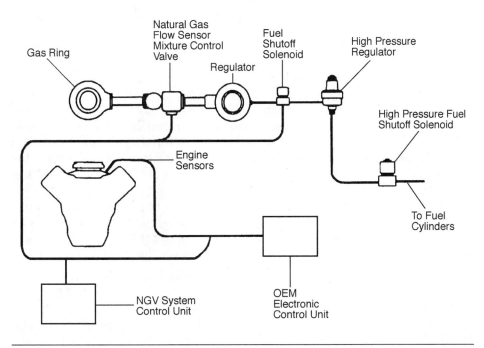

Figure 2.25 Diagram of Example #2

Example #2

Example #2 is a microprocessor-based engine management system utilizing the gas mass measuring method. This is the same method used by most automobile manufacturers in original equipment. The onboard signals are transferred to the computer (NGV system control unit) along with a signal from a gaseous fuel mass flow sensor of natural gas into the engine. The computer processes the signals to provide a precise natural gas/air mixture. An electrical interface module is inserted between the vehicle's computer and the NG computer. It includes adaptive learning capability which adjusts for variations among engines, long-term changes in operating conditions, and degradation in the engine or conversion system. The system is available for both NG and propane.

Components:

• electronic control unit (ECU)

• high/low pressure fuel shutoff solenoid

• high/low pressure regulators

• air temperature sensor

• natural gas flow sensor

• mixture control valve (fuel injectors)

• gas distribution ring

Figure 2.25 is a diagram of Example #2.

Example #3

This type of system electronically meters fuel, controls spark advance, and registers natural gas fuel storage pressure on the OEM fuel gauge. A combination of OEM and NG sensors is used to monitor the engine and environment to provide closed loop control of fuel. This system is designed to automatically return the engine to gasoline operation when the fuel storage pressure drops below a minimum level. The system is fully programmable by way of an external personal computer. It uses a speed-density calculation for both fuel flow and air flow and calculates for air/fuel mixture based on a stoichiometric value of the fuel composition in the area of operation. Speed-density calculations are based on temperature, pressure, fuel absolute pressure, and fuel regulated temperature. These sensors are located in a metering valve (injector manifold). The intake air temperature sensor is mounted in the intake system, and a manifold skin temperature sensor is mounted on the intake manifold.

A high pressure natural gas line supplies fuel to a single-stage regulator. The regulator reduces pressure to approximately 100 psi. Once the fuel flows through the regulator, the natural gas is passed on to a special fuel filter and into the computer/metering valve (CompuValve). The CompuValve then regulates fuel flow by means of a series of electronically controlled solenoids and injectors. After flowing through the CompuValve, the natural gas is sent to a spray discharge unit(s) located in the engine's air intake.

This system is also available for propane conversions. The difference is that the system uses six solenoids for propane conversions and only five for natural gas conversions, and includes an additional vaporizer section for conversion of liquid propane to a gas.

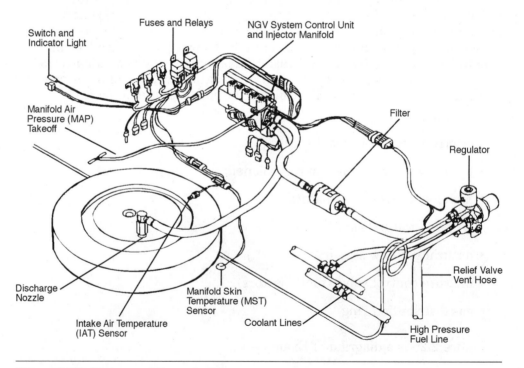

Figure 2.26 Diagram of Example #3

Components:

- CompuValve (NGV system control unit and injectors mounted together)

- filter

- regulator

- manifold skin temperature (MST) sensor

- intake air temperature (IAT) sensor

- discharge nozzle(s) or spray bar

- switch and indicator light

- fuses and relays

Figure 2.26 is a diagram of Example #3.

Example #4

Example #4 is a fuel injection system incorporating an electronic calibrator module that provides optimized performance and fuel economy for General Motors engines converted to operate on compressed natural gas. The module is installed in the original engine electronic control module (ECM) in existing pin sockets and is specifically designed to optimize natural gas vehicles by increasing engine power, improving driveability, and extending vehicle range. The module is fully compatible with

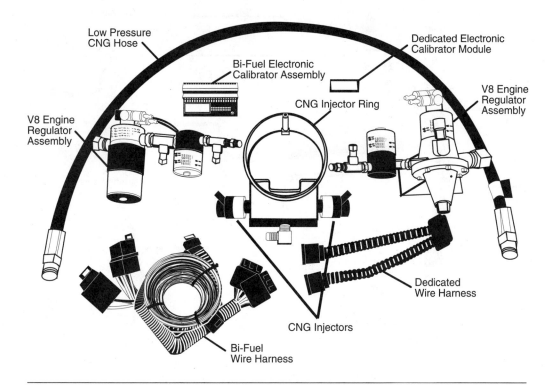

Figure 2.27 Diagram of Example #4 *(Courtesy Baytech Corporation)*

the ECM, eliminating the need for additional external systems commonly used for spark advance control and diagnostic code capability.

The bi-fuel module software provides specific natural gas engine calibration parameters when operating on natural gas without affecting operation on gasoline. The module has demonstrated 20% to 30% increases in fuel economy. In some applications the module has demonstrated horsepower increases of 5 hp to 10 hp over the stock gasoline engine before conversion. The fuel calibration mode is selected via an external switch or relay.

The module meets federal and California emissions standards and is certified by the California Air Resources Board (CARB) when installed as part of the CARB-approved conversion systems for bi-fuel and dedicated NGVs. Figure 2.27 is a diagram of Example #4.

Example #5

Example #5 is a closed loop, stand-alone engine control system that works independently of the vehicle's original equipment computer, and is compatible with all other original control functions. When switched to the natural gas mode, the controller activates the relays that disconnect the gasoline fuel injectors and fuel pump and activate the natural gas fuel system. A time delay is provided for the transition both into and out of the natural gas mode to account for transport delay time of gasoline compared to natural gas and to provide smooth switching between fuels.

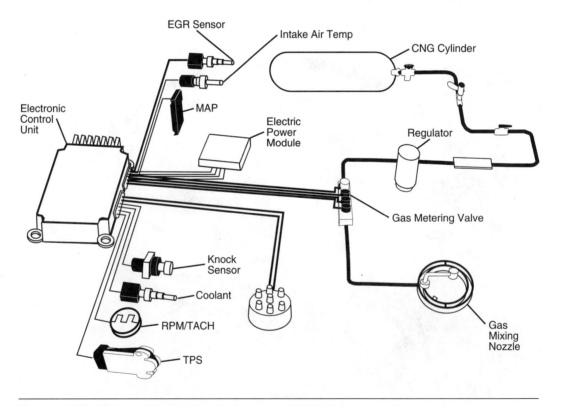

Figure 2.28 Diagram of Example #5 *(Courtesy MESA Environmental)*

Fuel metering is based on speed-density calculations. The fuel is metered through pulsewidth modulated injectors, fired in sequence to provide a near continuous flow of fuel to the engine. Fuel pressure is regulated by a single high pressure regulator. Example #5's processor can compensate for differences in Btu content between fuels and control within 35% of stoichiometric. The system can also be used on propane-fueled and lean-burn engines. Other Example #5 system features include self-diagnostic capability and sensor default to ensure "limp-home" capability.

Components:

- electronic control unit with EEPROM (NGV) system control unit

- power module (fuses and relays)

- gas metering valve (fuel injectors) with master fuel shutoff solenoid

- in-line coalescing filter

- high pressure regulator with temperature and pressure sensors

- gas mixing ring or nozzle

Figure 2.28 is a diagram of Example #5.

Example #6

Example #6 is an O_2 sensor-driven feedback system. It maintains an ideal air/fuel ratio that fulfills the OEM computer expectations. It has a four-stage, thermostatically controlled, pneumatic flow control regulator. It includes automatic priming and electronic shutoff. Mixers are either in-line, fixed-gap, or special fixed venturi designs. A dash-mounted fuel selector switch and gauge uses an LED display with an electronic transducer sending unit and is available with an automatic gasoline start override. Example #6 also has a vented valve that eliminates the "bagging" of cylinders located in enclosed areas. In the event of a system failure, the OEM computer diagnostic will turn on the Check Engine light and will record the fault code(s).

Components:

- four-stage regulator

- gaseous fuel control valve

- air/gas mixer

- fuel selector switch

- fuel control processor (NGV system control unit)

- optional high pressure lockoff

- vented cylinder valve

- computer "fixes" (injector, knock sensor emulator)

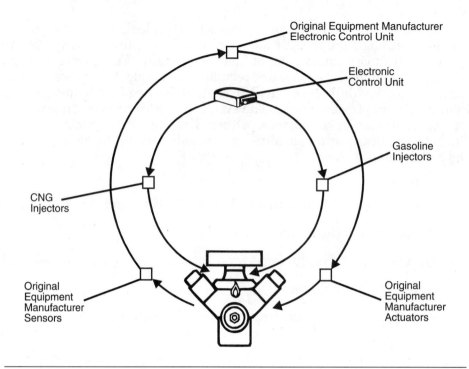

Figure 2.29 Diagram of Example #7 *(Courtesy Synchro-Start Products, Inc.)*

Example #7

The Example #7 system employs the engine manufacturer's control system instead of utilizing a new controller. It determines the fuel demand parameters of the engine by monitoring the existing electric signal that is sent from the OEM electronic control module to the gasoline fuel injectors. Then this signal is translated to operate a metering valve to provide the equivalent amount of natural gas. To tailor the system for use on a particular engine, a personal computer downloads individualized calibration curves to an EEPROM in the system's microprocessor. Changes in the engine's spark timing are also incorporated through the NGV system control unit. Diagnostic functions are also built in. This same technology can be transferred to lean-burn diesel, propane, or alcohol fuels. Figure 2.29 is a diagram of Example #7.

Example #8

Example #8 is a high pressure gaseous injector. It can be located in a multipoint, sequential, or throttle body application. Currently, it is used on OEM spark-ignited engines. NGV conversion systems are available. The system includes an electronic control unit and software (NGV system control unit). It can compensate for variations in gas quality (energy content), and has adaptive learn capability for real-time system self-adjustments to maintain emissions performance. Altitude compensation and timing control are also included.

Example #9

Example #9 is a multistage regulator that fits into the cylinder (where the valve traditionally is) and modulates pressures from the high cylinder pressure down to atmospheric, if needed. The regulator is for mono-, bi-, and dual-fuel natural gas vehicles. The two-stage series features a pressure relief, high pressure solenoid, environmental cover, pressure relief valve, and straight 90 degree hose fittings. The product uses infinite-life springs, conventional pintles, a rolling diaphragm, and a high-capacity 40-micron filter. The three-stage series of zero-pressure differential regulation is for mono-, bi-, and dual-fuel NGVs using carburetion. It carries many of the same features as the two-stage regulator and comes with its own dashboard-mounted controller.

TRENDS AND PURCHASING

The traditional mechanical-based systems will probably lose their popularity as the more complex, efficient, and higher performing closed loop fuel injection systems become established. The number of interactive electronic components will increase (with the sensor and control circuitry of the vehicle). It will become more difficult to differentiate between the electronic natural gas and OEM electronics of a bi-fuel vehicle.

Much like other purchases, shopping around can pay off. Be aware that the conversion time is a major factor in calculating the total cost of an NGV conversion. Certain systems may be less expensive, but the increased installation time may offset these savings. Experience is the best guide in selecting a system. Contact a reputable conversion specialist for specific answers to questions you may have. Availability of a system for the specific vehicle and the availability of parts, if replacement is ever needed, should be a consideration.

Warranty coverage is changing; it has traditionally been one year for parts and/or labor with optional extended warranties of three years to five years. New EPA regulations specify that the conversion emission warranty must be comparable to existing gasoline OEM warranties. Ultimately, these warranty options will be reflected in the price of the conversion system.

Finally, be familiar with the natural gas industry organizations that test and certify components and systems.

PRE-INSTALLATION CNG SAFETY GUIDELINES

PROPERTIES OF THE FUEL

As a motor fuel for vehicles, natural gas should typically contain 80% to 95% methane. The rest is small amounts of ethane, propane, butane, other hydrocarbons, and only trace amounts of sulfur or other contaminants. When burned, this chemical composition produces significantly fewer noxious emissions than does gasoline. The simple hydrocarbons that make up natural gas tend to have a more complete combustion, which produces mostly carbon dioxide and water vapor.

Although natural gas is primarily methane (CH_4), it also contains ethane and paraffins. Natural gas becomes liquid at -259°F at a pressure of 1 atm. On a Btu/gal basis, natural gas contains approximately 22% the Btu/gal of gasoline. The autoignition temperature of natural gas is higher relative to gasoline, reducing the likelihood of explosion or kindling point fires. The flame point temperature is a slightly lower combustion temperature relative to gasoline. The flash point temperature is a very low temperature. The flammability limits of natural gas range from 5% to 15% (vol. % in air).

TOXICITY

Natural gas is nontoxic and poses considerably less health hazard than gasoline or diesel fuel. Natural gas is believed to be noncarcinogenic. The only known danger of inhaling natural gas is that it can be an asphyxiant if it is present in sufficient quantities to displace a large fraction of the oxygen in air.

EXPLOSION POTENTIAL

The risks of explosion or fire for natural gas are less than gasoline. Since methane mixes rapidly with air and is less dense than air, it should disperse quickly in open spaces. The risk of outdoor explosions should be less for methane than for conventional fuels. Inside a natural gas fuel cylinder there is essentially no risk of explosion since there is no air inside. The chief source of fire or explosion hazard from natural gas is fuel leakage from defective equipment.

CONVERSION SAFETY

Natural gas is not harmful to skin or eyes unless suddenly released from high pressure. The sudden expansion of the gas results in rapid cooling that can cause freezing. It is also important to realize that, under the right circumstances, a high pressure leak can act as a cutting edge capable of cutting through clothing and skin. Keep in mind the following:

- Always open all valves slowly.

- Your eyes and ears are particularly sensitive to great changes in pressure.

- Always be aware of what direction the gas is moving (to and from), where the pressure relief devices are aimed, and other points of possible massive leaks that could lead to a great deal of natural gas being vented on explosion.

- Safety glasses and leather gloves are recommended for handling NGV cylinders.

- Safety devices in valves or pressure relief devices should not be tampered with and should be verified for proper use and pressure ratings.

- Product identification labels or decals should not be removed or altered. Color of the cylinder should not be changed.

- The cylinder decal or label is the only positive way to identify the gas contained in a cylinder; all cylinders should be properly labeled.

CONSIDERATIONS FOR WORKING WITH HIGH PRESSURE NATURAL GAS

Technicians (including trainers and trainees) should know and understand the properties, uses, and safety precautions of compressed natural gas before working with the gas and/or associated equipment. There are special considerations for working with any gas stored at high pressure.

When working with components that have high and low pressure ports, pay close attention to where connections are made. It is possible, and rather easy, to connect the fuel lines to a pressure regulator backwards. Close attention should be given to pressure testing. Be sure to tap into the right inlet or outlet port for the pressure range of the gauge you are using.

Never substitute components unless you can verify that they meet or exceed the applicable specification. Check all components for compatibility with the system working pressure (e.g., a 2,400 psi pressure relief device on a 3,000 psi cylinder valve). Also, inspect all components for defects *prior* to assembly. Pay especially close attention to all new cylinders and inspect each cylinder to ensure that it is free of defects.

Always purge the fuel lines before any components are removed or replaced. The easiest way to do this is to shut off the fuel (either at the cylinders or the quarter-turn valve) and run the engine until it stops.

Plans should be developed to cover *any* emergency situation that might arise. Trainers should be especially familiar with all emergency procedures and equipment necessary to deal with leaking cylinders and control equipment.

In addition to special natural gas considerations, every technician should know the location and proper operation of available emergency and safety equipment. They should know the location and operation of fire extinguishers and phone numbers of local emergency facilities.

According to a report issued by the Gas Research Institute, two incidents involving ruptured fuel cylinders in GM pickups occurred in early 1994, and another occurred in August 1993. All were utility vehicles. The first incident occurred in a bi-fuel passenger car in Michigan. The other two were dedicated GM pickups and occurred in Minnesota and California. A gas industry task force was immediately appointed to examine the full range of cylinder technology available for use in NGVs.

The cause of the GM pickup failures was acid-induced stress corrosion cracking of the cylinders. A combination of stress during normal cylinder wear and immersion of the uncoated, fully wrapped cylinders in an acidic solution caused accelerated degradation of the overwrap. The source of the acid in California was batteries carried in the bed of the truck. The acid solution dripped from the bed of the pickup onto the underbody cylinders via bolt holes in the truck bed, and was held in direct contact with the cylinders by a stone shield. The source of the Minnesota case is undetermined. Contrary to some reports, water and road salt, in and of themselves, were not the causes of the premature failures. The cause of the third cylinder failure in Michigan was due in part to mechanical damage of the overwrap. The overwrap on the trunk-mounted hoop-wound cylinder was compromised. Cylinder recertification/inspection may not have been performed. The cylinder was being reused for multiple vehicles.

As a result of the incidents, a number of issues were investigated. The results of the investigation indicate that cylinder failure can be prevented by: (1) modifying stone shields to not allow the cylinders to sit in liquid solution by drilling drainage holes as needed (with cylinders removed from vehicle); (2) using special protective coatings and alternate overwrap systems to make cylinders more resistant to attack; and (3) informing more NGV users about the effects of acid on composite wound cylinders, especially for non-OEM vehicles.

During the course of inspection following the two GM cylinder ruptures, it became apparent that cylinder recertification or visual inspections were not being routinely performed. Cylinders were suffering from various levels of damage from mechanical rubbing, improper installation, or misuse. Users had the feeling that NGV cylinders were indestructible. Users should immediately inspect cylinders using cylinder manufacturer guidelines or Compressed Gas Association C-6.2, specifically looking for stress corrosion cracking.

FUEL CYLINDER HANDLING

Cylinders should be assigned to a definite, isolated area for fuel storage, and the area should be posted with the name of the gas stored. The area should be dry, cool, well ventilated, and preferably fire resistant. Cylinders should be protected from excessive temperatures by storing them away from radiators or other sources of heat. In general, cylinders must be secured while in storage. Cylinders containing compressed natural gas should be stored away from other combustible materials. Empty and full cylinders should be stored separately and properly labeled.

Dragging or sliding cylinders, even for short distances, should be avoided. Cylinders should be moved by using a hand truck or similar device. Cylinders should not be dropped or permitted to strike each other violently. When cylinders are moved, they should not be subjected to abnormal mechanical shocks which may cause damage to their valves, to their safety devices, or to the cylinders themselves.

Cylinders containing natural gas should be properly grounded when they are being vented. This is necessary since a static charge may be produced due to the friction of the gas passing through restricted openings. The accumulation of static charge can produce sparks. This situation is particularly acute for composite fuel cylinder(s).

INSTALLATION OF NGV FUEL CYLINDERS

This operation is often the single most difficult installation. Not only are the cylinders bulky but the space is often confining. Special consideration should be given to the mounting surfaces.

IMPORTANT CONSIDERATIONS INVOLVING THE NGV FUEL CYLINDER

Great effort has been invested in designing safe storage. Because natural gas is typically stored at a pressure of 3,000 psi, fuel cylinder(s) are built to resist high temperatures, forceful impacts, and possible punctures.

Other considerations in cylinder design include obtaining maximum fuel capacity while minimizing cylinder weight. Cylinders often weigh from 25 pounds to 275 pounds, depending on their size and the material used. Three materials, (1) aluminum, (2) steel, and (3) composites, are commonly used to manufacture NGV fuel cylinders. Aluminum cylinders wrapped in fiberglass are popular because they weigh less and cost less than steel cylinders.

All new cylinders purchased today are certified by the United States Department of Transportation. A DOT stamp of approval along with psi capacity, serial number, manufacturer's name, and date of manufacture should be located on the cylinder. NGV cylinders must be recertified periodically by hydrostatic testing for maximum pressure, leaks, and stress cracks. Fiberglass wrapped cylinders must be recertified every three years, and all-steel cylinders every five years. Currently, new NGV-2 standards will allow longer test intervals.

SAFETY STANDARDS FOR CNG CYLINDERS

NGV-2 is the primary cylinder safety standard and has been adopted by the National Highway Traffic Safety Administration (NHTSA) and the Department of Transportation.

Under the new Federal Motor Vehicle Safety Standard: "Compressed Natural Gas Fuel Container Integrity" (FMVSS 304), the NHTSA sets criteria for a pressure cycling test to measure a cylinder's durability, a burst test to measure strength, and a fire test to evaluate pressure relief characteristics. The rule also established labeling requirements for CNG containers. It became effective March 26, 1995.

In the burst test, manufacturers must meet a safety factor of 2.25 times the working pressure in pounds per square inch. The entire container, including the mounting straps, must be inspected every 36 months, or at the time of any reinstallation, for external damage and deterioration. For composite-wrapped cylinders (types NGV2-2, NGV2-3, and NGV2-4), the areas beneath the mounting straps must also be thoroughly inspected. Documentation of the inspection must be maintained and provided upon request to the authority having jurisdiction. Alternatively, containers may be inspected in situations using a nondestructive test (NDT) method, provided that the ability of the procedure to detect injurious defects, as defined by the manufacturer, has been documented.

With composite-wrapped cylinders, the deterioration is often found under the mounting straps, at locations where either the metal of the straps or their mounting supports comes in contact with the composite, or where foreign materials trapped underneath the straps are in contact with the composite. A proper visual inspection cannot be made without removing the straps and also looking at the backside of the cylinder.

Alternatively, an NDT method, such as acoustic emission, could be applied to containers *in situ* (in place) to ascertain their condition.

Users should inspect cylinders immediately upon installation using cylinder manufacturer guidelines or Compressed Gas Association C-6.2, specifically looking for stress corrosion cracking. Cylinder installation should preclude, and users be informed to avoid, corrosive fluid contact with the cylinder. Cylinders should be mounted such that they are not exposed to continuous immersion in fluids. Cylinders should be periodically reinspected according to the cylinder manufacturer's recommendations. Cylinders should be periodically inspected for cuts, abrasion, dents, and heat or fire damage using the cylinder manufacturer's recommended visual inspection guidelines. Chassis members, brake cables, brackets, or attachments used to fasten cylinders to the vehicle should not be able to damage the cylinder. Users/drivers should be informed about the safe treatment and handling of NGV cylinders. When using cylinders, installation should be in accordance with NFPA 52. Cylinders should be mounted such that they are protected from impact damage that may occur during normal use of the vehicle. Cylinders must be protected from ultraviolet (UV) damage.

Acoustic emissions testing is included in new NGV-2 standards as an alternative to hydrostatic testing. Acoustic emissions testing eliminates the need to remove the cylinder from the vehicle, which can result in damage to an otherwise acceptable cylinder, as is necessary with hydrostatic emissions testing. Acoustic emissions testing is done *in situ* in approximately 45 minutes and does not jeopardize cylinder integrity. It works with steel, wrapped, and all composite cylinders. During testing, two or more sensors are put on the cylinder which is then pressurized in a series of incremental pressure steps. At each step, signals are recorded for four minutes to determine if cracks are present and to what degree (Figure 2.30).

INSTALLING THE FUEL CYLINDER(S)

NGV cylinders usually are mounted in convenient locations on the vehicle; this often results in less available cargo space. Many NGV conversion specialists try to avoid this problem by mounting the cylinders on

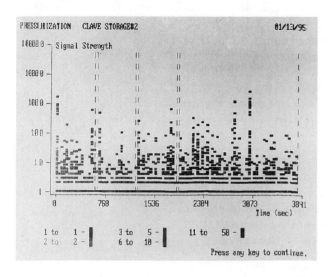
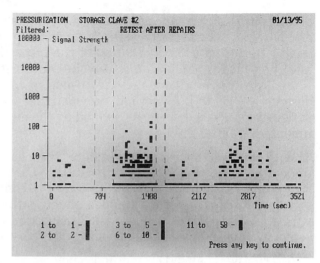
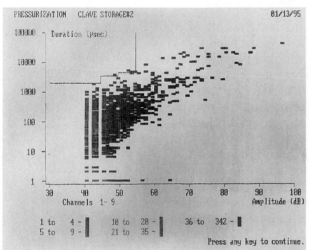
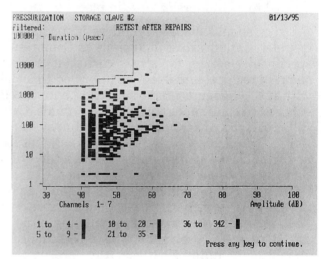

Figure 2.30 Acoustic emissions test results *(Courtesy Spencer Testing of West Virginia)*

the underside of the vehicle or in other nonobstructive locations. It is best to install the fuel cylinder(s) in open areas, avoiding, if possible, closed areas such as the trunk of a car or back of a van. Closed areas may restrict leaking gas from escaping into the atmosphere and therefore must be vented. Fumes entering the passenger compartment have the potential to cause asphyxiation. Wherever fuel cylinders are mounted, an equal weight distribution in the vehicle should be maintained. The following suggestions should be considered before mounting the cylinders:

- Mount where there is adequate space.

- Mount the cylinder(s) on a rigid, rust-free surface.

- Make sure the valve on the cylinder(s) is accessible.

- Keep the cylinder(s) at least eight inches from the exhaust system or powertrain components or shield.

- Protect the cylinder(s) from road or cargo hazards.

- Provide adequate ground clearance as specified in NFPA 52, Section 3-3.12.

After identifying satisfactory locations, proceed to mount the cylinder brackets. The brackets hold the cylinder securely, preventing it from rotating or jarring loose. Therefore, they must be mounted using all fasteners and reinforcing plates provided (and maybe a few more). A rubber belt provides a cushion and a nonskid surface between the brackets and the cylinder.

The next step is to attach the valve to the cylinder; make sure there is a pressure relief device (PRD). If the cylinder is 65 inches long or longer, two PRDs may be required. Use pipe thread compound approved for high pressure on all NPT connections. Place the compound on the male thread of the valve and tighten according to manufacturer's recommendations. Rubber O-rings seal the valve on aluminum cylinders.

The fuel cylinder is now ready to be installed on the mounting brackets. Place the fuel cylinder on the bottom set of the brackets and rotate it until the valve is positioned where it can be serviced easily. Make sure the fuel cylinder label is visible. Then secure the top bracket to finish the cylinder installation.

A cylinder installed in a confined area must be vented for added safety. Natural gas could leak from a burst disc or fittings around the relief valve. To prevent possible harm to passengers, a plastic bag, referred to as a *vent bag,* is placed around the neck of the cylinder. The vent bag is

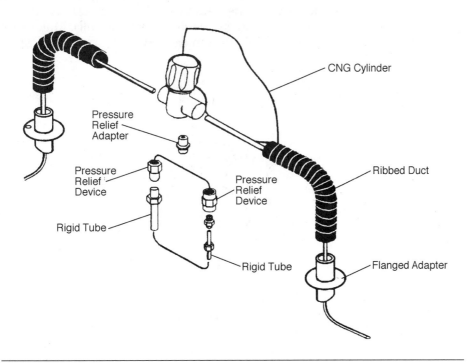

Figure 2.31 Enclosed integral venting system *(Courtesy GFI Control Systems, Inc.)*

connected to a boot that directs any vented natural gas through a hole in the body of the vehicle to the outside where it can dissipate into the atmosphere.

Another vent system uses metalized tubing and internal vent passages cast into the cylinder valve (Figure 2.31). An enclosed integral venting system allows for clean, compact, and safe installations inside closed vehicle areas such as trunks and vans. The system eliminates the need for venting bags. The valve provides manual cylinder shutoff with an exposed knob. Venting is incorporated internally by means of precast vent paths built into the valve. The gas then flows through ducting to sealed flanged adapters that discharge outside the vehicle. The high pressure supply/delivery lines are routed through standard high pressure tubing. The pressure relief device discharges from a separate port through a piece of metalized tubing routed to the outside of the vehicle.

The following is the step-by-step procedure for the installation of an NGV fuel cylinder(s).

Step 1: Location of Mounting Brackets

Before drilling the first bolt hole for a bracket, check and verify that each part of the fuel cylinder assembly will fit into the selected location. Start by placing the cylinder into the selected location. Position the cylinder and valve to accommodate the fuel line. Will the cylinder be secure according to the eight-times-the-weight-of-the-filled-fuel-cylinder guideline that NFPA 52, Section 3-3.3 specifies?

Step 2: Guards and Venting Bags

Make sure that any guards fit in the space. Place them in the selected location and verify that there is a clear path for accessing the mounting bolt holes. Vent to a location on the vehicle that is unrestricted (i.e., a place that will not retain the leaked gas, such as a wheel well). Make sure the vent bags or tubes are not kinked, compressed, or obstructed (Figure 2.32).

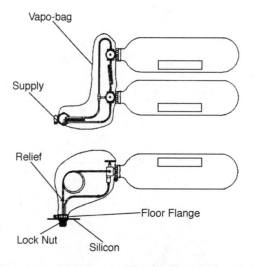

Figure 2.32 Bag-type ventilation system *(Courtesy GFI Control Systems, Inc.)*

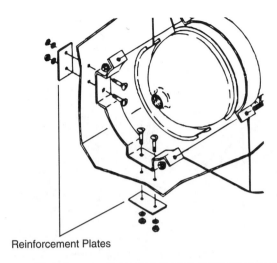

Reinforcement Plates

Figure 2.33 Reinforcement plates *(Courtesy CNG Cylinder Company)*

Step 3: Bracket Mounting Bolts

Look to see where the fuel cylinder mounting bolt holes should go. What is on the other side? Are the surfaces solid and free of rust? Will there be enough space for reinforcement plates (Figure 2.33)? Will the plates need to be altered?

Step 4: Fuel Lockoff

Canadian regulations require a safety interlock solenoid valve near the fuel cylinder. This is a device that is similar to the vacuum fuel lockoff between the primary and secondary regulators. If you are installing this device, make sure it fits and that the control lines are unobstructed. Will the fuel lines fit in the selected space?

Step 5: Mounting Requirement for Brackets

Hold the brackets into the selected location and verify that there is an unobstructed, solid mounting surface for the brackets.

Step 6: Location for Ease of Service

Allow adequate access to the cylinder valve for future needs. If safety laws require access to the fuel cylinders, can you get to them? It is better to measure twice and cut once.

Step 7: Mount Bracket(s)

Once it has been determined that there are adequate solid surfaces for the fuel cylinder and the brackets, mount the brackets. Some brackets and mounting setups require that the fuel cylinder be bolted into the brackets and moved into the location to prevent the half bracket from obstructing the fuel cylinder installation (Figure 2.34).

Step 8: Drill Holes for Brackets

Check to see what is on the other side before drilling. Drill pilot holes and check clearance. If everything looks good, then drill the holes for the brackets. Reinforcement of drilled holes is required in some applications.

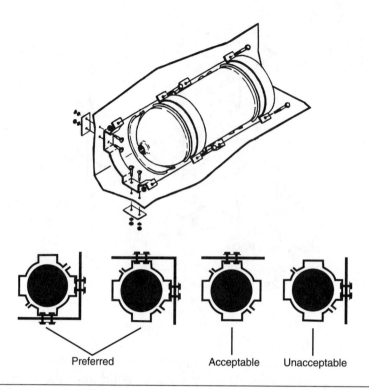

Figure 2.34 Proper and improper cylinder mounting procedures *(Courtesy CNG Cylinder Company)*

Reinforcement plates are installed at this time. Some standards specify a minimum square surface area (e.g., seven square inches) for these plates.

Step 9: Rubber Belting Strips for Mounting Brackets

Glue belting on both upper and lower brackets to protect fiberglass reinforcement of fuel cylinders. According to NFPA 52, the mounted fuel cylinder(s) must be able to withstand a force eight times the weight of the filled fuel cylinder in all directions. This also means being able to withstand being pushed out of the brackets.

Step 10: Mount Half Bracket

Once the holes are drilled and the plates are in place, mount half the bracket.

Step 11: Mount Valve on Fuel Cylinder

Before placing the fuel cylinder into the brackets, install the fuel cylinder valve.

Note: Do not use pipe wrench on cylinders.

Step 12: Install Fuel Cylinder in Brackets

Install the fuel cylinder in the brackets. Position the cylinder so the valve handle is facing in a direction that is both protected and accessible. The serial number and test date stamp must be visible (Figure 2.35).

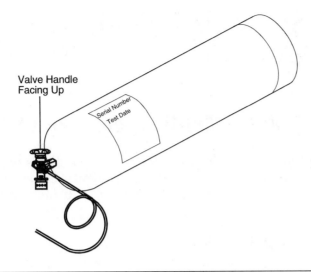

Figure 2.35 Cylinder with serial number and test date label

Step 13: Mount Other Half Bracket

Once the fuel cylinder(s) is properly oriented, install the second half of the bracket. Tighten the bracket bolts and check to make sure the installation is sound. Follow the manufacturer's specifications on torque for the fuel cylinder bracket bolts.

Step 14: Label Fuel Cylinder

The DOT and NFPA 52, Section 2-4.2, require the labeling of the fuel cylinders. The labels should be a permanent part of the cylinder and included with the cylinder (Figure 2.36).

Note: Some installations require that the fuel cylinder(s) be mounted in the brackets first and then the entire assembly placed. If this is the case, make sure the date stamp and valve are correctly oriented. This procedure may make installing the fuel line more difficult.

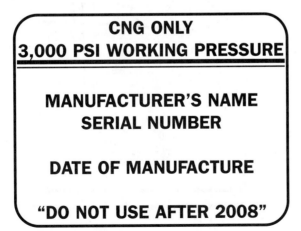

Figure 2.36 Cylinder labels

INSTALLATION OF MANUAL SHUTOFF VALVE, REGULATORS, AND FUEL LOCKOFF

INSTALLATION OF MANUAL SHUTOFF VALVE

The manual shutoff valve is a quarter-turn valve that is typically located near or around the driver's door. This valve must be easily accessed in an emergency, such as an accident or engine fire. It must also be clearly labeled.

Step 1: Location of Manual Shutoff Valve

Review the location planned for the manual shutoff valve (Figure 2.37). Check for a suitable mounting surface using the same considerations as for the fuel cylinders and fuel lines. Be sure that the fuel line route accommodates the placement of the manual shutoff valve. Consider installing a guard or shield to protect the manual shutoff valve.

Step 2: Connect to Fuel Line

Include the stress loops and/or bulkheads needed before and after the manual shutoff valve.

Step 3: Apply Safety Sticker

A decal must be placed on a visible surface to identify the exact location of the manual shutoff valve.

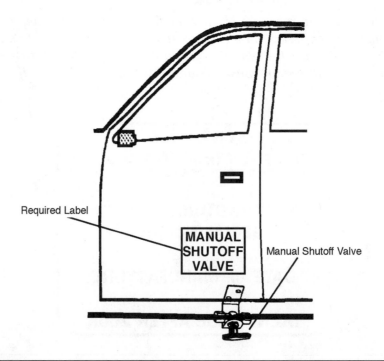

Required Label

MANUAL SHUTOFF VALVE

Manual Shutoff Valve

Figure 2.37 Typical location of manual shutoff valve and label

INSTALLATION OF REGULATOR(S)

The next task is the installation of the regulators. Many system providers supply the regulators with prefabricated bracket assemblies to simplify this process.

The fuel cylinder pressure of natural gas must be reduced to attain proper air/fuel mixing and combustion. This reduction in pressure usually occurs in one stage; however, some NGV systems may use two, three or four pressure reduction stages. The component used to reduce pressure of compressed gas is called a *regulator*. During the first stage of pressure reduction, natural gas flows through the high pressure regulator where it is reduced from the fuel cylinder pressure to 40–100 psi. In mechanical mixer systems, the fuel then enters the low pressure regulator which further reduces it to the required mixing pressure.

Important Considerations Involving the NGV Pressure Regulator(s)

Regulators are important components of the compressed natural gas fuel system and must be mounted according to specifications. As with other NGV installation procedures, quality and craftsmanship are imperative for improving efficiency and safety. The following are suggestions for mounting the regulators.

Installing the NGV Regulators

- Fasten mounting brackets securely to a rigid part of the vehicle.

- On systems that have low pressure regulators, mount the regulator with the diaphragm parallel to the length of the vehicle to prevent surges caused by vehicle stop-and-go motions.

- Make sure the regulator is easily accessible for making adjustments.

- Mount the regulator as close as possible to the mixer.

- If possible, mount the regulator back toward the fire wall for added protection in case of accidents.

- Locate the regulator in a cool, protected spot away from exhaust pipes and away from belts or pulleys.

After identifying a proper location and securing the mounting brackets, you are ready to install the regulator. Install the fill valve, check valve, pressure gauge, and shutoff valve to the regulator as required by the manufacturer.

The second-stage regulator is installed similarly. Depending on the conversion system manufacturer, it may be necessary to install the natural gas solenoid valve between the regulators. A unit called a *multistage regulator* may have all three components already assembled. When installing the connection fittings of the second-stage regulator, it is important to be aware of the correct direction of flow on both regulators so you do not confuse inlets and outlets.

Connecting the heater hoses is the last step in installing the regulators. Heater hoses help maintain proper temperatures and prevent freezing when natural gas passes through the regulators. A "T" connector must be spliced into the original heater hose and connected to the regulator as recommended by the system manufacturer.

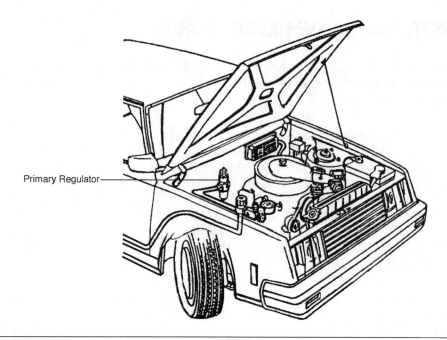

Primary Regulator

Figure 2.38 A mounted location of a primary regulator

Installing Primary Regulator

Step 1: Location for Regulator

Revisit the location selected for the regulators earlier. Before drilling the first hole, verify that the mounting space is dry and free of obstruction, excessive vibration, and heat. If there are serious obstructions, it may be necessary to relocate components such as the battery, windshield washer reservoir, and engine coolant reservoir (Figure 2.38).

Step 2: Fuel Line Locations for Primary Regulator

Take a moment and review where you planned to run the fuel lines in and out of the regulator (this may include using the second inlet as a "T" location from the fill block). Are there good, clear paths with sound mounting surfaces and room for loops?

Step 3: Coolant Line Locations for Primary Regulator

Review the design layout to locate how you plan to run the coolant lines to the regulator. Make sure there are clear paths with sound mounting surfaces and access to the heater lines.

Step 4: Mount Brackets for Primary Regulator

NFPA 52, Section 3-8.3, requires the use of mounting brackets. Double-check the position of the brackets and what is on the other side of the surface (use plates if needed).

Step 5: Mount Primary Regulator

Install the primary regulator into the brackets. Make sure that it is secure and that there is a clear path to access all the needed adjustments and inlets.

Step 6: Connect Coolant Lines to Primary Regulator

Splice into the coolant lines with "T" or "Y" connectors. Run lines to and from the regulator. Make sure the lines are secure and do not leak. Make sure there is no air trapped in the circuit and that the coolant is flowing freely and not restricting the designed coolant flow for the engine

Installing Secondary Regulator

If required in your system, review the selected surface for mounting the secondary regulator. Make sure the mounting surface is sound.

Step 1: Fuel Line Locations for Secondary Regulator

If required in your system, review the planned route for the fuel line in and out of the secondary regulator. Be sure to consider the rotation of the engine under load when routing the vapor hose between the mixer or venturi and the secondary regulator. Is there a maximum length limitation for the vapor hose?

Step 2: Mount Brackets for Secondary Regulator

If required in your system, double-check the position of the brackets and think of what is on the other side of the surface. Does the surface require the use of reinforcement plates?

Step 3: Mount Secondary Regulator

If required in your system, install the secondary regulator into the brackets. Make sure that it is secure and that there is a clear path of access to all the adjustments and connections. Label the secondary regulator, and label the setting on the outside. Orient the secondary regulator so that the oil drain plug is down. Remember to check the orientation of the secondary regulator so that inertial forces will not affect the performance of the regulator.

INSTALLATION OF FUEL LOCKOFF

Review the selected surface for mounting the fuel lockoff valve. Make sure the mounting surface is sound.

Step 1: Fuel Line Locations for Fuel Lockoff

Review the planned route for the fuel line in and out of the fuel lockoff and the control line. If it is a mechanical lockoff that requires a vacuum line, make preparations for routing a line to the intake manifold. If it is a solenoid fuel lockoff, follow the manufacturer's recommendations for the electrical wiring.

Step 2: Mount Brackets for Fuel Lockoff

Mount brackets for the fuel lockoff. Double-check the position of the brackets and know what is on the other side of the surface (use reinforcement plates if needed).

Step 3: Mount Fuel Lockoff

Install the fuel lockoff valve into the brackets. Make sure that it is secure with clear access to all the needed adjustments and connections. Install the vacuum line and/or electrical wiring that controls the fuel lockoff.

INSTALLATION OF FUEL LINES

STAINLESS STEEL TUBING, FITTINGS, AND SEALANT

The system manufacturer should have provided approved stainless steel tubing, fittings, and fitting sealant with the system. There are two different types of connectors: (1) NPT (National Pipe Thread) and (2) high pressure compression fittings. Usually, fuel cylinder(s), valves, gauges, and regulators use NPT threads and the fuel line connectors use compression fittings. All NPT threads will have to be taped, sealed, or both, with an approved high pressure gas sealant. Be sure you have all the necessary sealants, tools, and bending mandrels before you begin.

Note: Some aluminum fuel cylinders use an SAE O-ring fitting instead of NPT threads. Do not use sealant on the SAE O-ring fittings.

Having mounted the fuel cylinder, manual shutoff valve, and the regulators, you can now install the fuel line to connect the major components of the system (Figure 2.39). Running fuel lines can be an art form. Bending lines and dealing with long pieces of bent lines can give you a new outlook on life.

MAJOR TASKS REQUIRED FOR INSTALLING THE FUEL LINE

The fuel line extends from the fuel cylinders to the high pressure regulator. It generally consists of quarter-inch stainless steel seamless

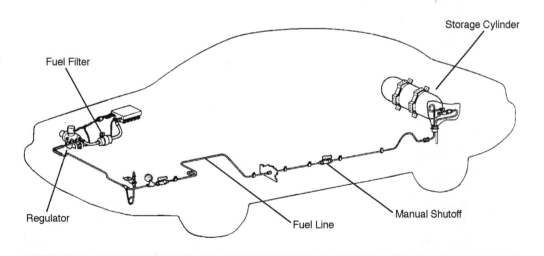

Figure 2.39 Components of fuel line system *(Courtesy GFI Control Systems, Inc.)*

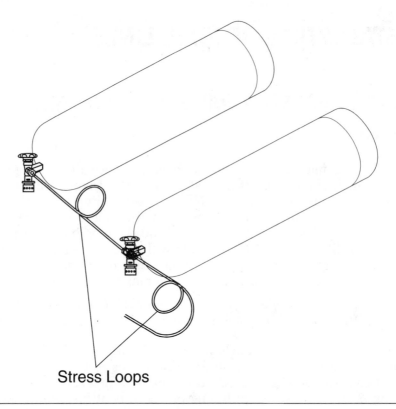

Stress Loops

Figure 2.40 Fuel line with stress loops

tubing connected to all components with stainless steel high pressure fittings. The line may be inserted into vinyl tubing for added protection. To reduce the chances of leaks, use a sealant on all NPT fittings, but *never* on the compression fittings.

The fuel line usually runs along the underside of the vehicle and is fastened to the frame with clamps that have an interior rubber cushion. Wherever the fuel line passes through a floor or wall panel, grommets or bulkheads should be used to protect the line from possible damage. Another safety feature built into the fuel line is stress loops. These loops are approximately three inches in diameter and are placed in the fuel line wherever it connects to another component. Stress (vibration) loops absorb any tension or compression forces exerted on the fuel line during the normal operation of the vehicle (Figure 2.40).

Common components installed along the fuel line include the fill valve, manual shutoff valve, and pressure gauge. The method of filling determines where the fill valve should be located. Under the hood is ideal for the fast-fill method. On the front of the grill or near the rear fender is a common place for vehicles using the slow-fill method. The manual shutoff valve typically is installed after the NGV fuel cylinders to isolate them from other components. It should be labeled and easily accessible in emergencies. The pressure gauge should be installed downstream from the master shutoff valve.

The first step for installing the fuel line is to estimate the required length, including bends and stress loops. Add approximately 12 inches per stress loop to the estimated length. The line can then be cut and the ends cleaned of all burrs. Before installing, use proper pipe-bending equipment to place all bends. The line can then be connected to the various system components; use approved sealant on all NPT fittings. The last step is to secure the line to the vehicle, using cushioned clamps every two feet or less.

Review the planned route for the fuel lines. Look for suitable surfaces for mounting the line clamps. The fuel lines should be fastened at least every 24 inches. Check the locations of planned alterations in the vehicle body. Again, keep in mind the rotational torque of the drivetrain and frame flex which may shear off the fuel line. Most important, always keep the fuel lines protected by using the form of the vehicle's frame. This could include running the fuel line inside a channel or fold in the frame.

Routing of Fuel Lines

Things To Keep In Mind When Working With the Fuel Line

- Always deburr the tubing after cutting (inside and out).

- Blow out the tubing before installation.

- Keep the installation design as professional as you can.

Installing Fuel Lines

Step 1: Measure Approximate Length of Tubing

Measure the planned route. Add extra length to accommodate stress loop(s). Use extra tubing; it is easy to cut off extra and impossible to stretch if too short. Make a set of second precise measurements for the placement of bends and loops.

Step 2: Cut and Bend the Fuel Line

Based on the measurements, use the appropriate tube bending tools (refer to the *Instrument Tube Fitters Manual* for help in forming the fuel lines). Plan on spending a bit of time comparing the bends in the tube to the planned route on the vehicle. Hold it in place and see what you have. Use stress loops when the fuel line is attached to independent body components or body and frame elements. Each bulkhead should have a stress loop. Good judgment is all that's required; but it is better to have too many stress loops than too few.

Step 3: Body Modifications for Fuel Line Bulkheads

Before making the first cut, verify what is on the other side of the surface. Use a bulkhead connector to save snaking a long bent tube into place. If everything checks out, drill the hole and install the bulkhead connection (Figure 2.41).

Step 4: Install Fuel Line

Consider placing the stainless steel tubing inside a rubber hose for added protection. Install the fuel line in sections: (1) fuel cylinder-to-emergency shutoff valve, (2) manual shutoff valve-to-primary regulator,

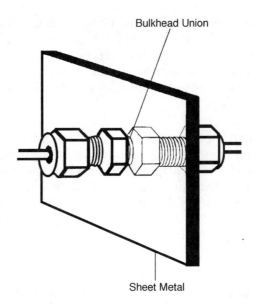

Bulkhead Union

Sheet Metal

Figure 2.41 Bulkhead connector

and (3) filling connection "T" and the fuel receptacle assembly. Mount any line clamps (hangers or fuel line support brackets) after installing the fuel line. See NFPA 52, Section 3-5.6, for minimum spacing requirements between line clamps.

Step 5: Connect Fuel Lines to Fuel Cylinder Valve

Use approved fitting sealant where appropriate. There should be stress loops between each fuel cylinder and the main fuel line.

Step 6: Install Vent Bags and Guards

Install vent bags and guards as planned. Use clamps rather than adhesives for holding bags in place.

Step 7: Connect Fuel Lines to Pressure Gauge and Coolant Lines to Primary Regulator

Use approved fitting sealant where appropriate. If a secondary regulator is included in your conversion, connect fuel lines to it.

Step 8: Connect Fuel Lines to Manual Shutoff Valve

Include stress loops as needed before and after the manual shutoff valve.

Step 9: Build the Refueling Assembly and Mount

Install the filling connector with a stress loop to isolate any body flexing that may occur.

INSTALLATION OF MIXER AND FUEL INJECTION SYSTEM

The layout for the mixer is primarily concerned with two questions: (1) Is there room for the mixer? and (2) How will the fuel line be routed? Remember, the EPA rules specify that air cleaner integrity must be maintained. Also, a PCV air intake placed after (under) the mixer will suck a fuel mixture into the crankcase; this may have undesirable consequences.

COMPONENTS NECESSARY FOR AIR/FUEL MIXING

Air/fuel mixing is accomplished by a device called a *mixer* or *fuel injector*. Mixers vary greatly among system manufacturers and vehicle types. Older vehicles with carbureted engines require a modified carburetor, or mixer, which usually is placed over the existing carburetor. Newer vehicles with fuel injected engines generally require injectors to introduce fuel into the airstream of the intake manifold or directly into the throttle body. All air/fuel mixing components should be installed in a location consistent with the manufacturer's recommendations.

After securing the mixer, connect the gas line from the regulator to the mixer. Connect all vacuum hoses to the mixer according to manufacturer's recommendations. A "T" connection may be needed for splicing into existing vacuum hoses. Although the mixer can be installed before the system wiring, it may be easier to complete the wiring without the mixer in the way.

Position, Height, and Placement of Mixer

The system manufacturer should provide mounting apparatus. This could be a modified air cleaner or a cast piece to offset the position of the air cleaner mount. Lack of clearance between the hood and the top of the air cleaner is a common problem. The best way to check these points is to set the mixer assembly into place and look it over very carefully.

Step 1: Mount Mixer

Examine the mounting materials included with the mixer and make sure that they are complete. Before mounting, refer to your initial design layout and double-check hose routes and space requirements. Assemble the pieces and mount the mixer.

Note: Air leaks are critical, so be certain you have a tight fit that seals well.

Step 2: Connect Vapor Hose

The vapor hose should be connected to the secondary regulator and should be labeled. Make sure the route is sound, with no kinks or crushed spots, and that there is a little slack. Each manufacturer will have a recommended maximum length for the vapor hose.

Step 3: Connect Vacuum Line(s)

Connect vacuum line(s) as necessary between the mixer, intake manifold, and/or fuel lockoff.

Step 4: Connect Solenoid to the NGV Mixer (Bi-Fuel)

If lines (to the fuel lockoff) also included an electrical solenoid shutoff, make these connections now.

INSTALLATION OF FUEL INJECTION SYSTEM

The layout for the injector(s) is primarily concerned with two questions: (1) Is there room for the injectors or spray nozzles? and (2) Where will the fuel line be routed? Spray nozzles or bars are mounted above (before) the throttle body. Direct injection systems will require a modified intake manifold. Because of tight spaces above the engine, routing the fuel line may involve additional planning and innovative ideas.

INSTALLATION OF ELECTRICAL COMPONENTS AND WIRING

New vehicles feature digital electronic systems and the tolerances of the electrical signals must be tighter. In most cases electrical problems will be due to poor connections. Figure 2.42 illustrates various inputs to a modern closed loop system. A more in-depth discussion of NGV electronics will follow in Chapters 3 and 4; however, this section will provide an overview of installation procedures.

If necessary, make a schematic of the electrical system before you wire it. Make notes on that schematic as needed. If maintenance is later required (in months or years), the schematic will save you hours of wire tracing.

MAJOR TASKS INVOLVED IN THE ELECTRICAL WIRING FOR AN NGV CONVERSION

The additional electrical components needed for a vehicle to operate on natural gas depend on the type of vehicle being converted. Common components on a bi-fuel vehicle include: a fuel selector switch, a relay to electronically signal the natural gas solenoid to turn on or off, a natural

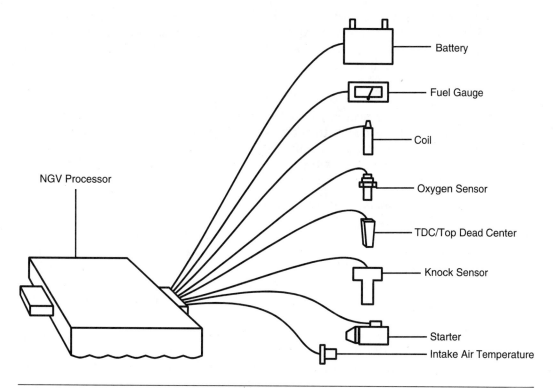

Figure 2.42 Electrical components

gas fuel gauge, and a timing modification unit. The timing modification device advances engine ignition approximately 15 degrees when running on natural gas and returns the engine ignition to the OEM timing curve when operating on gasoline. A computer signal modification device, or computer fix, is necessary if the vehicle contains a computer diagnostic system. This device interacts with the vehicle's computer to monitor and control engine and emission systems. (As discussed previously, vehicles that use computer feedback devices are called *closed loop systems*. Those without computer electronic feedback systems are called *open loop systems*).

The fuel gauge and fuel selector switch should be installed on an easily seen and accessed location in the dash.

Whenever possible, mount electrical components on the fire wall in a dry location away from all heat sources. All electrical connections should be made according to manufacturer's specifications using rosin core solder and heatshrink tape or special weather-tight connectors. All exposed wires should be enclosed with split-loom tubing.

Note: The other electrical components (computer modification device, relay, and timing adaptation devices) should be sealed using a silicone sealant before installation. This will help prevent moisture from entering and possibly damaging the device.

Location for Brackets and Electrical Components

Review the layout for the electrical connections. Check for: (1) availability of suitable mounting surfaces for electrical components, (2) areas easy to guard and shield from moisture, heat, vibration, and induction problems, (3) room enough to work where splices must be made, (4) neat wire routing (use OEM schematics), (5) accessibility of the timing apparatus, (6) proper placement of the dashboard meters (i.e., that they are in clear sight of the driver and that they can actually be mounted where you want to put them), and (7) that the switches needed are placed where they can be reached but not accidentally tripped or damaged.

Step 1: Mount Electrical Components

When making preparations for mounting the control unit's brackets remember (1) to check to make sure they will be mounted in a secure place and (2) to mount in place *after* the connections are made. Leave extra wire for all connections to be made, so that there is extra loose wire for routing the wire. Route and mount.

Make appropriate electrical connections allowing extra wire. Mount any wire harness hangers and conduits before tightening the computer signal modification device. Use good quality connectors, preferably Weather Pak, or solder and shrinkwrap all connections. If conversion schematics don't match or are not available for the particular vehicle you are converting, make your own. A picture is worth a thousand words, and another technician working on the vehicle will appreciate this information.

Step 2: Install Relay

Relays are used for such things as switching injectors and controlling the fuel lockoff. Always consider accessibility, protected locations, and good grounds before installation.

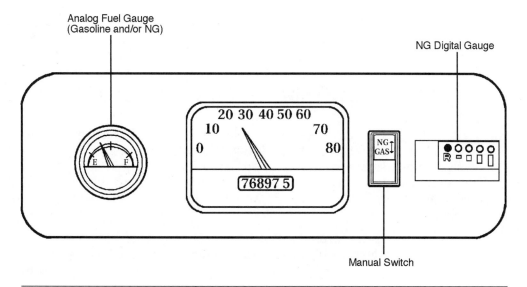

Figure 2.43 Dashboard with fuel switch and gauges

Step 3: Install Fuel Selector Switch

Review the selected location for the fuel selector switch(es), and verify that it is a good location. If both automatic and manual fuel selector switches are being used, double-check your plan and clearly document the connections. Review the planned wiring route and mount the switch (Figure 2.43).

Step 4: Install Fuel Gauge

The fuel gauge indicates the amount of fuel based on the pressure in the fuel cylinder(s). The gauge uses a pressure transducer which produces an electrical signal.

Review the selected mounting surface for the fuel gauge and the signal line to the pressure transducer. If the surface is suitable, mount the fuel gauge. Follow the manufacturer's wiring schematic closely for the connections between the sending unit and the gauge. Some require separate grounds; others are included in the wiring harness.

ENGINE TESTING

FILL NGV TO SYSTEM WORKING PRESSURE

After all systems have been assembled and attached, perform a pressure-up test to see if there are any leaks. Big leaks are obvious. There will be signs like a hissing sound. Use an ammonia-free liquid or electronic leak detector on all fittings and look for bubbles. If you detect a leak, purge the system of all natural gas and seal the leak before operating the vehicle.

The engine testing procedure includes: (1) test all of the natural gas components for leaks, (2) make initial adjustments on components, (3) start and troubleshoot, and (4) tune the running engine to run smoothly.

VERIFY ELECTRICAL CONNECTIONS

Follow the methods recommended by the manufacturers. Make appropriate adjustments.

Now, start the vehicle! How do you first start a vehicle, and what are the most common problems in getting it started?

The recommended settings from the manufacturer should be close enough to get the engine started, but it will probably need some tuning. After the engine is running, make the initial tuning settings. Switch between fuels to verify that both systems are operational if it is a bi-fuel system.

TUNING THE VEHICLE

After completing a conversion, the vehicle should be tested and tuned according to state and federal regulations for emissions and performance expectations. The vehicle can be tuned for optimizing horsepower, fuel economy, or emissions. However, optimizing one standard affects the other two. A compromise tuning may be necessary to satisfy performance and emission demands.

Tuning the vehicle involves adjusting the air/fuel mixture (mixer), gas pressure (regulators), and ignition timing (timing modification device). Because natural gas has an octane rating between 120 and 130, the engine can operate at a compression ratio as high as 16:1 without pinging. This compression ratio may result in improved mileage and power, compared to the same engine operating on gasoline. The regulators, mixer, and timing modification device should be adjusted to the system manufacturer's recommendations. A dynamometer is very helpful for tuning the system, but a four-gas analyzer is more common. The ultimate fine tuning should occur in the emissions testing stage.

TEST DRIVE VEHICLE

Review pre-conversion test drive information to get a feeling for how the vehicle should perform. Once the vehicle has been tuned as close as possible in the shop, it should be ready for a test drive. Have some tools with you to make adjustments, if needed. Once the vehicle is running well, you should be ready to validate the engine over its operating range.

SUMMARY

- A conversion should be planned out both on paper and mentally as much as possible to help minimize problems.

- Section 3.3 of NFPA suggests safety guidelines that should be followed regarding fuel cylinder installation.

- The most vulnerable element of the fuel cylinder mount is the cylinder valve.

- Natural gas is stored at pressures between 2,400 and 3,600 psi, depending on the system components.

- Due to the size and weight of the fuel cylinder, numerous factors must be taken into consideration when deciding on the fuel cylinders' placement to ensure a safe and secure mounting location.

- The three types of fuel cylinders available are: (1) steel, (2) aluminum/steel composites, and (3) full composites.

- High pressure lines should be welded or seamless stainless steel, normally 1/4- or 3/8-inch diameter.

- When determining the location of any conversion component, the routing of the fuel line must be taken into consideration before mounting.

- The manual shutoff valve is a 1/4-turn valve that needs to be located so that it is easily accessible and with the label clearly visible from the outside; normally located under the driver's door.

- The primary (high pressure) regulator reduces the CNG from its storage pressure down to approximately 100 psi on most systems.

- Natural gas absorbs heat as its pressure is reduced; therefore, coolant lines are routed through the high pressure regulator to prevent freezing.

- The fuel lockoff device is a safety device that is designed to stop the flow of natural gas when the engine is not running or cranking.

- The lockoff device can be controlled either electronically or using engine vacuum, and can be placed in the high or low pressure lines.

- The secondary regulator (if needed) reduces the pressure of natural gas from the high pressure regulator to 3–5 ounces of pressure in a variable venturi system and close to zero in a fixed venturi system.

- The secondary regulator is normally mounted parallel to the length of the vehicle to prevent driveability problems due to sudden acceleration or deceleration, so it is important to follow manufacturer's instructions on installation.

- Location of the mixer, spray bar, nozzle, or injector assembly is normally restricted only by the space in the engine compartment or accessibility of fuel hose routing.

- Emission components cannot be removed or modified.

- The PCV inlet filter must be routed upstream of the fuel mixer because there is fuel present in the air downstream of the mixer.

- Location of the electrical components must be accessible, visible, and protected from damage or accidental tripping.

- Early conversion systems were open loop type, had no computer controls to ensure compliance with acceptable emissions level standards, and needed frequent adjustments to maintain acceptable engine performance.

- Closed loop systems incorporate the use of the OEM or a stand-alone natural gas computer to maintain proper air/fuel ratio and perform timing modifications. Some even contain self-diagnostic capabilities.

- Conversion systems that are designed specifically for a particular vehicle are normally more expensive but easier to install, and provide for better performance than systems that have more universal applications.

- Natural gas is nontoxic and poses considerably fewer health hazards than gasoline.

- The risk of explosion of natural gas is less than that of gasoline.

- Natural gas is less dense then air and therefore disperses quickly in open spaces.

- Special precaution must be taken when handling natural gas due to the high storage pressure.

- Fuel cylinders (full or empty) should be handled with care and stored in a cool, dry, well-ventilated space which is protected from sunlight.

- Fuel cylinders should be grounded while venting to prevent personal injury due to sparks that may be created from static charges.

- CNG fuel cylinders are certified by the Department of Transportation (DOT) and must be clearly labeled with a DOT stamp of approval, pounds per square inch capacity, serial number, manufacturer's name, and the date of manufacture.

- NGV-2 is the fuel cylinder safety standard approved by NHTSA and DOT.

- Based on the type of construction, NGV fuel cylinders must be either recertified, inspected, or discarded periodically.

- Recertification can be done either hydrostatically or by means of acoustic emissions.

- Fiberglass reinforced tanks must be recertified every three years.

- Steel tanks must be recertified every five years.

- Full composite tanks require a complete visual inspection every three years and have a service life of fifteen years.

- All fuel connections located in enclosed areas must be bagged and vented to the atmosphere in a safe location in case of leakage.

- The step-by-step procedure for fuel cylinder installation should be closely followed, in order to make sure that the cylinder installation is safe, secure, and meets all NFPA requirements.

- Regulators should be mounted in such a manner that they are protected in case of accident, and that adjustments and connections are all accessible.

- Fuel line connections will be either: (1) National Pipe Thread (NPT) requiring special thread sealant, (2) high pressure compression fitting requiring a special tightening procedure, or (3) SAE O-ring fitting (found on some aluminum fuel cylinders) which doesn't require sealant to be used.

- Fuel line that runs a span of more than two feet should be secured every 24 inches.

- Stress loops need to be used when the fuel line is attached to independent body components, and between body and frame components.

- Common electrical components include: a fuel selector switch, a relay to turn on or off the natural gas solenoid, a natural gas fuel gauge, and either a timing modification device or a computer modification device.

- All electrical connections should be made following manufacturer's recommendations—normally either a connection soldered with rosin core solder that is wrapped with heat shrink tubing or a special weather-tight connector is used to prevent future problems.

- The engine testing procedure includes: (1) testing all components for leaks, (2) making initial adjustments on components, (3) starting and troubleshooting, and (4) tuning engine to run smoothly and cleanly.

REVIEW QUESTIONS

1. List the three different types of CNG fuel cylinders currently being used and state their required service intervals or service life.

2. Describe the safety restrictions that must be met when deciding on how and where to mount a CNG fuel cylinder in a vehicle.

3. Describe the factors involved when planning and installing the fuel lines and fuel line connectors.

4. Describe the factors involved when planning and installing the fuel lockoff device.

5. Describe the factors involved when planning and installing the manual shutoff valve.

6. Describe the factors involved when planning and installing the primary and secondary regulators.

7. Describe the factors involved when planning and installing the fuel mixer or fuel injection assembly.

8. Describe the factors involved when planning and installing the conversion system wiring and electronics.

9. Explain the safety characteristics of CNG and what rules or precautions must be followed to ensure a safe environment when servicing, refueling, or operating a CNG vehicle.

10. Describe the testing procedures that should be followed both before and after performing a CNG conversion.

CHAPTER 3

NGV Electronics and Control Systems

OBJECTIVES

- Understand the three factors a technician must consider when troubleshooting complex problems.
- Understand the fundamentals of electricity.
- Understand the fundamentals of computer operation.
- Identify the basic input sensors of a computer system and how they operate.
- Identify the basic outputs of a computer system and how they operate.
- Understand the importance of onboard computer systems.
- Determine the methods in which an NGV computer and OEM computer can work together.
- Understand the difference between closed loop and open loop systems.
- Identify some of the closed loop conversion systems available.

KEY TERMS

Conductors

Nonconductors

Semiconductors

Transistors

Base

Emitter

Collector

Forward-biased

Reversed-biased

Logic gates

Electromagnetism

Dual incline packages (DIPS)

Quad pacs

Read only memory (ROM)

Programmed read only memory (PROM)

Random access memory (RAM)

Reference voltage

Discrete sensor

Variable sensor

Thermistor

Potentiometer

Throttle position sensor (TPS)

Manifold absolute pressure sensor (MAP)

Barometric pressure sensor (BARO)

Vacuum differential sensor (VAC)

Electronic spark control (ESC)

Injector driver

Speed-density

DIAGNOSTIC INTEGRATION METHODS FOR NGVs

INTRODUCTION TO ELECTRONIC SYSTEMS PROBLEM RESOLUTION

Vehicle diagnosis and repair is extremely challenging for the technician. To the uninitiated, the solving of automotive problems appears to be a simple task at first glance: a vehicle breaks down and a technician has to repair it. So, of course, the technician finds the appropriate tools and starts repairing the vehicle according to well-defined procedures. After cleanup and proper inspection of the parts, the vehicle starts and operates perfectly.

Some vehicle problems are straightforward. When they are, they're so routine they're often considered preventative maintenance procedures and not really "problems." However, few problems are this simple. Most vehicle problems are rather complex due to the interaction of subsystems.

Automotive electrical systems and components have become increasingly more complex. The application of automotive electrical systems and components is limited only by the engineer's imagination and public demand. Electronic voltage regulators and ignition systems started the revolution. The demand for reduced emissions and increased fuel economy led to more electronic control of engine functions and the integration of electronic control with add-on systems. These functions include fuel, ignition, and charging systems. The entire vehicle has become more of an

Figure 3.1 Three factors exist

integrated system with climate, suspension, transmission, and ignition functions controlled by onboard computers that communicate with engine controls. Smaller displacement engines and components, as well as reduced weight, demand higher operating efficiency.

Generally, any time technicians attempt to solve a complex problem they must consider these three factors: (1) mechanical aspects (the source of the problem), (2) resources (includes information as well as tools and parts), and (3) technician skill level/ability (especially troubleshooting skills) (Figure 3.1).

When a problem occurs with a vehicle, it is often not a simple mechanical, resource, or troubleshooting problem. The interaction of a number of independent subsystems makes it more difficult to diagnose problems. In other words, a whole set of problems is usually involved. It is the critical thinking skills of a technician that are central to resolving the problem. The problem resolution process includes identifying the problem, analyzing alternatives, and proposing solutions (Figure 3.2).

In order for the technician to correctly define a problem, he must be a skilled analyst. Deciding that a problem actually exists, and then determining what it is, can be a tricky matter. This is especially true in today's automotive service industry where improper diagnosis can increase customer dissatisfaction with the product and technical support. Before a problem can be solved, there must be an understanding of what the problem is, what its possible causes are, and what can be done about the problem.

Figure 3.2 Master technician troubleshooting a problem

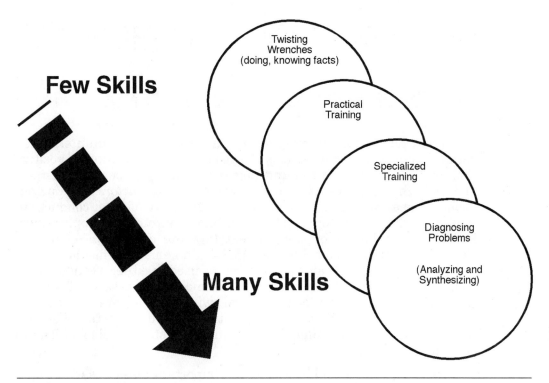

Few Skills

Many Skills

Twisting
Wrenches
(doing, knowing facts)

Practical
Training

Specialized
Training

Diagnosing
Problems

(Analyzing and
Synthesizing)

Figure 3.3 Multiple skills, knowledge, and abilities are all required to diagnose vehicle problems

In basic automotive classes, electricity and electronics are introduced and discussed. Automotive systems have progressed from mechanical controls to electronic controls. The skill, knowledge, and ability needed by the technician include knowing basic facts about electronics and control systems (Figure 3.3).

ELECTRONIC SYSTEMS REVIEW

REVIEW OF ELECTRICITY FUNDAMENTALS

Current flow is the movement of electrons through an uninterrupted path, such as a copper wire. It is the result of the attraction of positive charges to negative charges and negative charges to positive charges. Materials that promote current flow are called *conductors*. Conductors include copper, gold, iron, and silver. Given the price of other conductors, copper is the conductor of choice in most automotive applications. Materials that hinder or stop current flow are called *nonconductors*. Nonconductors, such as rubber and glass, can be used as insulators and to direct current flow. Materials that can be used as either a conductor or an insulator are called *semiconductors*. Semiconductors serve effectively as one-way current valves and electrical switches. They are used as logic circuits in onboard computers. In addition to switching, the effects of current flow include heating, lighting, and magnetizing, all of which are put into practical use.

Voltage, amperage, and resistance are important measures in automotive electronics. Voltage, the measure of electrical pressure, is an indication of the pressure exerted on each electron in a circuit by a source of electrical potential, such as a car battery. Amperage, the measure of total current, is an indication of the number of electrons flowing past a given point in a circuit. The ohm, a unit of resistance, is used to express the differing ability of various materials to support current flow. Ohm's law shows the relationship between voltage (in volts), amperage (in amps), and resistance (in ohms) (Figure 3.4).

If one quantity (voltage, amperage, or resistance) changes, then at least one other must also change. In automotive applications, most problems are caused by the following two conditions of Ohm's law:

VOLTAGE	RESISTANCE	AMPERAGE
+	−	+
+	0	+
+	+	0
0	−	+
0	0	0
0	+	−
−	+	−
−	0	−

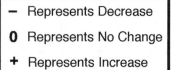

− Represents Decrease

0 Represents No Change

+ Represents Increase

Figure 3.4 Ohm's law—relationship between voltage, resistance, and amperage

1. When the resistance of a circuit remains constant and the voltage applied to that circuit increases, then the amperage will increase.

2. When the voltage in a circuit remains constant and the resistance decreases, then the amperage will increase.

Electromagnetism

Electromagnetism occurs whenever current flows through a conductor, such as a copper wire formed into a coil. These electromagnets can be turned on or off by turning the current on or off. The polarity can be changed by reversing the current flow, and the strength can be changed by changing the current flow or the number of loops in the coil. Electricity and magnetism control the operation of control devices including thermocouples, transducers, solenoids, relays, and actual onboard computers.

Semiconductors

Semiconductors behave in a certain way when voltage is applied. By adding such materials as phosphorus, antimony, or arsenic to semiconductor material, a negatively charged carrier, or *N-type* semiconductor, is produced. The addition of aluminum, indium, or boron results in a positively charged carrier known as a *P-type* semiconductor.

In most automotive applications, semiconductors are used in combination to form diodes and transistors. N- and P-type semiconductors joined in three layers are called *transistors*. Diodes are used to change alternating current (AC) to direct current (DC). Special types of diodes help to control the voltage output of alternators. The diodes can be placed into the circuit to either allow the current to flow or prevent the current from flowing. If the diode permits current flow, it is said to be *forward-biased*. If the diode restricts current flow, it is said to be *reversed-biased*.

N- and P-type semiconductors joined in two thin layers are called *diodes*. Transistors are two diodes sharing a center layer; therefore, one of the diodes will always be reversed-biased and the other will be forward-biased. The outside layer of the forward-biased diode is the *emitter*. The outside layer of the reversed-biased diode is the *collector*. The shared center is the *base*. Each layer has its own connections into the electrical circuit. The transistor is basically an amplification device and is also used to make logic gates—the basic building blocks of an onboard computer microprocessor. An example of an application of a transistor is the use of a solid-state ignition system, which allows reduced voltage and improved spark plug performance in the system.

REVIEW OF COMPUTER FUNDAMENTALS

The onboard computer in an automobile uses information coded in the binary numbering system (0s and 1s). For example, the numbers eight and ten are written as 1000 and 1010, respectively, in binary form. Each of these binary representations is called a *bit*. Eight bits comprise one *byte*. The size of a computer's memory is stated in terms of bytes, such as 5 Mbytes (5 million bytes or 40 million bits). Bit patterns, such as 1000

Binary (8421 Code) Hexadecimal Representation of Decimal Numbers

DEC	BINARY								HEX
	8	4	2	1	8	4	2	1	
1	0	0	0	0	0	0	0	1	01
2	0	0	0	0	0	0	1	0	02
3	0	0	0	0	0	0	1	1	03
4	0	0	0	0	0	1	0	0	04
5	0	0	0	0	0	1	0	1	05
6	0	0	0	0	0	1	1	0	06
7	0	0	0	0	0	1	1	1	07
8	0	0	0	0	1	0	0	0	08
9	0	0	0	0	1	0	0	1	09
10	0	0	0	0	1	0	1	0	0A
11	0	0	0	0	1	0	1	1	0B
12	0	0	0	0	1	1	0	0	0C
13	0	0	0	0	1	1	0	1	0D
14	0	0	0	0	1	1	1	0	0E
15	0	0	0	0	1	1	1	1	0F
16	0	0	0	1	0	0	0	0	10
17	0	0	0	1	0	0	0	1	11
31	0	0	0	1	1	1	1	1	1F
47	0	0	1	0	1	1	1	1	2F
255	1	1	1	1	1	1	1	1	FF

Figure 3.5 Code inversion chart

or 1010, usually indicate high and low voltages, on-off circuits, or regions of opposite magnetic polarity. These 8-bit patterns can also be represented by hexadecimal numbers. Instead of using the numbers one through ten (the decimal system), the hexadecimal system uses the numbers zero through nine and represents the numbers ten through fifteen with the letters A through F. The chart in Figure 3.5 gives conversions for numbers in binary and hexadecimal form.

An important part of the onboard computer is the logic gate. Logic gates, used for manipulating bits, are electrical devices that produce a given output bit pattern for a given input. Types of logic gates include AND, OR, NAND, NOR and EXCLUSIVE-OR gates. The inputs to the gates are high- and low-voltage pulses. High can be referred to as *positive, 1,* or *true;* low-voltage pulses are called *negative, 0,* or *false.* The outputs from the logic gates can be determined by looking at each gate's truth table. A truth table is a computer decision-making device (Figure 3.6). It allows the computer to decide what the output of certain operating conditions will be according to the input conditions.

The circuitry of the logic gate is designed by using combinations of diodes, transistors, and resistors. The combination of logic gates produces the basic circuits used to perform such functions as comparison, selection, addition, and storage.

A combination of resistors, capacitors, integrated circuits (I/Cs), and other electronic components soldered onto a printed circuit board (PCB) makes up an onboard computer. The PCB is nothing more than a piece of phenolic-type material with an etched copper covering on one or both sides. The etchings on the PCB are called *traces.* The traces act much like copper wire carrying electrical signals and eliminate the need for actual

Truth Table for AND Gate

B	A	Y
Off	Off	Off
Off	On	Off
On	Off	Off
On	On	On

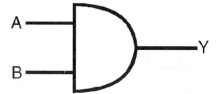

Truth Table for NAND Gate

B	A	Y
Off	Off	On
Off	On	On
On	Off	On
On	On	Off

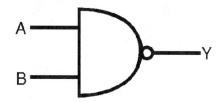

Truth Table for OR Gate

B	A	Y
Off	Off	Off
Off	On	On
On	Off	On
On	On	On

Truth Table for NOR Gate

B	A	Y
Off	Off	On
Off	On	Off
On	Off	Off
On	On	Off

Truth Table for XOR Gate

B	A	Y
Off	Off	Off
Off	On	On
On	Off	On
On	On	On

Truth Table for XNOR Gate

B	A	Y
Off	Off	On
Off	On	Off
On	Off	Off
On	On	On

Figure 3.6 Logic gates and respective truth tables

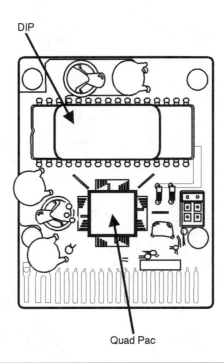

DIP

Quad Pac

Figure 3.7 DIPs and quad pac within onboard computer *(Courtesy General Motors Corp.)*

wires. A combination of the basic circuits on a single chip produces an I/C (Figure 3.7). These chips are black, rectangular housings, usually called *dual inline packages* (DIPs). In newer computers, these chips are square with pins protruding from all four sides, and are referred to as *quad pacs*.

The content of these I/C chips can be the microprocessing unit (the unit which controls the onboard computer), a clock circuit, or a number of other circuits. Its basic memory is very limited within the microprocessor and is used only for temporary storage of the information being processed. Different memory systems are used to store large amounts of information used by the onboard computer. The memory systems used in onboard computers are usually semiconductor devices. These memory systems are classified as ROM, PROM, and RAM.

Both ROM (read only memory) and PROM (programmable read only memory), just as their names state, can be read only and cannot be changed. Automotive onboard computers use ROM areas for storing basic operation instructions.

RAM (random access memory) is used by the automotive onboard computer to store space for information that is to be held temporarily while the computer is performing other functions. RAM or R/W (read/write) memory is easily accessible to store ever-changing data, but most information will be lost when the car is turned off, unless there is an additional supply of power to the RAM. Read and write controls are used to read and write information in and out of memory. These controls are basically decoders, a combination of logic gates allowing the microprocessor to read or write information stored in a specific memory location.

AUTOMOTIVE ONBOARD COMPUTER SYSTEMS

Onboard computer programs or software are the instructions that tell the onboard computer what to do. They are written in a computer language such as C or FORTRAN. For example, the program might be designed to monitor changes in automotive functions, such as ignition timing, or to initiate changes when appropriate. The program is converted into binary form (machine code) so that the onboard computer can process the information. For the programs to run, they require specific information, or inputs. These inputs provide the programs with the variables they need to control functions such as monitoring the oxygen levels in the NGV. Each input device converts a physical condition or state into an electrical signal representative of its present status. Some devices produce only two states (either on or off), but others have varying voltages as their physical state changes. In order for the computer to distinguish a change, it must use a known *reference voltage*. The computer compares the present state (voltage) of the input device, such as a sensor, to the reference voltage, enabling it to assign a numeric value to the present physical state of the device.

Figure 3.8 is a schematic that shows a typical layout of the components and functions of an onboard computer. The figure is labeled as follows:

A. Clock—a circuit that regulates the flow of data through the computer.

B. Input—a method in which data flow into the computer, such as from a sensor circuit.

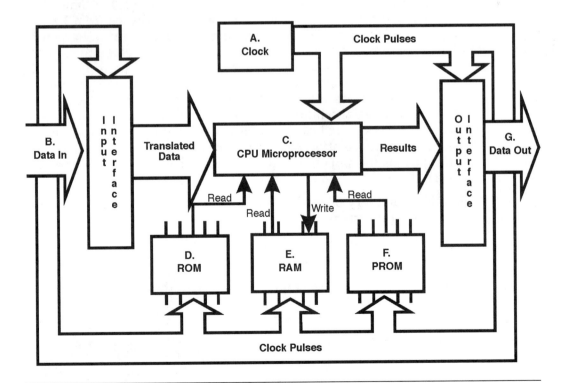

Figure 3.8 Typical layout and functioning of an onboard computer *(Courtesy General Motors Corp.)*

C. Microprocessor—the circuit that processes the data from the automobile using a computer program.

D. ROM—memory about the automobile that cannot be changed, such as the basic operation instructions.

E. RAM—memory about the automobile that can be changed, such as the current temperature of the engine.

F. PROM—memory about the automobile that can be reprogrammed by a technician; allows for the same memory chip to be used for a variety of automobiles.

G. Output—a method that uses the processed data to change the engine operating conditions, such as solenoids and relays.

All of the computer's functions are monitored by the clock circuit. Every function is timed according to clock pulses. Data goes into the computer at the input. The input interface translates the data and sends it to the microprocessor. The microprocessor processes the information according to preprogrammed instructions. It uses information stored in the ROM, PROM, and RAM to complete the instructions. Sometimes the microprocessor will store data in the RAM, but this information may be lost when the automobile is turned off. After the data is processed, the results are transferred as output to the various engine parts being controlled.

The following example illustrates how the onboard computer receives input from the oxygen sensor of the vehicle: When the oxygen sensor is exposed to oxygen, the outside plates (made of platinum) become positively charged. The voltage of the oxygen sensor can range from 1 millivolt (mV) to more than 900mV, depending on the amount of oxygen to which the sensor is exposed—leaner mixtures produce voltages near 900mV; richer mixtures produce voltages near 100mV. These voltage values are sent to the onboard computer, which examines these states and makes the appropriate adjustments. After the program receives the input and processes the information, it then sends the information to perform the necessary adjustment. For example, if the onboard computer has received information that the ignition is turned on, it will then send out signals (output) to the fuel cylinder solenoid to allow the natural gas to flow.

Here is a summary of the basic operation of the automotive onboard computer control system:

1. Input: The onboard computer receives voltage signals from sensors located around the engine.

2. Process: The onboard computer measures the voltage signals and converts them into sets of electrical states. The onboard computer "processes" the information by use of a program.

3. Output: The onboard computer sends out signals to the control devices (switches, solenoids, etc.) which make the necessary modifications.

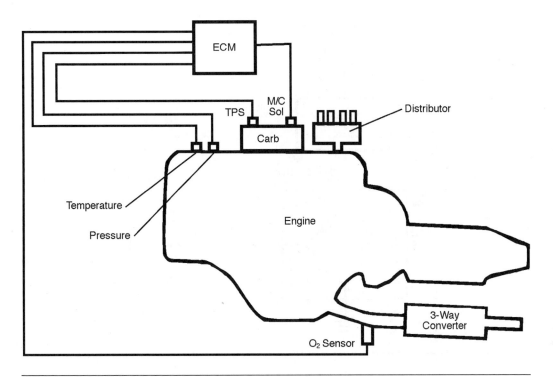

Figure 3.9 Typical layout of engine operating condition sensors *(Courtesy General Motors Corp.)*

Automotive Onboard Computer Input Sensors

A sensor is a transducer, an electrical device that converts a physical quantity into its electrical equivalent. These sensors are one of two kinds:

1. *Discrete sensor*—indicates one of two conditions. For example, this type of sensor indicates whether the car door is open or closed, or whether the air conditioning is on or off.

2. *Variable sensor*—indicates a wide range of conditions. Oxygen level and engine temperature are indicated by this type of sensor.

Figure 3.9 identifies the automobile's onboard computer (ECM) and some of the typical engine operating condition sensors: temperature sensor, pressure sensor, throttle position sensor (TPS), electronic spark monitoring and control sensors (M/C sol), and the oxygen sensor.

Temperature Sensors

The engine temperature is typically measured by a thermistor that controls the signal voltage to the computer. A thermistor is simply a resistor that varies with temperature. Depending on the type of temperature measurements to be done, the thermistor can be either a positive temperature coefficient sensor, in which the resistance increases as temperature increases, or a negative temperature coefficient sensor, in which the resistance decreases as temperature increases. The computer applies a voltage to the sensor and concurrently the voltage from the sensor is

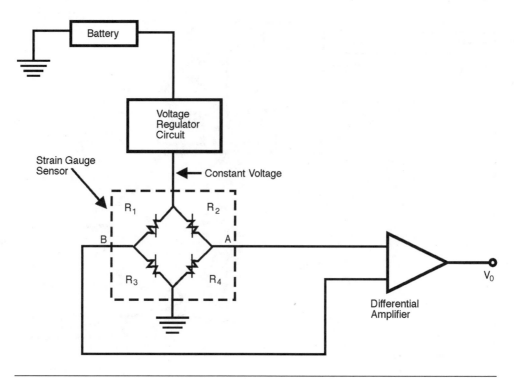

Figure 3.10 Pressure sensor circuit *(Courtesy General Motors Corp.)*

monitored within the computer. When the engine is cold, the thermistor resistance is high, and the computer registers a high voltage signal. When the engine is warm, the thermistor resistance is low and the voltage signal drops. At normal engine operating temperature (85°C to 95°C) the computer will read a voltage measurement of about 1.5 volts to 2.0 volts, with a 5-volt reference signal.

Pressure Sensors

Pressure sensors, such as manifold absolute pressure (MAP), barometric pressure (BARO), and vacuum differential (VAC) sensors measure pressure or lack of pressure. Engine load and altitude measurements are provided to the computer by pressure sensors. Sensor location is generally in the engine compartment. The computer sends a reference voltage to the sensor; then, corresponding to various loads, a voltage signal is sent back to the computer (Figure 3.10). The computer compares the value to a look-up table located in its ROM and uses the information to adjust the spark timing.

Throttle Position Sensor

The throttle position sensor (TPS) is a potentiometer, a resistor that changes resistance according to position. It provides a voltage signal that changes in relation to the throttle angle. Signal voltages will vary from a low voltage at idle to a high voltage at wide open throttle. The TPS signal is one of the most important inputs used by the computer for fuel control and for most of the computer control outputs. The TPS is connected to the throttle shaft and is controlled by the throttle mechanism. A reference signal is sent to the TPS by the computer. As the throttle valve angle is changed (accelerator pedal moved), the resistance of the TPS also changes. At a closed throttle position, the resistance of the TPS is high, so the output voltage to the computer will be low. The computer can determine fuel delivery based on the throttle valve angle by monitoring the output voltage from the TPS.

Electronic Spark Monitoring and Control Sensors

The electronic spark control (ESC) module is used to detect spark knock and to retard ignition timing. The system uses a detonation, or knock, sensor mounted in the engine block. Vibrations caused by detonation are sensed by the detonation sensor. The small voltage which is produced by a vibration is sent by the detonation sensor to the ESC, which evaluates the sensor signal and sends a command signal to the computer (Figure 3.11). The onboard computer normally sends an 8-volt to 10-volt reference signal to the ESC. The ESC module grounds the reference signal from the sensor when spark knock (detonation) occurs. If the computer notices the reference voltage pulled low, it typically starts to retard spark timing in 4° increments until the normal signal level has been maintained. While the reference voltage is returning to its normal level, the onboard computer slowly advances the spark timing.

Hall Effect Switch

Engine speed and crankshaft position can be provided to the computer by different means. The information can be translated by an ignition module or sent directly to the computer by a Hall effect switch. The Hall effect switch identifies the top dead center (TDC) position of each cylinder. It is mounted in the distributor above the normal pickup coil and

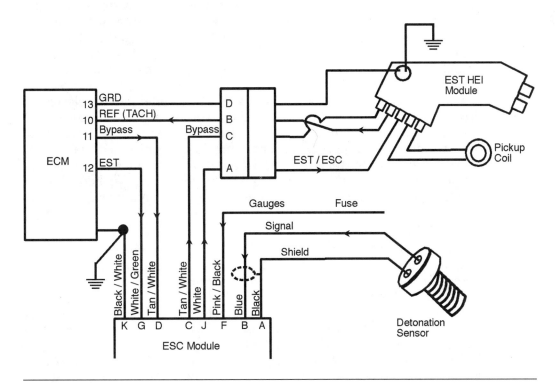

Figure 3.11 Typical electronic spark control layout *(Courtesy General Motors Corp.)*

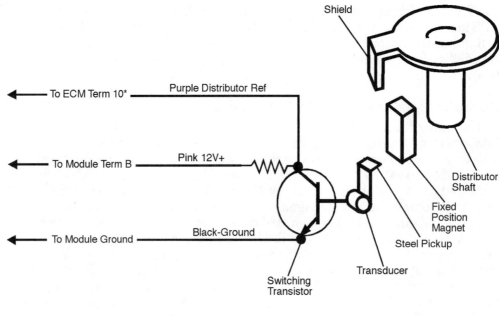

To ECM Term 10* — Purple Distributor Ref

To Module Term B — Pink 12V+

To Module Ground — Black-Ground

Shield

Distributor Shaft

Fixed Position Magnet

Steel Pickup

Transducer

Switching Transistor

* To ECM Term. J1-2 on 2.5L EFI

Figure 3.12 Hall effect switch *(Courtesy General Motors Corp.)*

module assembly. It contains a small magnet located very close to the electronic circuit for the switch. As the rotor turns, each of the steel vanes, or shutter blades, mounted on the rotor (the number depends upon the number of cylinders) passes through the small opening between the magnet and the electronic circuit. In general, a transistor is connected into the circuit with its collector connected to the onboard computer and a 12-volt signal, its emitter connected to ground, and its base connected to a transducer controlled by a magnetic field. When the magnetic field strikes the electronic circuit, it turns the transistor on, resulting in voltage less than 1V at the collector. When the magnetic field is cut off by a vane or shutter blade passing between the magnet and the electronic circuit, the transistor is turned off and the voltage at the collector is 12V. The resulting voltage at the collector determines the signal sent to the onboard computer (Figure 3.12). The signal is then processed by the computer to help control fuel delivery. In addition to fuel control, it is also one of the primary inputs for electronic ignition timing. Without the reference signal, the computer will not energize electronic spark timing.

Oxygen Sensor

The oxygen sensor acts as a small battery, continuously giving feedback to the onboard computer. It consists of zirconium between two plates of platinum. One of the platinum plates is exposed to the outside air, and the other plate is exposed to the exhaust gases (Figure 3.13). The oxygen sensor must be hot (i.e., 600°F) before it will send a signal that will cause the computer to respond. Until the oxygen sensor has reached 600°F it is operating in open loop mode. When the zirconium is heated to 600°F and comes in contact with oxygen, it becomes an electrical conductor. This causes the platinum plates to become positively charged. The platinum plate exposed to the outside air will attract positive

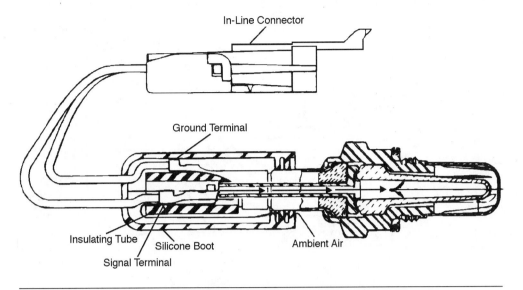

Figure 3.13 Cutaway of the oxygen sensor *(Courtesy General Motors Corp.)*

charges from the oxygen and remain constant, while the plate exposed to the exhaust gas will not attract as many positive charges and will vary according to O_2 content. The electrical difference between the two plates can range from 1mV to 1,000mV, depending on the amount of oxygen that comes in contact with the plate exposed to the exhaust gas. The onboard computer reads voltage from the oxygen sensor and makes adjustments to engine operating conditions.

Most of the components that the onboard computer controls are solenoids and relays. Typically, solenoids are used where there is lower current flow, and relays are used where there are higher currents. The solenoids and relays controlled by the onboard computer receive their power from the ignition switch. The computer will energize or de-energize these components based upon data it receives from the input sensors. The output instructions for the computer are typically stored in the PROM chip.

The following are some of the components controlled by the onboard computer: electronic spark timing, fuel metering solenoid, and fuel cylinder solenoid.

Electronic Spark Timing

The electronic spark advance is controlled automatically through the onboard computer. In many automobiles, the onboard computer controls a pickup coil and pole piece assembly and the ignition module (Figure 3.14). The onboard computer will receive a signal representing the engine speed. Inputs from the ESC module and pressure sensors are also sent to the computer. The computer uses all of this information to determine whether to adjust the spark advance.

In a carbureted system, the onboard computer uses a solenoid to regulate the amount of fuel entering the carburetor. An energized fuel-metering solenoid restricts the amount of fuel flowing into the main metering circuit by magnetic force, delivering a lean fuel mixture to the

Automotive Onboard Computer Outputs

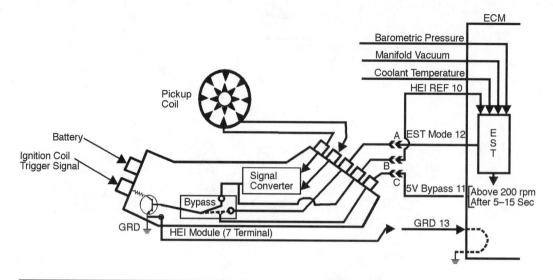

Figure 3.14 Typical electronic spark control layout *(Courtesy General Motors Corp.)*

engine. When the solenoid is de-energized, a richer mixture flows to the engine. Energizing and de-energizing are performed by the onboard computer. The computer energizes the solenoid for the amount of dwell time depending on the reading from the TPS, MAP, oxygen, and other sensors. The computer monitors the solenoid dwell time and is capable of maintaining the desired fuel ratio.

Fuel Cylinder Solenoids

In a typical NGV, a two-way electric solenoid is mounted on each fuel cylinder (Figure 3.15), and both are tied into the fuel control circuit. The

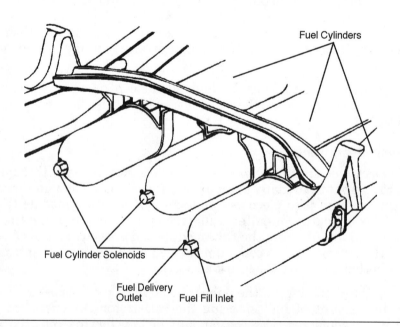

Figure 3.15 Fuel cylinder solenoids *(Courtesy General Motors Corp.)*

onboard computer will allow each of the solenoids to open and permit fuel to flow when the fuel pump relay receives an "ignition on" signal.

Now that the basics of computer control have been discussed, it is possible to look at some examples of computer-controlled automotive systems. Two excellent examples are the computer-controlled carburetion system and the computer-controlled fuel injection system.

Examples of Applied Computer-Controlled Automotive Systems

Computer-Controlled Carburetion System

The onboard computer operates the computer-controlled carburetion system in the following modes:

1. *Shutdown Mode*—This mode makes sure no current is supplied to the mixture solenoid and/or fuel injectors when the engine is stopped or when insufficient voltage is supplied to the onboard computer (which allows proper operation of the mixture solenoid). Operation under 200 rpm and battery voltage of less than 9 volts will put the system into the shutdown mode.

2. *Start-Up Enrichment Mode*—This mode provides a rich signal to the solenoid for a short time after any start-up. The length of this mode determines the temperature of the coolant sensor when started. It overrides the next three modes.

3. *Open Loop Mode*—This mode occurs during the engine warm-up period when the engine and oxygen sensor are not at operating temperature. The onboard computer provides a mixture command that regularly changes as the engine warms up. Whenever an engine is started, it is always in open loop mode.

4. *Closed Loop Mode*—This mode occurs when the engine is at proper operating temperature. At this point, the oxygen sensor is warm enough to generate a working signal to the onboard computer, after a predetermined amount of time has elapsed. On some cars, a few minutes idling will cause the oxygen sensor to cool and the system will go back to open loop. The system may switch back and forth.

5. *Enrichment* or *Near WOT Mode*—When the system is in an open or closed loop mode and the throttle is opened to near wide open throttle (WOT), the onboard computer sends a steady power enrichment signal to the mixture solenoid. Start-up and enrichment operation may be referred to as *adaptive modes*.

Computer-Controlled Fuel Injection System

The two basic types of fuel injection systems are the *port fuel injection* and the *throttle body injection*. There are also variations of both types. The location of the injectors usually determines the type of system. Port fuel injection refers to the injectors being located very near the intake valve. This system usually has one injector per cylinder and is very advantageous in the fine control of fuel delivery. Throttle body fuel injection, also known as *central fuel injection,* refers to an injector placed in a throttle body above the intake manifold. When this type of injector is turned on, it sprays its controlled amount of fuel at the throttle valves in a manner similar to a carburetor.

Since the injector is a solenoid, it has a voltage and a ground. It is controlled on its negative side, and the positive side is kept constant. In terms of the volt source, manufacturers have a couple of different options. In some cases the 12 volts are supplied by an ignition circuit, and in other cases by a relay controlled by the onboard computer. Such relays may be called either a *fuel pump relay,* an *automatic shutdown relay,* or a *control relay.* In certain cases the relay will be energized by the onboard computer after the computer sees a reference signal from the distributor or crank sensor.

The grounded side of the injector is used to control the length of time the injector is held open. This is controlled by the onboard computer through a device known as an *injector driver.* The computer instructs the injector driver as to the length of time the injector should be on. The injector driver responds by opening and closing the ground circuit of the injector. When the injector is de-energized (ground circuit opened with no current flowing through the solenoid wire coils), the plunger remains seated, preventing fuel from flowing through the nozzle. When the injector is energized (ground circuit closed with current flowing through the coil), the plunger moves off its seat, allowing pressurized fuel present at the nozzle to spray into the engine.

Usually measured in milliseconds (ms), *pulsewidth* is the length of time that the ground circuit to the injector is left on. Injector pulsewidth typically can vary between 40 ms (rich command) and 0.5 ms (lean command). The pulsewidth of the injector is determined by the onboard computer's input. The onboard computer must know the amount of air entering the engine, the engine temperature, engine speed, exhaust oxygen content, barometric pressure, throttle opening, and other input data before it can determine the pulsewidth of an injector.

The initial operation of the injector before the engine is cranking is known as the *primer shot mode.* The computer anticipates the starting of the engine by an initial shot from the injector(s). The pulsewidth of this varies according to coolant temperature. The colder the engine, the longer the primer shot will last, resulting in more fuel.

Importance of Onboard Computers

Electronic control of the functions of automobiles has made the NG vehicle an integrated system, with ignition, suspension, and transmission systems controlled by onboard computers. The advantages of the onboard computer are that it takes up less space under the hood, allows for control over a wide range of conditions, and can be reprogrammed as necessary. Many NG conversion systems are programmable through the use of a laptop computer. The laptop computer is the interface between the mechanic and the automobile.

Soon the reprogramming of the NG system will fall into the hands of shop mechanics who will need to know the basics of automotive computer control. This includes understanding how computers function and what their applications in the automobile are.

The various NG conversion systems on the market utilize the onboard computer in different ways. Some use OEM components and their own

Figure 3.16 Steps for onboard computer

aftermarket computer to translate the signals from gasoline to NG. Others replace system sensors and other components to run the vehicle on NG. It is important for the mechanic to understand how these systems function and the difference between them in order to be successful in the selection, installation, and troubleshooting of NG systems. Learning about computerized automotive control will give the mechanic a background in how the computer "thinks" (i.e., how the computer takes the information from the various components of the vehicle and makes decisions about engine operating conditions).

To perform its job of controlling engine operations, the onboard computer follows three steps (Figure 3.16):

Basic Operation of the Onboard Computer

1. *Input:* The computer receives input data from the sensors located around the vehicle. These sensors include pressure sensors (MAP, VAC, BARO), temperature sensors (MST, IAT), oxygen sensor, throttle position sensor, and others.

2. *Process:* The computer then processes the information it has received from these sensors using programs stored in its memory (PROM). These programs tell the computer what changes to make in engine conditions depending on the information it receives from the sensors.

3. *Output:* After the information is processed, the computer sends out signals to such devices as solenoids and relays. These devices adjust engine operating conditions according to instructions from the computer.

The closed loop conversion system uses an NGV system control unit. This unit allows a more precise control of both emissions and performance. The NGV system control unit continuously monitors various sensors such as the O_2 sensor and the throttle position sensor. The NGV system control unit then uses the information obtained from these sensors to adjust fuel flow and other engine conditions. Emissions feedback systems vary in their complexity, but typically the more interactive the system is with the engine sensors, the greater the vehicle's level of performance.

Closed Loop NGV Systems

Some conversion systems require an aftermarket control unit to allow the vehicle to run on NG, while others use the OEM control unit. In general, the NGV may require additional electronic equipment to allow the vehicle to run on NG. This equipment includes:

- computer signal modification device

- timing modification device

- fuel gauge

- NG/gasoline switch

- diagnostic link adapter

- NG conversion system control unit

Electrical and Electronic Faults

Symptoms of electrical and electronic circuit failures in an NGV are usually caused by an open circuit or a short circuit. In order to quickly and efficiently determine the cause of malfunctioning devices, troubleshooting should be thought out in advance.

ELECTRONIC CONTROL SYSTEMS

USE OF COMPUTERS FOR FEEDBACK CONTROL SYSTEMS

Automobiles possess a variety of automatic feedback controls which automatically adjust the operation of various functions in the vehicle in response to changing conditions. Onboard computers are being used as automatic feedback control units because: (1) they offer control over a wide range of circumstances, (2) they enable placement of large amounts of information into smaller spaces, and (3) they can be reprogrammed.

The use of onboard computers for feedback control systems eliminates the need for large mechanical control devices because onboard computer operation simply depends on the programs contained in small electronic circuits. The same basic onboard computer can be used to write different programs for monitoring devices (e.g., the oxygen sensor and the system voltage regulator) for different engines and operating conditions. In order to understand the basic functioning of the automotive computerized control system, automotive technicians need to learn more about the relationship between OEM control units and alternative fuel system control components.

The systems discussed here were chosen because of the different ways they interact with the OEM electronics and because they are common in the conversion industry. A number of systems meet these criteria for the purpose of this training. The treatment of these systems, as with all references to commercial products contained herein, is not intended to endorse or to criticize a particular product.

The interaction between the control system of any conversion system and the control system of the OEM can be described in three basic ways (Figure 3.17). First, the conversion system control unit can piggyback

THREE WAYS IN WHICH ALTERNATIVE FUEL SYSTEM AND OEM COMPUTER CONTROLS CAN WORK TOGETHER

1. Piggyback on signals
2. Tricking the unit with inserted signals
3. Creating a shift in true signals

Figure 3.17 Relationship between alternative fuel system and OEM computer controls

onto the signals sent by the OEM control unit; second, it can trick the OEM control unit into thinking it is receiving accurate data; third, it can shift the OEM signals in ways that are understood by the conversion system control unit.

Control Philosophy

As with all engine control computers, data are collected by polling the sensors on a timed basis. For example, consider a second hand on a watch. The second hand strikes a second mark for each of the 60 seconds in a minute. Imagine that each second mark on the watch face is a connection to other data. The mark in the third position might provide data on tank pressure, the 20th position might provide data on O_2 limits, and so on. As the engine data arrive at the control computer, the microprocessor interprets the data stream. The data may represent performance or conditions within an acceptable range. The microprocessor will then determine what, if any, additional action is necessary. The general control philosophy determines the nature of these control decisions.

Consider the following example of a decision-making philosophy. If a family taking a driving vacation has a drive philosophy of only driving on roads where there are ice cream stands, then the routes they take to reach their destination probably would be different from that of a family who has a philosophy based on fuel economy. Both families will arrive at the same destination. In fact, one philosophy may be as good as another, depending on what "good" means to a family.

OPEN LOOP NGV SYSTEMS

Open loop conversion systems provided an acceptable level of performance for vehicles that did not have onboard computer controls. One drawback was that these systems could be adjusted so that the vehicle's emissions levels violated mandated emissions levels. The venturi mixer systems that relied on vacuum signals to initiate the flow of natural gas were the most common open loop systems.

CLOSED LOOP NGV SYSTEMS

Closed loop conversion systems incorporate a method of monitoring the oxygen sensor and adjusting fuel flow according to the exhaust gas oxygen readings. This allows a more precise control of both emissions and performance. Many manufacturers use a computer during installation to customize the system to a particular engine/vehicle classification, making the system tamper-proof. The majority of the closed loop systems are controlled by an NGV system control unit. This control unit is wired into the OEM electronic control unit and system sensors. The following are examples of various closed loop systems.

ANGI

Figure 3.18 is a computer-controlled (NGV system control unit) closed loop, adaptive learn conversion system. Utilizing the speed-density principle (a means of determining how much natural gas is entering the

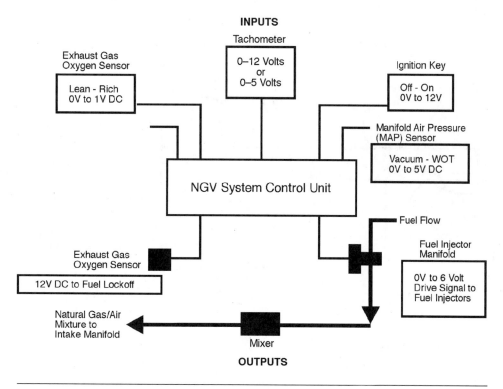

Figure 3.18 Closed loop adaptive learn system *(Courtesy Automotive Natural Gas, Inc.)*

intake manifold by measuring the difference in pressure and temperature for a given rpm), the computer adjusts the fuel metering valve position (in the gas flow) to preset oxygen sensor switch points for different engine speeds and loads. It incorporates an automatic fuel selector (which automatically switches between natural gas and gasoline) using the existing dash gauge for bi-fuel applications. This system uses a standard D-type regulator package that includes a first stage and a second stage with a fixed venturi mixer ring or nozzle combination.

IMPCO

Figure 3.19 is a microprocessor-based engine management system which uses the gas mass measuring method. This is the same method used by most automobile manufacturers in original equipment. Signals are transferred to the onboard computer (NGV system control unit) along with a signal from a gaseous fuel mass flow sensor of natural gas into the engine. The onboard computer processes the signals and determines a precise natural gas/air mixture. An electrical interface module is inserted between the vehicle's onboard computer and the NG onboard computer. It includes adaptive learning capability which adjusts to variations among engines, long-term changes in operating conditions, and degradation in the engine or conversion system.

GFI

The system in Figure 3.20 electronically meters fuel, controls spark advance, and registers natural gas fuel storage pressure on the OEM fuel gauge. A combination of OEM and NG sensors is used to monitor the engine and environment to provide closed loop control of fuel. This system is designed to automatically return the engine to gasoline operation

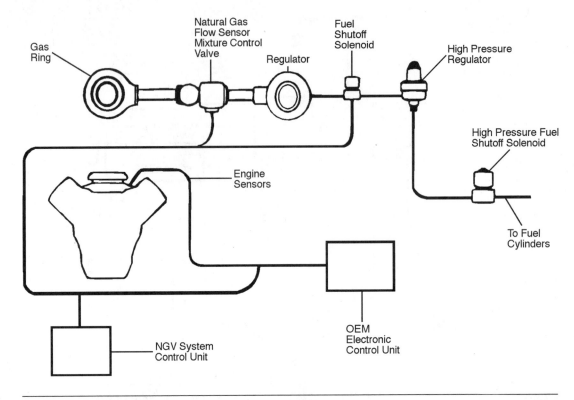

Figure 3.19 Closed loop, gas mass measuring system

when the fuel storage pressure drops below a minimum level. The system is fully programmable by way of an external personal onboard computer. It uses a speed-density calculation for both fuel flow and air flow and calculates the air/fuel mixture based on a stoichiometric value of the fuel composition in the area of operation. Speed-density calculations are based on temperature, pressure, fuel absolute pressure, and fuel regulated temperature. These sensors are located in a metering valve (intake manifold). The intake air temperature sensor is mounted on the intake system, and the manifold skin temperature sensor is mounted on the intake manifold. An onboard computer/metering valve regulates fuel flow by means of a series of electronically controlled solenoids and injectors.

A high pressure natural gas line supplies fuel to a single-stage regulator. The regulator reduces pressure to approximately 100 psi. Once the fuel flows through the regulator, the natural gas is passed on to a special fuel filter and into the computer/metering valve (CompuValve). The CompuValve then regulates fuel flow by means of a series of electronically controlled solenoids and injectors. After flowing through the CompuValve, the natural gas is sent to a spray discharge unit(s) located in the engine's air intake.

Baytech

Baytech is a fuel injection system that incorporates an electronic calibrator module that provides optimized performance and fuel economy for General Motors engines converted to operate on compressed natural gas. The module, which is installed in the original engine onboard computer

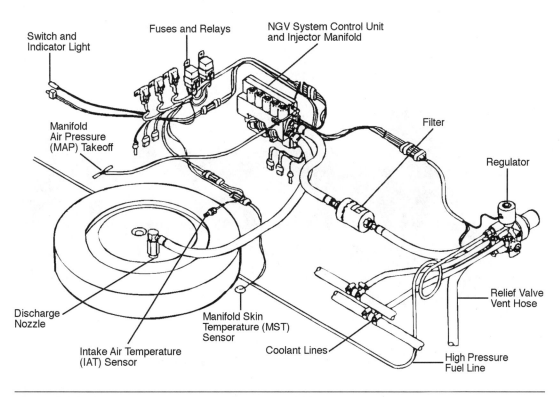

Figure 3.20 Closed loop, electronically metered bi-fuel system

in existing pin sockets, is specifically designed to optimize natural gas vehicles by increasing engine power, improving driveability, and extending vehicle range. The module is fully compatible with the engine control module, eliminating the need for additional external systems commonly used for spark advance control and diagnostic code capability.

The bi-fuel module software provides specific natural gas engine calibration parameters when operating on natural gas without affecting operation on gasoline. The module has demonstrated 20 to 30 percent increases in fuel economy. In some applications, the module has demonstrated horsepower increases of 5 to 10 hp over the stock gasoline engine before conversion. The fuel calibration mode is selected via an external switch or relay.

MESA GEM

This is a stand-alone engine control system that works independently of the vehicle's original onboard computer, and is compatible with all other original control functions. When switched to the natural gas mode, the controller deactivates the relays that connect the gasoline fuel injectors and fuel pump and activates the natural gas fuel system. A time delay is provided for the transition both into and out of the natural gas mode. The fuel is metered, based on speed-density calculations, through pulsewidth modulated injectors, and fired in a sequence that provides a nearly continuous flow of fuel to the engine. This system's processor can compensate for differences in Btu content between fuels and control within 35 percent of stoichiometric efficiency. This system also can include self-diagnostic capability and sensor default to ensure "limp-home" capability.

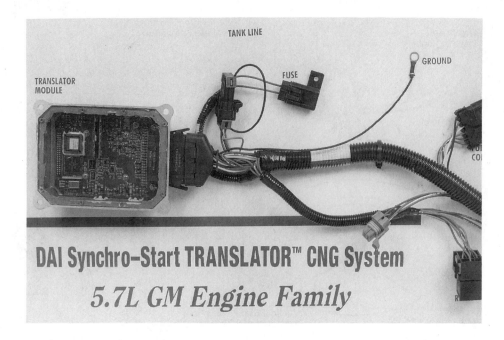

Figure 3.21 DAI Synchro-Start Translator CNG System

MOGAS

This closed loop system is an oxygen sensor-driven feedback system. It maintains an ideal air/fuel ratio that fulfills the OEM onboard computer expectations. It has a four-stage, thermostatically controlled, pneumatic flow control regulator. It includes automatic priming and electronic shutoff. A dash-mounted fuel selector switch and gauge uses an LED display with an electronic transducer sending unit and is available with an automatic gasoline start override. In the event of a system failure, the OEM onboard computer diagnostic will turn on the Check Engine light and will record the fault codes.

DAI/Synchro-Start

This closed loop system employs the engine manufacturer's control system instead of a new controller. It determines the fuel demand parameters of the engine by monitoring the existing electrical signal that is sent from the OEM onboard computer to the gasoline fuel injectors. Then this signal is translated to operate a metering valve to provide the equivalent amount of natural gas. To tailor this system for use on a particular engine, a personal onboard computer downloads individualized calibration curves to an EEPROM in the system's microprocessor. Changes in the engine's spark timing are also incorporated through the NGV system control unit. Diagnostic functions are also built in (Figure 3.21).

SPI

This system is composed of a high pressure gaseous injector. It can be located in a multipoint, sequential, or throttle body application. Currently, it is used on OEM spark-ignited engines. NGV conversion systems are available. The system includes an electronic unit and software (NGV system control unit). It can compensate for variations in gas quality and has adaptive learn for real-time system self-adjustments to maintain emissions performance.

SUMMARY

- The three factors a technician must consider when solving a complex problem are: (1) mechanical aspects, (2) resources, and (3) technician skill level/ability.

- Ohm's law states that it takes one volt of electrical pressure to push one amp of electrical current through one ohm of resistance.

- If one quantity changes (voltage, amperage, or resistance), then at least one other quantity must change.

- In automotive applications most electrical problems are caused by one of the following conditions: (1) resistance of a circuit remains constant; an increase in the amount of applied voltage results in an increase in amperage, or (2) voltage remains constant; a decrease in the resistance of the circuit results in an increase in the circuit amperage.

- Electromagnetism occurs whenever current flows through a conductor which is formed into a coil.

- In most automotive applications semiconductors are used in combination to form diodes and transistors.

- Logic gates are electrical devices that produce a given output for a given input.

- Both ROM and PROM can be read only and cannot be changed. They are used for storing basic operating instructions.

- RAM is used to temporarily hold information while the computer is performing other functions.

- Input devices convert a physical condition or state into an electrical signal representative of its physical status.

- Temperature sensors are typically thermistors that control the signal voltage to the computer based on changes in temperature.

- MAP, BARO, and VAC sensors are pressure sensors that provide the computer with a voltage signal corresponding to the relative pressures.

- The TPS is a potentiometer that provides a voltage signal in relation to the throttle angle.

- Different means can be used to provide information to the computer on engine speed and crankshaft position, the most common type being a Hall effect switch.

- The oxygen sensor acts as a small battery sending a changing voltage signal (1–900mV) based on the content of oxygen in the exhaust, which changes based on the air/fuel ratio.

- The computer uses inputs from the oxygen sensor to determine the implied air/fuel ratio.

- Most of the components that the computer controls are solenoids or relays.

- Some of the components controlled by the computer include: electronic spark timing, the fuel metering solenoid, and the fuel solenoid valve (injector).

- The basic operating modes of the computer-controlled carburetion system are: shutdown mode, start-up enrichment mode, open loop mode, closed loop mode, and enrichment or near wide open throttle mode.

- To perform its job of controlling engine operations, the onboard computer follows three steps: input, process, and output.

- Some conversion systems require an aftermarket control unit to allow the vehicle to run on natural gas, while other systems use the OEM control unit.

- Normally, NGVs require the following additional electronic equipment: (1) computer signal modification device, (2) timing modification device, (3) natural gas fuel gauge, (4) fuel selector switch, (5) diagnostic link connector, and (6) natural gas conversion system control unit.

- Symptoms of electrical and electronic circuit failures in an NGV are usually caused by an open circuit or a short circuit.

- Onboard computers are being used as automatic feedback control units because: (1) they offer control over a wide range of circumstances, (2) they enable placement of a large amount of information into smaller spaces, and (3) they can be reprogrammed.

- The interaction between the conversion and the OEM control systems can be accomplished using any of the following methods: (1) piggybacking signals sent by the OEM system, (2) tricking the OEM system, and (3) shifting the OEM signal.

- Open loop systems do not have onboard computers and may not always maintain satisfactory performance and emissions levels.

- Closed loop conversion systems incorporate a method of monitoring the oxygen sensor and adjusting fuel flow accordingly.

- The majority of closed loop systems are controlled by a separate NGV control unit wired into the OEM control and system sensors.

- The ANGI conversion system is an adaptive learn system that consists of an independent computer-driven system which utilizes the speed-density principle to maintain the proper air/fuel ratio by means of adjusting the fuel metering valve position, and an automatic fuel selector to control which fuel is used.

- The IMPCO system uses the gas mass measuring method, has adaptive learning capabilities, and has a separate microprocessor which interfaces with the OEM computer.

- The GFI system is a fully programmable electronic conversion system which uses speed-density calculations for air and natural gas inputs—the air/fuel ratio is controlled using a CompuValve (a combination of a computer, natural gas solenoids, and injectors).

- The Baytech conversion system is designed for select General Motors vehicles, and allows the use of the OEM computer control strategies to provide self-diagnostic capabilities and improved power and fuel economy.

- The MESA GEM conversion system is an independent speed-density type system which offers self-diagnostics and "limp home" capabilities.

- The MOGAS conversion system uses a four-stage pressure regulator and incorporates the self-diagnostic capabilities of the OEM computer while in natural gas operation.

- The DAI/Synchro-Start system "piggybacks" the OEM computer to operate a metering valve which controls the air/gaseous fuel ratio and has self-diagnostic capabilities. Modifications for specific vehicles are performed with a personal computer.

- The SPI system is a high pressure fuel injection system currently being used by some vehicle manufacturers. The system has adaptive learning capabilities, self-diagnostics, and can compensate for changes in natural gas quality.

- External computers are used during installation to customize the conversion system for use on a particular engine/vehicle combination by many conversion system manufacturers.

REVIEW QUESTIONS

1. Describe the three factors involved in the process of troubleshooting a complex problem.

2. Describe the two conditions of Ohm's law that cause most electrical problems in automobile applications.

3. List the three different types of memory and explain how they are used in automotive computer systems.

4. Explain the basic steps of operation used in an automotive onboard computer.

5. Describe the purpose of the six different types of input sensors described in this chapter and briefly explain how they operate.

6. List the three basic outputs of a computer system and explain what they are used for.

7. Explain the advantages of using an onboard computer system in the automobile.

8. Explain the three ways in which an alternative fuels computer system and the OEM computer system can work together.

9. Explain the difference between open loop and closed loop operating systems.

10. List the eight different types of closed loop conversion systems based on their operating strategies.

CHAPTER 4

System Specific Electronics

OBJECTIVES

- Identify three typical closed loop conversion systems using speed-density calculations.
- Identify the basic electronic components specific to the ECO conversion system.
- Understand the basic operating principles of an ECO conversion system.
- Understand which parameters of an ECO conversion system can be reprogrammed to meet specific vehicle demands.
- Understand the basic diagnostic procedures of the ECO system.
- Identify the basic electronic components specific to the MESA GEM conversion system.
- Understand the basic operating principles of a MESA GEM conversion system.
- Understand the basic diagnostic procedures of the MESA GEM system.
- Identify the basic electronic components specific to the GFI conversion system.
- Understand the parameters that can be used in the calibration of the GFI system to meet specific vehicle demands.
- Understand the basic operating principles of a GFI conversion system.
- Understand the basic diagnostic procedures of the GFI system.

KEY TERMS

ECO FMS

"Smart cable"

WARM_O2

O2_WARMUP_DELAY

DEF_SERVO

MIN_TPS

START_RPM

BASE_RPM

MIN_FUEL

MIN_FUEL_ADD

FG_MIN, FG_MAX

EMPTY_BLINK_T

MIN_LED_BRIGHT

Timing optimizer

NGP (natural gas pressure)

NGT (natural gas temperature)

CompuValve

Kit characterization

Application calibration

Field calibration

MST (manifold skin temperature)

FMON (field monitor)

DMAP (delta manifold absolute pressure)

FAP (fuel absolute pressure)

FSP (fuel storage pressure)

FRT (fuel regulated temperature)

TMIX (mixture temperature)

CLCF (closed loop correction factor)

LTAR (target lambda)

NMFF (normalized mass fuel flow)

SYSTEM SPECIFIC ELECTRONICS

FUEL MANAGEMENT SYSTEMS

Automobile fuel management decisions are based on two common control philosophies: mass air flow and speed-density calculation.

When the ECO fuel system is installed, technicians can access engine management data from both the OEM computer and the ECO computer. Standard scan tools can be used to access the OEM system for fault codes, settings, and performance data. A laptop computer can be used to access similar data directly from the ECO fuel management system (FMS) component (Figure 4.1).

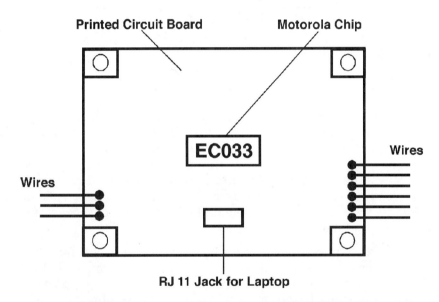

Figure 4.1 Inside the FMS

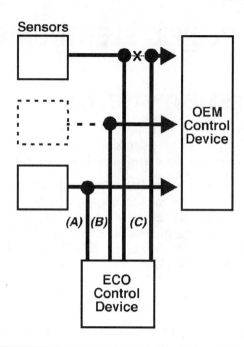

Figure 4.2 Control information flow

Of course, the goal is to establish an operating environment for the engine to run efficiently while keeping emissions at acceptable levels. The data sampling of the control system happens in a normal way. Transducers and sensors provide information to the control system. However, whether control signals are sent from the OEM control unit or the conversion system control unit is another matter. Information between the OEM computer system and the ECO computer system flows in the directions shown in Figure 4.2.

Two typical conversion systems that execute the speed-density calculation in slightly different ways are the ECO system and the GEM system. They differ in what data they gather and how they process it, but both make decisions based on verification of speed-density philosophy. The following is a closer look at the data points considered by the ECO system fuel management system. Like all microprocessor-based control systems, fast-paced change defines the products.

ECO Program System

Diagnostics are performed on the ECO system by connecting the serial port of an IBM PC-AT compatible laptop to the FMS via a "smart cable" (this cable has some electronic circuitry in its connection to the computer) and then running the FMS Diagnostic Support software. The only additional software required is a standard terminal emulation or communications program such as *Procomm Plus* or *Terminal EXC*. These programs are supported by the FMS.

Once the ECO system is installed and tested, the performance of the electrical system can be investigated further through proprietary diagnostic software and a laptop computer. The connection is made by inserting a twisted-pair cable with an RJ 11 connector on the end into the ECO fuel management system (FMS).

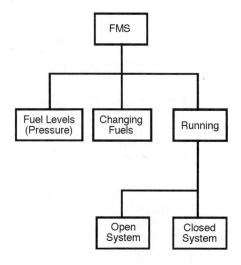

Figure 4.3 Three primary control responsibilities of the ECO FMS system

The ECO system is a closed loop system. The brain of the system is the fuel management system. The FMS performs three distinct functions; it monitors fuel levels, the changing of fuels, and engine performance (Figure 4.3). Figure 4.4 shows the basic electronic system components.

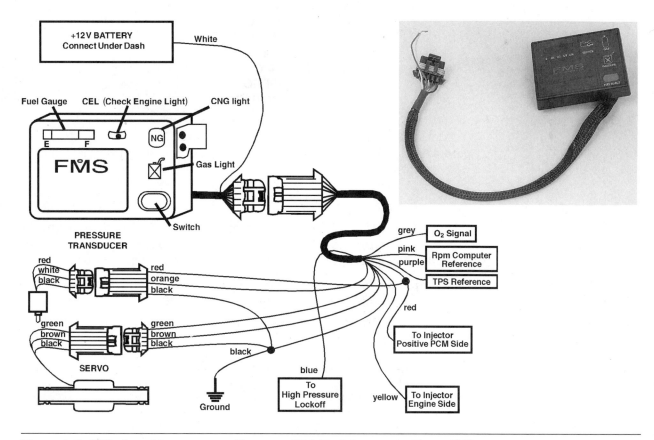

Figure 4.4 ECO closed loop system *(Courtesy ECO Fuel Systems). Photo:* FMS

- BASE_O2
- LIMIT_O2
- WARM_O2
- O2 WARMUP DELAY
- O2_FLIMIT
- O2_INIT_DELTA
- DEF_SERVO
- MIN_TPS
- DELTA_MIN_TPS
- DMD_TPS
- GASOLINE TO GAS DELAY
- GAS TO GASOLINE DELAY
- STEP SIZE 1
- STEP SIZE 2
- STEP SIZE 3
- STEP SIZE 4
- START_RPM
- BASE_RPM
- NO. OF CYLINDERS
- RPM_FACTOR
- DEAD_TIME 1
- DEAD_TIME 2
- DEAD_TIME 3
- DEAD_TIME 4
- DEAD_TIME 5
- DEAD_TIME 6
- DEAD_TIME 7
- MIN_FUEL
- MIN_FUEL_ADD
- FG_MIN
- FG_MAX
- FG_SPEED
- EMPTY_BLINK_T
- MIN_LED_BRIGHT

Figure 4.5 ECO FMS monitors 34 parameters that are shown on the computer display

The ECO FMS is able to monitor various parameters and values in the NG system (Figure 4.5) through a smart cable. The FMS also has the capability of displaying the values for diagnostic purposes (Figure 4.6).

The FMS can determine or allow for modification of the values within a range of 0 to 255, with the following exceptions:

- the DEF_SERVO value is calculated within the range of 0000H to FFFFH

- the START_RPM value is calculated within the range of 0 to 9999

- the NO. OF CYLINDERS value is within the range of 0 to 13

VEHICLE START-UP

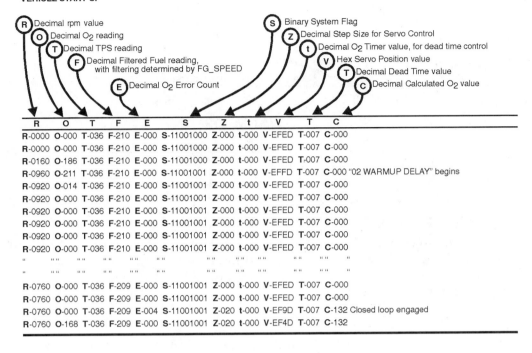

Legend:
- R — Decimal rpm value
- O — Decimal O$_2$ reading
- T — Decimal TPS reading
- F — Decimal Filtered Fuel reading, with filtering determined by FG_SPEED
- E — Decimal O$_2$ Error Count
- S — Binary System Flag
- Z — Decimal Step Size for Servo Control
- t — Decimal O$_2$ Timer value, for dead time control
- V — Hex Servo Position value
- T — Decimal Dead Time value
- C — Decimal Calculated O$_2$ value

R	O	T	F	E	S	Z	t	V	T	C	
R-0000	O-000	T-036	F-210	E-000	S-11001000	Z-000	t-000	V-EFED	T-007	C-000	
R-0000	O-000	T-036	F-210	E-000	S-11001000	Z-000	t-000	V-EFED	T-007	C-000	
R-0160	O-186	T-036	F-210	E-000	S-11001000	Z-000	t-000	V-EFED	T-007	C-000	
R-0960	O-211	T-036	F-210	E-000	S-11001001	Z-000	t-000	V-EFFD	T-007	C-000	"02 WARMUP DELAY" begins
R-0920	O-014	T-036	F-210	E-000	S-11001001	Z-000	t-000	V-EFED	T-007	C-000	
R-0920	O-000	T-036	F-210	E-000	S-11001001	Z-000	t-000	V-EFED	T-007	C-000	
R-0920	O-000	T-036	F-210	E-000	S-11001001	Z-000	t-000	V-EFED	T-007	C-000	
R-0920	O-000	T-036	F-210	E-000	S-11001001	Z-000	t-000	V-EFED	T-007	C-000	
R-0920	O-000	T-036	F-210	E-000	S-11001001	Z-000	t-000	V-EFED	T-007	C-000	
R-0920	O-000	T-036	F-210	E-000	S-11001001	Z-000	t-000	V-EFED	T-007	C-000	
"	" "	" "	" "	" "	" "	" "	" "	" "	" "	"	
"	" "	" "	" "	" "	" "	" "	" "	" "	" "	"	
R-0760	O-000	T-036	F-209	E-000	S-11001001	Z-000	t-000	V-EFED	T-007	C-000	
R-0760	O-000	T-036	F-209	E-000	S-11001001	Z-000	t-000	V-EFED	T-007	C-000	
R-0760	O-000	T-036	F-209	E-004	S-11001001	Z-020	t-000	V-EF9D	T-007	C-132	Closed loop engaged
R-0760	O-168	T-036	F-209	E-000	S-11001001	Z-020	t-000	V-EF4D	T-007	C-132	

Notice on the 'E' line when error reaches 255, the 7th status bit is set, indicating that the service light is set and the servo goes to its default position.

R	O	T	F	E	S	Z	t	V	T	C	
R-0800	O-000	T-038	F-206	E-193	S-11001001	Z-020	t-000	V-EDFD	T-007	C-132	
R-0800	O-000	T-038	F-206	E-197	S-11001001	Z-020	t-000	V-EDFD	T-007	C-132	
R-0800	O-000	T-038	F-206	E-201	S-11001001	Z-020	t-000	V-EDFD	T-007	C-132	
R-0800	O-000	T-038	F-206	E-205	S-11001001	Z-020	t-000	V-EDFD	T-007	C-132	
R-0800	O-000	T-038	F-206	E-209	S-11001001	Z-020	t-000	V-EDFD	T-007	C-132	
R-0800	O-000	T-038	F-206	E-213	S-11001001	Z-020	t-000	V-EDFD	T-007	C-132	
R-0800	O-000	T-038	F-206	E-217	S-11001001	Z-020	t-000	V-EDFD	T-007	C-132	
R-0800	O-000	T-038	F-206	E-233	S-11001001	Z-020	t-000	V-EDFD	T-007	C-132	
R-0800	O-000	T-038	F-206	E-237	S-11001001	Z-020	t-000	V-EDFD	T-007	C-132	
R-0800	O-000	T-038	F-206	E-241	S-11001001	Z-020	t-000	V-EDFD	T-007	C-132	
R-0800	O-000	T-038	F-206	E-245	S-11001001	Z-020	t-000	V-EDFD	T-007	C-132	
R-0800	O-000	T-038	F-206	E-249	S-11001001	Z-020	t-000	V-EDFD	T-007	C-132	
R-0800	O-000	T-038	F-206	E-253	S-11001001	Z-020	t-000	V-EDFD	T-007	C-132	
R-0800	**O-000**	**T-038**	**F-206**	**E-255**	**S-11001011**	**Z-020**	**t-000**	**V EFED**	**T-007**	**C-132**	**Service light on. Open loop Operation**
R-0960	O-167	T-039	F-206	E-255	S-11001011	Z-020	t-000	V-EFED	T-007	C-132	

OPEN LOOP OPERATION

The data stream indicates that there is no servo movement, no error generation and closed loop does not engage.

MONITOR MODE ENABLED

R	O	T	F	E	S	Z	t	V	T	C
R-0800	O-193	T-039	F-191	E-000	S-11001001	Z-000	t-000	V-EFBB	T-007	C-000
R-0760	O-191	T-039	F-191	E-000	S-11001001	Z-000	t-000	V-EFBB	T-007	C-000
R-0760	O-192	T-039	F-191	E-000	S-11001001	Z-000	t-000	V-EFBB	T-007	C-000
R-0760	O-187	T-039	F-191	E-000	S-11001001	Z-000	t-000	V-EFBB	T-007	C-000
R-0680	O-191	T-039	F-191	E-000	S-11001001	Z-000	t-000	V-EFBB	T-007	C-000
R-0720	O-187	T-044	F-191	E-000	S-11001001	Z-000	t-000	V-EFBB	T-007	C-000
R-0800	O-176	T-039	F-191	E-000	S-11001001	Z-000	t-000	V-EFBB	T-007	C-000
R-0720	O-197	T-039	F-191	E-000	S-11001001	Z-000	t-000	V-EFBB	T-007	C-000

Figure 4.6 ECO data stream *(Courtesy ECO Fuel Systems)*

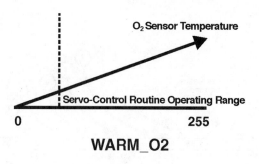

Figure 4.7 WARM_O2 operating range

Values That Can Be Altered

The following 17 values of those parameters monitored by the FMS can be altered by the technician to improve vehicle performance. The ranges in which they are monitored and other variables which affect them are also illustrated.

1. WARM_O2

This check verifies that the temperature of the O_2 sensor is in a given range.

The O_2 sensor temperature must be above the WARM_O2 value (represented by the dotted line) in order to engage the servo-control routine (Figure 4.7).

2. O2_WARMUP_DELAY

This value is the amount of time that the FMS is forced to wait before releasing the servo to closed loop operation.

3. DEF_SERVO

This value allows the technician to reset the position of the servo on initial start-up when the vehicle does not run due to a lean or rich mixture. The resetting of the servo allows for auto-setup (default system settings): at idle the system is in open loop and when not at idle the system is a closed loop.

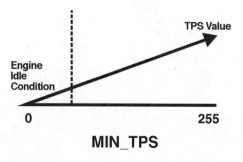

Figure 4.8 MIN_TPS value range

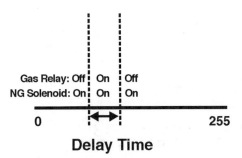

Figure 4.9 Gasoline to gas delay range

4. MIN_TPS

This check sets the minimum TPS value used to determine the engine's idle condition (Figure 4.8).

All TPS values lower than the MIN_TPS value (represented by the dotted line) indicate that the engine is idling. If the MIN_TPS is set too high, then the servo will be set to the DEF_SERVO position and the FMS will operate in open loop mode. If the MIN_TPS is set too low, the FMS will be in closed loop mode while the engine is idling.

5. GASOLINE TO GAS DELAY

This value indicates the time delay that occurs during the switch from gasoline to NG. It keeps the gasoline and NG relay or solenoid on simultaneously.

During switchover from gasoline to NG, the FMS will delay switching the gasoline relay off to allow time for the NG to reach the intake (Figure 4.9). This prevents stalling during fuel switchover. If the delay value is set too high, then the mixture will be too rich and may cause engine flooding. If the delay value is set too low, the fuel flow may be interrupted, causing the vehicle to stall under a lean condition.

6. GAS TO GASOLINE DELAY

This value represents the delay time during the switch from NG to gasoline. The computer shuts the gasoline relay and NG solenoid off simultaneously (Figure 4.10).

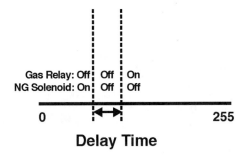

Figure 4.10 Gas to gasoline delay range

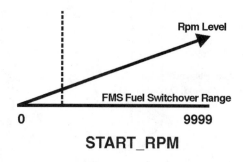

START_RPM

Figure 4.11 START_RPM range

During switchover from NG to gasoline, the FMS will delay switching on the gas relay in order to allow all of the NG to be depleted before allowing gasoline to flow. If the delay value is set too high, the engine may stall due to lack of fuel because of an excessive time delay during switchover. If the value is set too low, fuel overlapping may occur; this also causes engine stall due to a rich condition.

7. START_RPM

This value indicates the minimum rpm level that must be reached for the FMS switchover to operate after start-up.

In order for the FMS fuel switchover to occur (Figure 4.11), the engine speed must reach the value indicated by START_RPM (represented by the dotted line). If the START_RPM value is set too high, the system will continue operating on gasoline. If the START_RPM value is set too low, NG will be turned on, resulting in a rich condition and poor starting quality.

8. BASE_RPM

This value shows the minimum rpm level that the engine must maintain while running; it determines that the NG solenoid valves will be closed if the engine stops or stalls (Figure 4.12).

The rpm level must equal at least the BASE_RPM value (represented by the dotted line) to keep the NG solenoid valves open while the engine is running. If the BASE_RPM value is set too high, then the FMS may

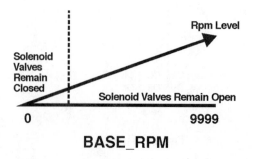

BASE_RPM

Figure 4.12 BASE_RPM range

rpm = (number of pulses in ½ second) x (RPM_Factor)

-or-

$$RPM\_FACTOR = \frac{rpm}{(number\ of\ pulses\ in\ \frac{1}{2}\ second)}$$

Figure 4.13 RPM_FACTOR equations

switch to gasoline during an engine idle condition and close the NG sole-noids. If the BASE_RPM is set too low, then the NG solenoid valves may not be turned off when the engine stops or stalls.

9. and 10. NUMBER OF CYLINDERS and RPM_FACTOR

The NUMBER OF CYLINDERS value allows for the selection of the correct number of cylinders between 1 and 12. Since manufacturers do not use the same pulse rate to describe rpm, the FMS uses a value called the RPM_FACTOR to account for an unusual pulse rate. When there is an unusual pulse rate, the technician sets the NO. OF CYLINDERS to 13 and then sets the appropriate RPM_FACTOR so that the FMS can read the rpm precisely. The equation that determines the RPM_FACTOR is shown in Figure 4.13.

11. MIN_FUEL

The MIN_FUEL value is the minimum fuel pressure level that must be reached to obtain a low fuel condition (Figure 4.14).

If the fuel pressure value falls below the MIN_FUEL value (repre-sented by the dotted line), the FMS will automatically switch over to gasoline operation. If the MIN_FUEL value is set too high, the FMS may switch over to gasoline while there is still an adequate supply of NG available. If the MIN_FUEL value is set too low, then the FMS may not switch over to gasoline operation before the NG supply is depleted.

12. MIN_FUEL_ADD

This value represents the needed increase in fuel for the FMS to

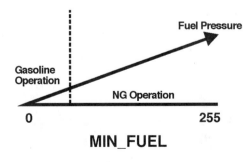

Figure 4.14 MIN_FUEL range

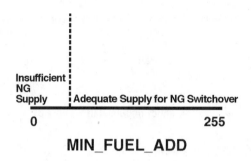

Figure 4.15 MIN_FUEL_ADD range

perform an automatic switchover on start-up after MIN_FUEL has been engaged (Figure 4.15).

If the MIN_FUEL_ADD level (represented by the dotted line) is not reached after MIN_FUEL has been engaged, then the FMS will not switch over to NG on start-up. This MIN_FUEL_ADD variable will prevent the switchover to NG when the fuel cylinder has not been filled.

13. and 14. FG_MIN and FG_MAX

The FG_MIN value is the minimum number achieved by the fuel pressure transducer. It is represented by "empty" on the NG fuel gauge. The FG_MAX value, represented by "full" on the NG fuel gauge, is the maximum number achieved by the fuel pressure transducer (Figure 4.16).

15. EMPTY_BLINK_T

This value indicates the number of seconds between blinks on the NG fuel gauge once the fuel pressure is below MIN_FUEL (Figure 4.17).

16. MIN_LED_BRIGHT

This value shows the minimum light intensity needed to control the LED on the NG fuel gauge (Figure 4.18).

17. TIMING OPTIMIZER

An additional device may be installed in the system to collect electronic data. This device makes decisions to optimize spark timing and/or

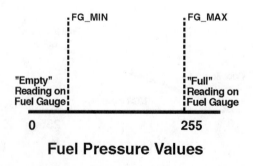

Figure 4.16 FG_MIN and FG_MAX range

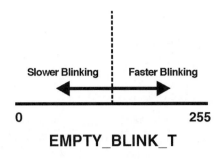

Figure 4.17 EMPTY_BLINK_T range

cycle other data collection processes to adjust other variables. The devices are programmed to collect data and make decisions for specific engine families in specific vehicles. Such devices are made by Autotronic Controls or A.E.B.

These supplemental devices are referred to by their manufacturers' product names. For example, Ford calls their product the "Gold Master," even though it is an A.E.B. product. Autotronic Controls produces devices with such names as "Super Fix," "Support," or "Magnum Advance."

The Magnum Advance is a timing device. The Super Fix connects to the engine control module in order to account for the necessary modifications. The Support is a multifunctional device that combines the Super Fix's capability to account for adjustments with the Magnum Advance's capability to advance timing.

MESA GEM System

The MESA GEM system (Figure 4.19) follows a decision-making philosophy based on a speed-density calculation. A general assessment of the difference of the ECO and GEM approaches to making the speed-density calculation can be based on the observation that the GEM system measures data (and bases decisions) on more data points than the ECO system. In the previous section, we reviewed the data inputs of the ECO system. The data collected and factored into decisions by the GEM system include those data points as well as the following measurements.

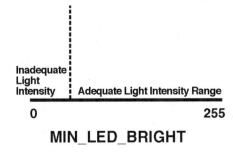

Figure 4.18 MIN_LED_BRIGHT range

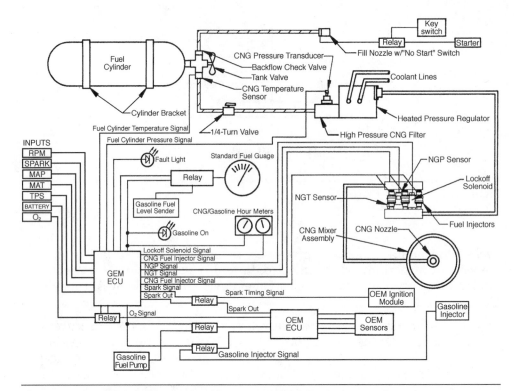

Figure 4.19 MESA GEM system *(Courtesy MESA Environmental)*

1. MAP

This is a measure of the manifold absolute pressure and is identified on the GEM diagnostic screen as MAP. The GEM control system displays the value in terms of psi (pounds per square inch). If the MAP is incorrect, there will either be no start-up on NG or a rough and unsteady idle (Figure 4.20).

2. MAT

This is a measure of the manifold air temperature, which is identified on the GEM diagnostic screen as MAT. The GEM control system displays the value in terms of °F (degrees Fahrenheit). An incorrect MAT will cause a rough or unsteady idle or low power and poor performance when running on NG (Figure 4.21).

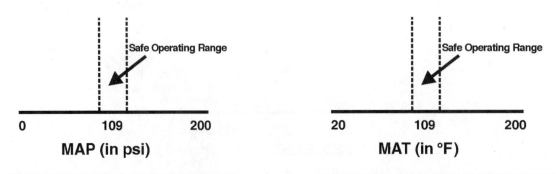

Figure 4.20 MAP safe operating range

Figure 4.21 MAT safe operating range

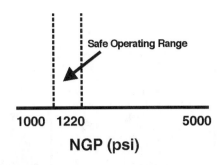

Figure 4.22 NGP safe operating range

3. NGP

This value is a measure of the natural gas pressure in the fuel cylinder and is identified on the GEM diagnostic screen as NGP. The GEM control system displays this value in terms of psi. This pressure is monitored for a rapid NG pressure relief if the NG pressure levels become unsafe (Figure 4.22).

4. NGT

This value is a measure of the temperature of the natural gas at the injectors and is identified on the GEM diagnostic screen as NGT. The GEM control system will display this value in terms of °F. This temperature is monitored for a rapid relief if the NG temperature level becomes unsafe. It also assists in fuel injector timing (Figure 4.23).

5. TankTemp

This value represents a measure of the temperature of the NG in the tank. It is identified on the GEM diagnostic screen as TankTemp. The GEM control system displays this value in terms of °F.

MESA GEM System Diagnostics

Diagnostics are performed on the MESA GEM system by first connecting the four-pin Weather Pak diagnostic link connector in the GEM wire harness (located near the GEM control unit) to the GEM diagnostic interface cable, and then plugging it into the COM port on a laptop computer.

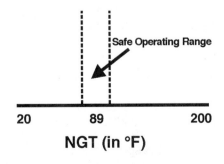

Figure 4.23 NGT safe operating range

GEM Control System Monitor   PROMID:1710-0050

Analog	HIGH	LOW	Operational Faults		ECU Faults	
NGT	14:OK	15:OK	EGO Open	13:OK	RAM	51:OK
TPS	21:OK	22:OK	NGP HighExp	41:OK	COP	55:OK
MAT	23:OK	25:OK	Spark Input	42:OK	Timing	55:OK
ECT	26:OK	27:OK	NGP_LowExp	43:OK	Execution	55:OK
EGR	31:OK	32:OK	EGO Lean	44:OK	Clocks	55:OK
MAP	33:OK	34:OK	EGO Rich	45:OK	Stack	55:OK
BP	35:OK	36:OK	Adapt-Limit	46:OK		
NGP	38:OK	39:OK	Adapt+Limit	46:OK		
NGI	64:OK	65:OK	Voltage	53:OK		
NGTP	66:OK	67:Ok	EGO Volts	63:OK		

Speed	1129 rpm	ECT_volts	0.06 Volts	RunTime	00:02:12
MAP	4.8 psia	MAP_volts	1.22 Volts	RichLean	LEAN
MAT	109° F	MAT_volts	2.92 Volts	CNG/Gasoline	CNG
NGP	122.6 psia	NGP_volts	2.96 Volts	RunMode	RUNNING
NGT	89° F	NGT_volts	2.51 Volts	ControlMode	CL+ADAPTIVE
TankPres	2701 psi	NGTP volts	2.69 Volts	FuelGauge	72%
TankTemp	87° F	NGrr_volts	3.90 Volts	ClsdLoop_Mult	-1.98%
EGO	0.186 Volts	TPS	0.59 Volts	Adapt_Mult	+3.25%
Voltage	14.4 Volts	EGR	5.00 Volts	PulseWidth	4.4ms

Figure 4.24 GEM diagnostic stream *(Courtesy MESA Environmental)*

A live data stream is displayed on the computer screen. These data, presented in the MESA GEM system manual, are reproduced in Figure 4.24.

The GEM diagnostic stream provides information on how close the system is to stoichiometric efficiency, and how well the MESA system is providing adjustments in response to the stoichiometric settings. The closed loop multiplier and the adaptive multiplier indicate this information to the technician.

GFI Fuel Management Strategy

The GFI system is a fully computerized natural gas fuel injection system. It uses speed-density calculations for both mass fuel flow (MFF) and mass air flow (MAF), with adjustments occurring with each spark event. A combination of base vehicle and GFI sensors is used to continually monitor the engine and environment to provide closed loop control of fueling (Figure 4.25). The computer is housed in a single package with the metering valve.

The original design philosophy of GFI was to build a single system that could have universal application. That goal has been met with a CompuValve capable of fueling engines from 1L to 8L on both natural gas and propane (Figure 4.26).

Calibration of the computer is programmable and consists of the following parameters:

1. *Kit characterization*—includes corrections for production variability in injectors, pressure transducers, and temperature sensors.

2. *Application calibration*—responsible for fuel demand and spark advance information. This is engine family specific and is installed at the factory or distributor/dealer.

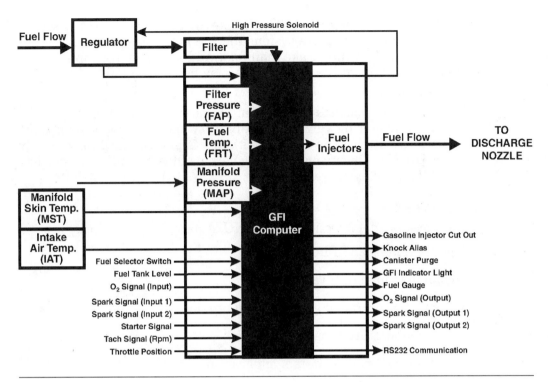

Figure 4.25 GFI fuel management system *(Courtesy GFI Control Systems, Inc.)*

3. *Field calibration*—specifies information required for the area of operation (e.g., fuel composition and fuel gauge calibration). This information is entered by the installer during installation.

Speed-density calculations are based on knowing the temperature and pressure of air and fuel. The manifold absolute pressure (MAP), fuel absolute pressure (FAP), and fuel rail temperature (FRT) are sensors

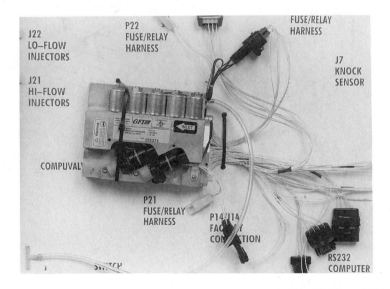

Figure 4.26 GFI CompuValve

located in the metering valve. The intake air temperature (IAT) sensor is mounted in the air intake system and the manifold skin temperature (MST) is located on the intake manifold. Additional sensor inputs, such as TPS or EGR, from the base vehicle may be used to tailor the fueling calculations.

The computer consists of a computer module inside the electronics cavity of the metering valve. For calibration and adaptive memory, the ECU uses EEPROM. The operating system is programmed in read only memory (ROM). The memory is nonvolatile and is neither reset nor lost when battery voltage is removed.

Components

The gaseous fuel injection (GFI) CNG system design comprises:

- gas regulator and filter

- combined metering valve

- computer controlled gas discharge nozzles

- two temperature sensors

- fuel selector switch (bi-fuel applications only)

Incorporated into the CompuValve are absolute pressure sensors (fuel and intake manifold) and a fuel temperature sensor. The discharge nozzles can be in the form of either a spray bar (port injection) or spray disks (throttle body). Newer systems may use a custom multiport manifold design for fuel delivery.

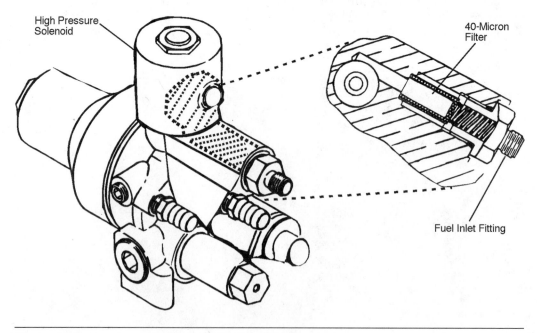

Figure 4.27 Regulator *(Courtesy GFI Control Systems, Inc.)*

The GFI CNG system uses a single-stage high pressure regulator (Figure 4.27). Natural gas enters the regulator at the inlet port and goes through a 40-micron filter or a coalescing filter. This filtered gas proceeds to the high pressure solenoid activated valve that is normally closed. A fuel system pressure (FSP) sensor generates a signal that is sent to the GFI computer which, in turn, sends a compatible signal to the base vehicle fuel gauge. The regulator section uses a proprietary spring diaphragm-pintle mechanism to regulate pressure in the outlet chamber. The outlet chamber is also connected to a 175 psig (psi, gauge) pressure relief valve. The regulator uses engine coolant for heat control to prevent line freezing under high flow, cold ambient conditions.

System Operation

Fuel from the fuel storage vessels flows to the high pressure regulator. The regulator provides a consistent operating fuel pressure (100 psi) for the system. The fuel is passed through a special fuel filter to the CompuValve. The CompuValve electronically meters fuel according to demand. The general formula is:

$$\text{Normalized Mass Fuel Flow} = \frac{\text{MAF} + \text{CLCF}}{\text{Stoichiometric Air/Fuel Ratio}} + \text{Biases}^*$$

* i.e., fuel composition, emission biases

Some aftermarket applications may use an additional module. These devices are generally used to prevent false Check Engine codes by sending compatible signal aliases to the base vehicle computer. Examples are: injector cutouts, O_2 signals, and exhaust gas temperature (EGT). The GFI system can generate some of these "alias" signals internally, or use either an external module developed by GFI or a third party module, depending on the application.

When natural gas mode is selected, the GFI computer intercepts the base vehicle fuel gauge signal and substitutes an appropriate signal to indicate the volume of natural gas in the fuel storage vessel(s). Finally, the fuel is introduced into the air intake system through the discharge nozzles.

System Diagnostics

Checking the system operation consists of determining that the vehicle operates properly when using natural gas. It is recommended that the standard base vehicle maintenance schedule be performed prior to checking the natural gas system. A base vehicle problem (such as a weak ignition system) can affect natural gas system operation before the problem becomes evident in gasoline mode. See the vehicle manufacturer's written procedures for both gasoline and NG schedules, and consult the GFI system manual.

Field Monitor

A PC-based diagnostic software program called *Field Monitor* (FMON) allows a dynamic graphical monitoring of the system installations. The program is designed for installers and end users that must do routine maintenance and diagnostics on vehicles that contain a GFI system.

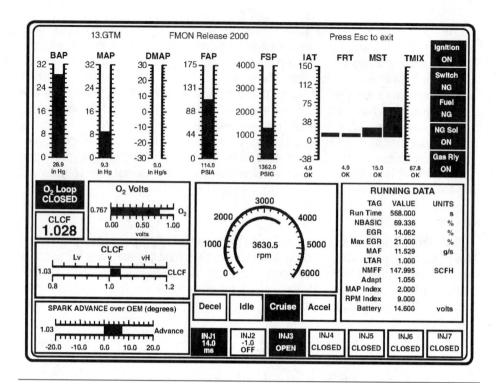

Figure 4.28 Field monitor screen *(Courtesy GFI Control Systems, Inc.)*

With proper connections established between a laptop and the CompuValve RS-232 diagnostic link, the monitor screen seen in Figure 4.28 will be displayed.

1. Pressures

The upper left block of information shows the various pressure sensor readings from GFI. The information is displayed via a graph barometer. Directly below the barometer is a text readout of the measurement (Figure 4.29). The measured pressures are:

- BAP—barometric absolute pressure. This display indicates the ambient outside air pressure. Measured in inches of mercury (in. Hg). Values will vary with altitude. High altitudes (e.g., Denver, Colorado) measure approximately 25 in. Hg. A lower altitude would be closer to 29 in. Hg.

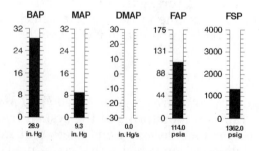

Figure 4.29 Pressure sensor settings *(Courtesy GFI Control Systems, Inc.)*

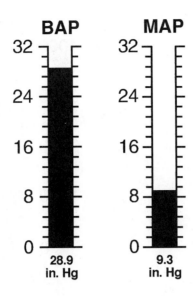

Figure 4.30 Barometric air pressure and manifold air pressure *(Courtesy GFI Control Systems, Inc.)*

- MAP—manifold absolute pressure. The difference between BAP and manifold vacuum. During closed throttle coast-down the MAP value will be low. Wide open throttle operation produces a high MAP value. The high value is produced when the pressure inside the manifold is almost the same as the pressure outside the manifold. This value is the opposite of that which is indicated on the vacuum gauge (Figure 4.30).

- DMAP—delta manifold absolute pressure. The rate of change of MAP measured in inches of Hg per second. *(Note: Unlike mechanical*

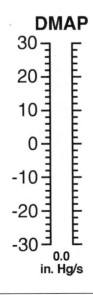

Figure 4.31 Delta manifold absolute pressure *(Courtesy GFI Control Systems, Inc.)*

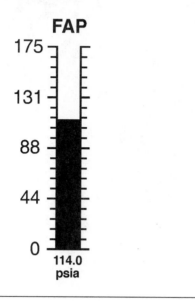

Figure 4.32 Fuel absolute pressure *(Courtesy GFI Control Systems, Inc.)*

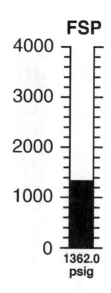

Figure 4.33 Fuel storage pressure *(Courtesy GFI Control Systems, Inc.)*

systems, the computer's ability to "predict" the trend in a value such as MAP enables it to provide the right amount of fuel ahead of the actual vehicle demand.) This value should be fairly steady (Figure 4.31).

- FAP—fuel absolute pressure. Measured between the regulator and the CompuValve (low pressure side). The standard delivery pressure is approximately 115 psia (psi, absolute) for CNG and 60 to 70 inches Hg for propane (Figure 4.32).

- FSP—fuel storage pressure. Tank pressure at the regulator inlet (high pressure side), measured in psig. For propane systems, FSP is replaced by Tank Level, which is based on a tank-mounted float sensor and reads 0–100% (Figure 4.33).

2. Temperatures

The temperature display is located in the upper right center of the screen. GFI uses temperature readings to determine air and fuel supply and fuel density. The key temperature status display will read "OK" if the temperature is in range (-38°C to 150°C), "HIGH" if above range, and "LOW" if below range (Figure 4.34). The key temperatures are:

- IAT—intake air temperature. An open sensor will read 100°C. On lean burn turbocharged systems, the IAT reads intake air/fuel temperature.

- FRT—fuel regulated (rail) temperature.

- MST—manifold skin temperature—may change.

- TMIX—mixture temperature. Calculated temperature of the engine heated air/fuel mixture.

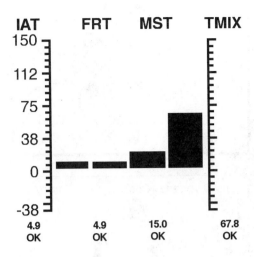

Figure 4.34 Temperature display *(Courtesy GFI Control Systems, Inc.)*

3. Closed Loop Correction Factor

This block provides the status of the closed loop fuel control. The upper left indicator shows whether the GFI system is in OPEN or CLOSED loop. Below this is a digital display of the current value of the closed loop correction factor (CLCF) (Figure 4.35). This is equivalent to GM's integrator/block learn. The bar graph shows where CLCF is on a scale of 0.8 to 1.2. CLCF can be thought of as a fueling multiplier. If CLCF < 0.9, GFI is correcting an excess fuel (rich) condition. If CLCF > 1.1, GFI is correcting an underfueling (lean) condition. During steady state idle or cruise, CLCF should remain within the 0.9 to 1.1 range. Transients may force CLCF outside this range. On a properly running system, CLCF will toggle above and below 1.00. CLCF is based on feedback from the oxygen sensor.

4. Oxygen Sensor Voltage

The oxygen sensor voltage is shown by the first horizontal bar graph (Figure 4.36). This is the actual signal output from the sensor. Normal operating range for an O_2 sensor is about 0.2 volts when lean and about 0.8 volts when rich. If the maximum O_2 voltage is less than 0.7, it may indicate a weak or failing O_2 sensor.

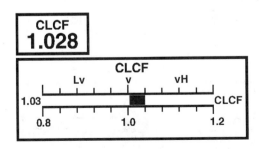

Figure 4.35 Closed loop correction factor *(Courtesy GFI Control Systems, Inc.)*

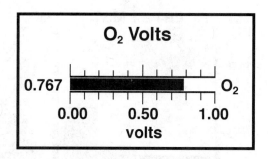

Figure 4.36 Oxygen sensor voltage *(Courtesy GFI Control Systems, Inc.)*

5. Spark Advance

Spark advance is shown in the lower left corner of the screen. If GFI is not advancing timing, this block will indicate "TDC BYPASSED." For emissions optimization, GFI may apply an emission retard value to spark advance. This retard value is not displayed. The value displayed represents the number of degrees GFI is *adding* to base vehicle timing (Figure 4.37). For propane, GFI may retard base vehicle timing. The best way to verify spark advance is to use a timing light.

6. TACH and Engine Mode

The central block of the monitor screen shows a familiar tachometer display of rpm (Figure 4.38). Below the tachometer is a set of indicators showing the current engine mode. These modes may not always seem appropriate, but GFI is constantly monitoring MAP and rpm fluctuations to anticipate mode switches, so brief mode changes are normal.

7. Injector Status

This block displays the status of the GFI fueling injectors (Figure 4.39). Injectors 1 and 2 are "low flow" injectors, which may be ON, OFF, or PULSED. If pulsed, the pulsewidth is shown in milliseconds (ms). The "high flow" injector status will be either OPEN or CLOSED. In all cases, an injector in use will be highlighted on the monitor. For propane systems, an eighth injector status is displayed.

8. Running Data

The final block of information collects several useful values (Figure 4.40). These are:

- Run Time—Elapsed time since engine start.

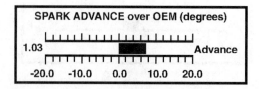

Figure 4.37 Spark advance *(Courtesy GFI Control Systems, Inc.)*

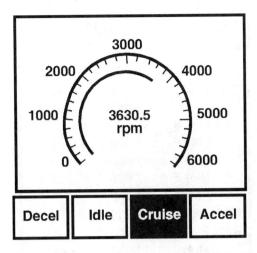

Figure 4.38 Tachometer and engine mode *(Courtesy GFI Control Systems, Inc.)*

- NBASIC—Current estimated volumetric efficiency. A higher number indicates a better breathing engine and a higher fuel demand.

- EGR—Estimated rate of EGR at the current operating point.

- Max EGR—The maximum EGR rate for this engine.

- MAF (mass air flow)—calculated based on speed-density.

- LTAR (target lambda)—1.00 indicates a stoichiometric target. Lean burn systems will typically display LTAR about 1.2 to 1.6.

- NMFF (normalized mass fuel flow)—This value indicates how much fuel GFI has calculated to deliver. Units are SCF/H (standard cubic feet per hour).

- Adapt—This indicates the current long-term adaptive learn value. A value below 0.8 or above 1.2 may indicate a past fueling or calibration problem. The main purpose for adaptive memory is to adjust for fuel consumption.

- MAP Index—The current operating point from 0 (low MAP) to 12 (high MAP).

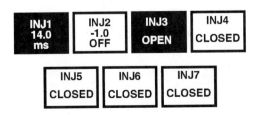

Figure 4.39 Injector status *(Courtesy GFI Control Systems, Inc.)*

RUNNING DATA		
TAG	**VALUE**	**UNITS**
Run Time	568.000	s
NBASIC	69.336	%
EGR	14.062	%
Max EGR	21.000	%
MAF	11.529	g/s
LTAR	1.000	
NMFF	147.995	SCF/H
Adapt	1.056	
MAP Index	2.000	
RPM Index	9.000	
Battery	14.600	volts

Figure 4.40 Running data *(Courtesy GFI Control Systems, Inc.)*

- RPM Index—The current operating point from 0 (low rpm) to 15 (high rpm).

- Battery—The actual voltage feed to GFI. This may be useful to diagnose hard starting conditions.

Summary

In addition to the monitor program described, GFI has developed two other programs that will allow the dealer/installer to load factory-released calibrations, and more recently, a program to facilitate cleaning of the CompuValve injectors.

The GFI II system has the ability to react immediately to large fluctuations in fuel requirements by opening the binary sequenced top injectors, in any combination, and "trimming" those with lower pulsed injectors. This unit, with only minor modifications, can be used for either natural gas or propane.

SUMMARY

- With the ECO system installed, technicians can access engine management data from the OEM and the ECO computers.

- A standard scan tool can be used for the OEM system, while a laptop computer must be used for the ECO system.

- The FMS (fuel management system) is the "brain" of the ECO system. Besides housing the microprocessor, the FMS also contains the CNG fuel gauge, the Check Engine light, the fuel indicator, and the manual fuel selector switch.

- The FMS performs three basic functions: (1) monitors fuel level, (2) controls the switching of fuels, and (3) monitors/controls engine performance.

- The basic electronic controls specific to the ECO system include: the FMS, fuel pressure transducer, fuel servo, and the high pressure fuel lockoff.

- The ECO system will display a data stream on its diagnostic screen.

- Seventeen of the thirty-four parameters monitored by the ECO system can be programmed by a service technician to meet specific vehicle demands.

- The ECO conversion system may incorporate one of three different timing optimizers.

- Diagnostics of the ECO system are performed with a laptop computer using the FMS Diagnostic Support software.

- The ECO system starts on gasoline and then switches to CNG after a programmed delay time. Automatic switchover back to gasoline occurs when CNG storage pressures fall below a preprogrammed value.

- The MESA GEM system utilizes more data inputs than the ECO system.

- The basic electronic controls specific to the MESA GEM system are: GEM ECU, CNG storage pressure transducer, CNG storage temperature sensor, NGT sensor, and the NGP sensor.

- The MESA GEM system is a closed loop conversion system which has adaptive learning, self-diagnostics, and "limp home" mode capabilities.

- The diagnostic procedures of the MESA GEM system include the use of a laptop computer to display all of the available data stream information on a single screen.

- The GFI conversion system is a closed loop system designed to be a more universal conversion system.

- The GFI conversion system has adaptive learning and self-diagnostic capabilities.

- The CompuValve (combination of computer, fuel injectors, fuel flow solenoids, fuel pressure sensor, fuel temperature sensor, and manifold absolute pressure sensor) is used in the GFI system to promote more universal applications.

- The basic electronic components specific to the GFI system include: the CompuValve, a manifold skin temperature sensor, and an intake air temperature sensor.

- The calibration of the GFI computer can be modified to match specific vehicle demands and consists of the following parameters: kit characterization, application calibration, and field calibration.

- The GFI system can provide single-screen display of serial data through the use of a laptop computer and Field Monitor (FMON) software.

- *Closed Loop Correction Factor* (CLCF) is the term the GFI system uses to display how much modification is being done to maintain a stoichiometric air/fuel ratio.

REVIEW QUESTIONS

1. List the electronic components specific to the ECO conversion system.

2. Describe the function of each electronic component specific to the ECO conversion system.

3. List what information is displayed on the diagnostic screen of the ECO conversion system.

4. List the electronic components specific to the MESA GEM conversion system.

5. Describe the function of each electronic component specific to the MESA GEM conversion system.

6. List what information is displayed on the diagnostic screen of the MESA GEM conversion system.

7. List the electronic components specific to the GFI conversion system.

8. Describe the function of each electronic component specific to the GFI conversion system.

9. List what information is displayed on the diagnostic screen of the GFI conversion system.

10. Which of the three conversion systems introduced in this chapter can be reprogrammed in the field to meet specific vehicle demands?

CHAPTER 5

Emissions

OBJECTIVES

- Identify what emissions are created by automobiles.
- Identify the impact of harmful pollutants on the environment and human health.
- Identify how the various emissions are created.
- Understand the difference between reactive and nonreactive hydrocarbons.
- Identify the two different ways in which NG is introduced into an engine.
- Identify current and future federal emissions standards.
- Define *mass emissions testing*.
- Define *steady-state* and *transient testing*.
- Understand the basic diagnostic procedures involved in using an exhaust gas analyzer.
- Understand the testing procedures of both the Federal Test Procedure (FTP) and Inspection/Maintenance 240 (I/M 240).

KEY TERMS

Methane hydrocarbons (CH_4)

Nonmethane hydrocarbons (NMHC)

Reactive hydrocarbons

Nonreactive hydrocarbons

Carbon monoxide (CO)

Oxides of nitrogen (NO_x)

Carbon dioxide (CO_2)

Stoichiometric

Lambda (λ)

Constant volume sampling (CVS)

National Ambient Air Quality Standards (NAAQS)

Mass emissions measurement

Grams per mile (GPM)

Clean fuel vehicle (CFV)

Federal Test Procedure (FTP)

Inspection/Maintenance 240 (I/M 240)

EMISSIONS OVERVIEW

EXHAUST GASES FROM NATURAL GAS VEHICLES

In order for NGV technicians to successfully perform NGV conversions, they must understand the components of an exhaust stream, i.e., emissions, and their impact on vehicle performance and the environment. The goal is to achieve the lowest levels of emissions while maintaining acceptable vehicle driveability and operating performance.

The United States Environmental Protection Agency (EPA) has identified three pollutants emitted in the exhaust streams of motor vehicles which it deems hazardous to human health and the environment: unburned hydrocarbons (HC), carbon monoxide (CO), and nitrogen oxides (NO_x). The amounts of these pollutants, measured in grams/mile (gpm), that vehicles legally can produce have been regulated since 1978 and have been reduced significantly since then. In the last 25 years, emissions from light-duty vehicles have been reduced by over 90 percent, according to the Motor Vehicle Manufacturers Association (MVMA) 1992 Annual Facts and Figures Report.

Unburned Hydrocarbons (HC)

Unburned hydrocarbons are hydrogen- and carbon-containing compounds that are not oxidized in the combustion process. The principal components of today's motor vehicle fuels, HC compounds come in many forms and are difficult to separate. They result from the quenching effects whereby the burning flame front of combustion is extinguished by the relatively cool surfaces of the combustion chamber. Because the quench zone contains more HC, an excessively rich air/fuel mixture can also contribute to unburned hydrocarbons.

Because of the many possible HC combinations, the measurement of HC for emissions regulation purposes is stated in "total mass" rather than measuring each individual compound. This measurement is usually referred to as *total hydrocarbons,* or THC.

While gasoline can have many different hydrocarbons in its makeup, natural gas is composed primarily of one hydrocarbon—methane (CH_4). For discussion purposes, methane comprises about 80 percent to 95 percent of natural gas. The NGV technician should be aware that the percent of methane in natural gas can vary among parts of the country or even the season of the year. Such variances in methane can affect engine performance. Discussions are under way in the United States to attempt to standardize the quality of natural gas as a vehicle fuel.

Unburned hydrocarbons are regulated for two primary reasons. First, some hydrocarbons are considered carcinogenic and, therefore, are health hazards. The gases can be inhaled or absorbed through the skin and reside there long enough to affect one's health. Second, many hydrocarbons are photochemically reactive in the atmosphere. Reactive hydrocarbons contribute to the formation of ozone and atmospheric smog, both of which are harmful to the environment and human health.

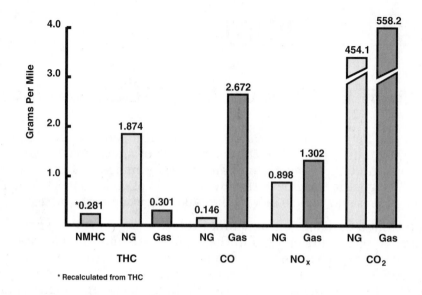

Figure 5.1 Comparison of emissions levels for a 1986 Ford Ranger 2.9L V6 running on gasoline versus NG *(Courtesy NCVESCS, Colorado State University)*

Methane hydrocarbons in the exhaust stream are generally considered the least reactive and do not contribute to smog formation. Although methane is a powerful greenhouse gas absorber in the atmosphere, it decomposes rapidly. Methane is also difficult to catalyze in conventional two-way and three-way catalytic converters. Special converter applications may be considered for NGV conversions in the future in order to reduce the amount of methane in the atmosphere.

Finally, it should be pointed out that in presentations of emissions test results of NGVs, two sets of hydrocarbon numbers may be shown. One is the total hydrocarbon (THC) count, which may be the same or higher than the THC of a gasoline vehicle. The other is the nonmethane hydrocarbons (NMHC), which should be significantly lower than the THC. The NMHC count will usually be the number cited when reference is made to emissions reductions due to conversion to NG fuel (Figure 5.1).

Carbon Monoxide (CO)

Carbon monoxide is a colorless, odorless gas that can be deadly to humans and animals if inhaled in sufficient quantities. Carbon monoxide is readily absorbed into the bloodstream, displacing the oxygen, which can lead to asphyxiation.

Carbon monoxide emissions are created by too little oxygen in the combustion process. This can result from a rich mixture of fuel or a restriction of available air. Under ideal conditions, if the chemical reaction started by the ignition of the air/fuel mixture were complete and the mixture were stoichiometric to begin with, then the only carbon/oxygen compound emitted from the tailpipe of a vehicle would be carbon dioxide (CO_2). However, real situations involve an incomplete oxidation of the air/fuel mixture, and the result is the formation of carbon monoxide. Incomplete combustion is caused by the poor mixing of the air and fuel in the combustion chamber or the lack of air, particularly oxygen (O_2), in the air/fuel mixture. This can also be attributed to high altitude operation, or misadjustment/failure of the fuel metering circuitry.

Since natural gas produces a better mixing of two gases (O_2 and NG) instead of a liquid/air combination, it has the potential for lowered carbon monoxide emissions *if* the conversion systems are properly designed and *if* they are correctly installed and adjusted. Typical test results of vehicles that have been properly converted and adjusted have shown significant reductions in CO over gasoline-fueled vehicles, positively impacting air quality. However, if vehicles have not been properly converted, then actual increases in CO emissions over gasoline are possible because of the rudimentary techniques used in some conversion systems.

Nitrogen oxides are a group of pollutants that are grouped together as one for measuring purposes. They include: NO, NO_2, NO_3, and others.

Some NO_x compounds are irritants to the eyes and respiratory system of humans, creating difficulty in seeing and breathing. These NO_x compounds can also damage plants, property, and react in the atmosphere to form photochemical smog and acid rain.

Nitrogen oxides are created in a very complex set of chemical reactions that take place primarily in the combustion chamber early in the combustion process. NO_x are believed to be caused during "rapid combustion" phases or premixed burn phases which usually prelude the high temperature point. NO_x production is somewhat sensitive to the air/fuel ratio in the combustion chamber. NO_x are even more affected by excessive timing advance. When the air/fuel mixture is lean (14–18 to 1), combustion temperatures rise dramatically and NO_x formation becomes high. Unfortunately, peak NO_x production occurs when HC and CO production

Oxides of Nitrogen (NO_x)

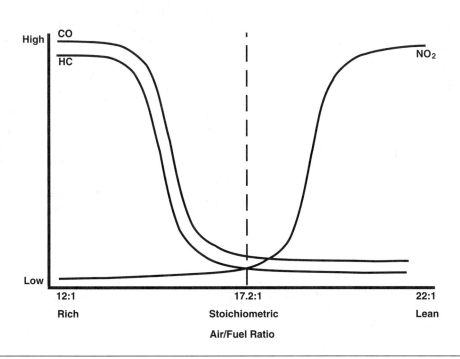

Figure 5.2 Emissions levels related to air/fuel ratio (methane) *(Courtesy NCVESCS, Colorado State University)*

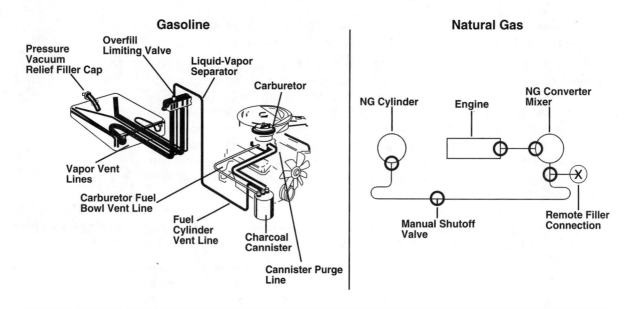

Figure 5.3 Gasoline and NG fueling system schematics *(Courtesy NCVESCS, Colorado State University)*

are low and combustion is good. Running lean has other problems, as well. Therefore, a compromise in the air/fuel ratio must be achieved in order to reduce all pollutants (Figure 5.2).

Evaporative Emissions

Evaporative emissions of unburned hydrocarbons occur in gasoline-fueled vehicles when the liquid fuel evaporates and escapes into the atmosphere. They are caused by limitations of the evaporative control system. Evaporative emissions are regulated because some are carcinogenic and photochemically reactive. One example of evaporative emission occurs during the refueling of gasoline-fueled vehicles. The filler cap is removed and the vapors escape from the cylinder. Also, a bad seal on the filler cap can result in a prolonged evaporative leak.

The NGV fuel system must be totally sealed so that no natural gas leaks out of the system under normal operating conditions (Figure 5.3). However, given the impact that methane has on greenhouse gases, and for safety, it is very important that the complete fuel system of every converted vehicle be pressure tested for system integrity. Leak detection and repair of the system is recommended on a periodic basis (once every 12 months) after the vehicle has gone into service. Few leaks ever develop during normal vehicle service, if the conversion has been done properly by qualified technicians.

EFFECTS OF AIR/FUEL RATIOS ON EXHAUST GASES

For hydrocarbon fuels such as NG, propane, and gasoline, the major hydrocarbon in each is as follows:

- For NG, the major HC is methane (CH_4).

- For liquefied petroleum gas, the major HC is propane (C_3H_8).

- For gasoline, one major HC is octane (C_8H_{18}).

In general, the following combustion reaction takes place inside the combustion chamber:

$$Fuel + Oxidizer = Combustion\ products$$

The equation for natural gas can be written ideally as:

$$CH_4 + (N_2 + O_2) = CO_2 + H_2O + N_2$$

But the reality of natural gas combustion is this:

$$CH_4 + (N_2 + O_2) = CO_2, H_2O, CO, HC, O_2, N_2, NO, NO_2, NO_3 +$$
$$other\ constituents$$

Common gasoline fuel mixtures contain over one hundred hydrocarbons; therefore, the chemistry involved in the combustion process becomes more complicated. There are, however, two important characteristics of the HC molecules for each fuel that should be noted:

1. As we move from methane and propane (gases) to gasoline (liquid), the molecules get larger. As HC molecules get very large they tend to be viscous liquids (oils) and solids (waxes and tars). This explains why NG is difficult to liquefy, propane is easier to liquefy, and gasoline is naturally liquid at cool room temperature.

2. The hydrogen-to-carbon ratio becomes lower with larger HC molecules. For methane, the H-to-C ratio is 4:1; for propane, the H-to-C ratio is slightly less than 3:1; and for gasoline, the H-to-C ratio is slightly more than 2:1. This shift is important because it lowers the percentage of carbon dioxide (CO_2) in the exhaust gas stream as NG or propane is substituted for gasoline in an engine.

The concentration reading for CO_2 at the tailpipe, as measured with a 4-gas analyzer, will be lower for NG and propane than for gasoline. Under ideal conditions, the CO_2 content in the gasoline-fueled exhaust stream would yield approximately 15.3 to 15.8 percent CO_2, whereas the NG-fueled exhaust stream would yield approximately 11 percent CO_2.

Catalytic Converter Reactions

A catalyst is a substance used to create and speed up a chemical reaction or chemical change. The catalytic converter, therefore, provides an additional area, after the combustion chamber, to oxidize, burn, and reduce the HC, CO, and NO_x. Catalytic converters have been installed on vehicles since the 1970s to help reduce tailpipe pollutants. Proper converter action will take these pollutants and change them to CO_2, N_2, and H_2O.

To assure the most efficient conversion of exhaust gases, the internal temperature of the converter must be between 1,200°F and 1,600°F, and the air/fuel mixture must be near the stoichiometric ratio. An excessively rich air/fuel mixture can cause CO to be formed; heat damage to the

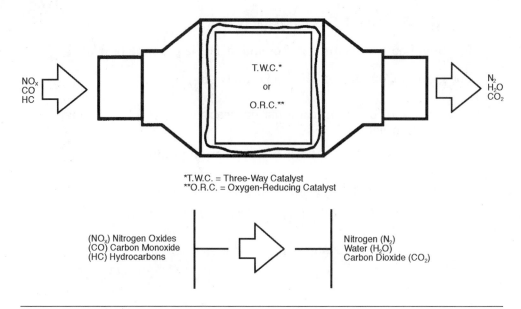

Figure 5.4 Exhaust catalyst reactions *(Courtesy NCVESCS, Colorado State University)*

converter can then result. The NGV technician must be aware of these consequences and must take steps to ensure that this situation does not occur.

Recent research on the ability of automotive three-way catalytic converters to catalyze the exhaust stream of NG-fueled engines has revealed, among other important information, that with current catalytic converters, it is difficult to catalyze methane under normal operating conditions. It has been suggested that the air/fuel ratio window for best converter efficiency on NGVs is smaller than the window for gasoline-fueled vehicles. In order to maintain converter efficiency, the NGV technician must make the system adjustments necessary to achieve the proper air/fuel ratio (Figure 5.4).

As converters age, their conversion efficiency decreases. Periodic inspection and adjustment of converted NGV fuel systems may be in order. This will ensure that catalytic converters will remain fully functional for their natural "useful" life. Converter aging and inefficiency might accelerate if the proper air/fuel ratio is not maintained. This can result in increased emissions and premature replacement of the converter.

NG Mixers and Gaseous Fuel Injection

Previous discussion has noted the necessity of maintaining a near ideal (stoichiometric) air/fuel ratio in NGVs in order to keep emissions at the lowest possible level and still maintain reliable performance. The type of alternative fuel management system installed on the vehicle plays an important part in how well these systems perform. These systems fall into two categories: mixer systems and gaseous fuel injection systems.

Mixer systems currently comprise the majority of systems in use. They are typically a carburetor configuration where the fuel vapor flows continuously into a mixing device and then passes the throttle plate where the total flow is regulated based upon engine and throttle demand. Mixer systems can be configured as closed loop systems and can be very efficient. Be aware, however, that they can also be of poor design. Most mixer systems are relatively low in cost and not extremely complex.

The second type of system is gaseous fuel injection. NG gaseous fuel injection systems are very similar to their gasoline counterparts. They may be either a throttle body injection (TBI) system or a ported fuel injection (PFI) system. Gaseous fuel appears to be the direction that the automakers have chosen for their OEM NG vehicles. These systems represent a significant improvement over mixer systems in fuel control precision and lower emission levels because of enhanced control mechanisms.

VEHICLE EMISSIONS INSPECTION

EMISSIONS STANDARDS AND NG VEHICLES

The history of motor vehicle emissions controls dates back to the early 1950s, when the first studies were done to determine the air pollution contributed by motor vehicles. These studies showed that motor vehicles were major contributors to urban air pollution and that strategies were needed to curb these contributions. Federal legislation addressing emissions from motor vehicles first appeared in 1955. Since then, additional legislation has been revised and broadened beyond the coverage of that original legislation.

The first significant piece of federal legislation that laid the groundwork for controlling motor vehicle emissions was the Clean Air Act of 1963. While it was very general in nature, it represented the first step in what has become a complicated effort to reduce air pollution.

The Clean Air Act Amendments of 1968 established the first emissions standards that auto manufacturers had to meet in order to sell vehicles to the U.S. public. These standards, 1.5 percent CO and 275 ppm HC as measured at idle by a 2-gas infrared analyzer, forced the automotive industry to build cleaner burning cars. These standards remained in effect for two years, 1968 and 1969.

In 1970 the National Emissions Standards Act was enacted as Title II of the Clean Air Act. This act established mass emissions standards for motor vehicles and a testing process to verify compliance. These emissions standards, now measured in grams per mile (gpm), represented a 90 percent reduction in motor vehicle emissions. These standards took effect in 1975.

The change in the measurement of emissions required a different technique to analyze the exhaust stream. The new testing process, constant volume sampling (CVS), is more complex. The test requires that the exhaust be collected over a period of time as the vehicle is being driven on a dynamometer and then analyzed to determine the weight of the pollutants in the sample. Once the analysis is complete, the results are recorded as a measurement in grams per mile. This is not possible with modern 2-, 3-, or 4-gas analyzers. The CVS test is also capable of analyzing NO_x emissions, which were also given a standard to meet in the new CAA amendments.

The Clean Air Act Amendments of 1977 mandated lower emission levels and provided for the phasing in of even lower levels over a period of several years (Figure 5.5). Heavy-duty engines were now subject to certification.

The 1977 amendments also introduced several additional approaches for controlling motor vehicle emissions. One was the establishment of the National Ambient Air Quality Standards (NAAQS). These standards were established for urban areas with populations of 200,000 or more and provided a target for improved air quality. It also identified areas

PASSENGER CAR/EXHAUST EMISSION REDUCTION PROGRESS
FEDERAL 49 STATE STANDARDS (Grams Per Mile)

Model Year	Hydrocarbons**		Carbon Monoxide		Nitrogen Oxides	
	Grams	Reduction	Grams	Reduction	Grams	Reduction
Precontrol*	10.60	--	84.0	--	4.1	--
1968-1971**	4.10	62%	34.0	60%	NR	--
1972-1974**	3.00	72%	28.0	67%	3.1	24%
1975-1976	1.50	86%	15.0	82%	3.1	24%
1977-1979	1.50	86%	15.0	82%	2.0	51%
1980	0.41	96%	7.0	92%	2.0	51%
1981-1982	0.41	96%	$3.4^{(1)}$	96%	$1.0^{(2)}$	76%
1983-1992	0.41	96%	3.4	96%	$1.0^{(2)}$	76%

* MVMA 1960 baseline data.
** Pre-1975 standards have been adjusted according to current test procedure, EPA data.
(1) Waivers allowed manufacturers to use 7.0 grams per mile CO for 1981-82 model years.
(2) Waivers allowed 1.5 grams per mile NO_x for light-duty diesel engines only through the 1984 model year.

Figure 5.5 Passenger car/exhaust emission reduction progress *(Courtesy U.S. Environmental Protection Agency)*

that were in nonattainment with the NAAQS. Another was the requirement to establish inspection and maintenance (I/M) programs in nonattainment areas. It also established penalties for tampering with emission control system (ECS) equipment on motor vehicles.

In November 1990, President Bush signed the newest amendments to the original Clean Air Act. Again, lower emissions levels were established for automakers to achieve beginning in the 1994 model year. These are known as *Tier I* standards. Cold start standards will also be implemented. If necessary, higher *Tier II* emissions standards will be phased in by 2004.

The amendments also established the enhanced I/M program criteria. Enhanced I/M will be implemented in nonattainment areas still struggling to reach attainment. These areas are contained in 20 states and the District of Columbia. Enhanced I/M testing will use CVS testing with a shorter, more aggressive driving cycle.

The 1990 Clean Air Act Amendments (CAAA) established the Clean Fuel Vehicle (CFV) program. This program requires the government to purchase clean fuel vehicles and provides private fleets with incentives to do the same. Natural gas has been classified as a "clean fuel." Consequently, activity in the NGV industry has escalated dramatically. It is imperative then that NGV technicians be proficient and exacting when converting, setting up, and adjusting these vehicles in order to assure compliance with applicable emissions standards.

The emissions reductions achieved by new motor vehicles over their 23-year-old predecessors is 96 percent—a very respectable reduction by anyone's standard. It also demonstrates the great technical advances that have occurred in automotive technology over the same time. A common question asked of air pollution control officials is: Given the reductions in pollution from motor vehicles that have been achieved, why do we still need more controls and tighter standards? Why do we still have dirty air?

The answer is two-fold. First, there are many more vehicles on the road today than there were 23 years ago. The population of the United States has grown from 200 million in 1968 to over 256 million in 1995. This means more people require more vehicles for transportation.

Second, we drive more now than before. Our society has become much more mobile. We live greater distances from work. We participate in more activities that require transportation. The term that is used with this phenomenon is *vehicle miles traveled* (VMT) (Figure 5.6). Transportation planners and air quality program officials are constantly monitoring VMT and planning strategies that will reduce air pollution.

The 1990 light-duty vehicle (LDV = GVWR < 8500 lbs.) federal emissions standards (in grams per mile) are the same as they were in 1981:

	NMHC	CO	NO_x
1990	0.41	3.4	1.0
Tier I (1994)	0.25	3.4*	0.4
Tier II (2004)	0.125	1.7*	0.2

*CO cold standard = 10 gpm

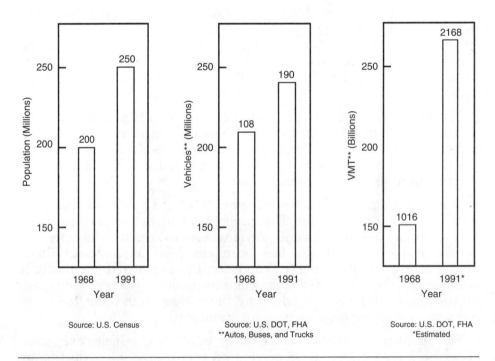

Figure 5.6 Factors affecting air quality in the United States *(Courtesy NCVESCS, Colorado State University)*

The cold CO standard will require the automaker to do additional testing at 20°F in order to certify the vehicle. Also, as specified in the final rule for cold CO emissions, the standard will be phased in over a period of three years. In 1994, 40 percent of each automaker's LDV sales volume must meet the standard; in 1995, 80 percent; and in 1996, 100 percent.

Tier II standards for LDVs will take effect in 2004, if they are adopted. These standards will be 0.125 gpm NMHC, 1.7 gpm CO at 75°F, 10.0 gpm CO at 20°F, and 0.2 gpm NO_x.

The NGV technician needs to be familiar with these standards for one other reason—many states with nonattainment areas have, or are in the process of adopting, regulations that require NG conversion systems to be certified. This usually means that a vehicle's emissions from natural gas, after a conversion, can be no more than what the vehicle emitted on gasoline. The NGV technician must understand the operation of the system and the consequences of his/her actions during installation and maintenance.

The Environmental Protection Agency issued final rules in September 1994 that govern tailpipe exhaust emissions of natural gas vehicles. The rules only require measurement of nonmethane hydrocarbons (NMHC), not total hydrocarbons. The regulations take effect with the 1997 model year and are designed, according to the EPA, to provide a "level playing field for gaseous-fueled vehicles, and to remove a potential barrier to their production."

After excluding methane emissions, the rules basically require that NGVs meet the same Tier I and later emissions standards that apply to vehicles that run on other fuels.

When the EPA proposed the rule, it recommended the NMHC-only standard for NGVs because, compared with other hydrocarbons, methane is not a major contributor to ground-level ozone.

The rule also provides procedures for measuring the fuel economy of light-duty cars, vans, and trucks that run on natural gas, allowing NGVs that comply with the regulations before 1999 to be included in an automaker's Corporate Average Fuel Economy (CAFE) calculation.

Manufacturers will be able to certify vehicles before model year 1997 for purposes of receiving CAFE credits and including medium- and heavy-duty vehicles in emissions-trading, banking, and crediting programs. Because NGVs receive significant CAFE credits and are capable of achieving superior emissions performance, manufacturers are expected to certify vehicles as early as possible.

Another provision of the new rule makes manufacturers, rather than installers of conversion systems, ultimately responsible for emissions performance. The original equipment manufacturer's emissions warranty on the rest of the system will continue to remain in effect as long as any degradation in performance is not attributable to the conversion system.

California LEV Standards

Historically, California, because of its severe air pollution problems (especially in southern California), has always had higher emissions standards than the federal standards. This has required that automakers produce two versions of each vehicle—one to meet federal standards and one to meet California standards. Even with the higher standards, parts of California are still in the severe nonattainment category for ozone levels. With that in mind, California has begun a program to bring low-emitting vehicles (LEV) into its state fleet.

The LEV program sets emissions standards for three classes of vehicles and provides for a schedule of implementation rates of these vehicles into the California fleet. The three classes of vehicles include: the transitional low-emitting vehicle (TLEV), the low-emitting vehicle (LEV), and the ultra low-emitting vehicle (ULEV). These three classes of vehicles, along with the zero-emitting vehicle (ZEV), will represent a major portion of the new car fleet in California by the year 2003.

Note: The zero-emitting vehicle class usually refers to electric vehicles, also included in the program implementation schedule.

Recently, several states in the Ozone Transport Region of the northeastern U.S. have adopted, or are attempting to adopt, the California standards for new vehicles sold in those states.

The California LEV standards (in grams per mile) are as follows:

	TLEV	LEV	ULEV
NMOG	0.125	0.075	0.04
CO	3.4	3.4	1.7
NO_x	0.4	0.2	0.2
Formaldehyde	0.015	0.015	0.008

California is using an NMOG (nonmethane organic gases) standard instead of NMHC because NMOG includes alcohols in its makeup, whereas NMHC does not. As of this writing, some automakers have introduced vehicles that meet the LEV standard.

California Air Resources Board (CARB) legislation pertains to mandates in the state of California and other areas and is currently under review and subject to change.

In May 1995, ANSI approved NGV3.1/CGA 12.3, which is the American/Canadian national standard for fuel system components for natural gas-powered vehicles. The standard details construction and performance criteria for the following natural gas fuel system components constructed entirely of new unused parts and materials: (1) check valves, (2) cylinder valves, (3) manual valves, (4) gas/air mixers for operation at differential pressures greater than or equal to 2 psi, (5) pressure measurement devices, (6) pressure regulators, (7) automatic valves, and (8) engine rotation sensors, intended for use on natural gas-powered vehicles.

According to the NGV3.1 standard, every component shall be designed to secure normal and reasonable conditions of handling and usage and minimize the possibility of incorrect assembly. NGV3.1 is primarily written for manufacturers of NGV components, but there are some new terms that apply to technicians. Compression fittings of only the double ferrule design may be used in CNG systems. In Canada, a "service valve" is used in addition to the 1/4-turn shutoff valve. It is usually located in conjunction with the fill receptacle and is used to isolate the underhood components for service. Also in Canada, the fuel lockoff device is located on the high pressure side of the system, and the vehicle will have an engine rotation sensor, which is an antenna around the coil or spark plug wire to sense rpm and trigger the fuel lockoff device.

SOURCES OF REGULATIONS

Since clean air is such a broad topic of interest, there are many regulatory entities that will have an impact on what you, as an NGV technician, will be doing with alternative fuel vehicles. These entities usually fall into one of three categories:

1. Governmental agencies

2. Environmental interest groups

3. Business and industry organizations

It is the responsibility of the NGV technician to be aware of which groups will impact his/her work. The following list is suggested as a starting point:

• State and local Departments of Health (health impact)

• State and local Departments of Natural Resources (environmental impact)

• State and local Departments of Transportation (vehicle codes)

• State and local Fire Protection Departments (refueling facility codes)

• National Fire Protection Association (NFPA) (vehicle fuel system codes)

• American Gas Association (AGA) (NG equipment standards)

VEHICLE TESTING

EXHAUST MEASUREMENT TECHNIQUES AND TESTING PROCEDURES

Over the years, air quality professionals have discovered that one of the hardest concepts for automotive technicians to understand is the concept of *mass emissions measurements* versus *concentrations measurements*. Technicians have used 2-, 3-, and 4-gas analyzers for many years and have tried to equate those concentration readings with mass emissions standards (or test results) to no avail. This requires some explanation.

Every technician should know that an engine is an air pump and during a given length of operating time the engine will pump a certain amount of air, which is measured in cubic feet. Since the exhaust gas components coming out of the tailpipe are made up of molecules and molecules have weight, then each cubic foot of exhaust gas will weigh a given amount depending upon the proportions of the various gases in the exhaust. This weight factor allows scientists to determine the amount of pollution, usually in tons, that is in the atmosphere or how much can be removed through various reduction strategies.

For example, take two engines with different cubic inch displacements, a 350 cubic inch displacement (CID) V8 and a 175 CID 4-cylinder, and run them for the same period of time at the same rpm and collect the exhaust in balloons. The volume of air pumped by each engine will be different. Let's say the V8 pumped 100 cubic feet of air and the 4-cylinder pumped 50 cubic feet. If each cubic foot of exhaust gas weighs 30 grams, then the gas in the balloon from the V8 will weigh 3,000 grams and the gas in the balloon from the 4-cylinder will weigh 1,500 grams (Figure 5.7).

Now take 10 percent CO (a concentration value seen on service department gas analyzers) times the weight value of each balloon. The result is two different weights. From this we can understand why 10 percent CO on one vehicle is not the same as 10 percent CO on another vehicle.

While 2-, 3-, and 4-gas analyzer concentration readings can give the technician an indication of the combustion efficiency of the engine, the technician should be careful about making assumptions about the correlation between idle concentration measurements and mass emissions measurements. The technician must consider all the variables affecting engine operation and their consequent results.

The Federal Test Procedure

The Federal Test Procedure (FTP) is the test process designed by the EPA and used by automakers to verify that engine and driveline combinations do not exceed the emissions standards set by the EPA. (These standards were discussed in the previous section.) It is essentially a two-part test: a driving-cycle exhaust measurement determination and an evaporative emissions determination. The test is time-consuming

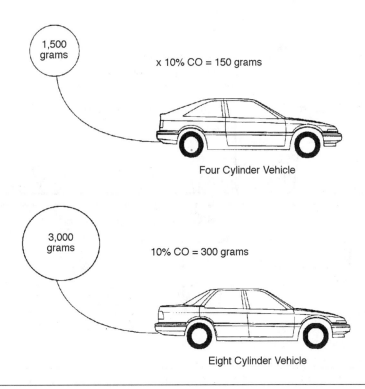

1,500 grams

x 10% CO = 150 grams

Four Cylinder Vehicle

3,000 grams

10% CO = 300 grams

Eight Cylinder Vehicle

Figure 5.7 Mass versus concentration; the impact of bigger cars *(Courtesy NCVESCS, Colorado State University)*

(approximately 24 hours) and very expensive (about $1,500). As a check to ensure compliance, the EPA will randomly pull vehicles from manufacturers' assembly lines for testing and perform tests on "in-use" vehicles.

When a vehicle is tested, it goes through the following process: Upon arrival, the fuel cylinder is drained and refilled to a 40 percent level with an EPA certified gasoline such as Indolene. Indolene is very similar to pump gasoline but with a known make-up of hydrocarbons. The vehicle is then driven through a prep cycle on an inertia weight type chassis dyno to condition the engine and fuel system and to purge the old gasoline out of the system.

Immediately following the prep cycle, the vehicle is put into a cold soak area where it must sit for between 12 and 36 hours. The ambient temperature in this area must be between 68°F and 86°F. Some time after the first 12 hours and before the end of 36 hours, the fuel is drained and refilled again with chilled fuel. A diurnal heat build-up is performed on the fuel cylinder. This simulates filling from an underground storage cylinder. The diurnal heat build up is performed with the vehicle inside a sealed room, lasting for one hour. This is the first part of the evaporative determination test, also known as the *Sealed Housing Evaporative Determination* (S.H.E.D). At the end of the diurnal heat build-up, the vehicle must be pushed onto the chassis dyno. The driving portion of the FTP can then begin.

The dyno uses a series of heavy steel flywheels attached to the dyno rolls to simulate the emissions test weight (ETW) of the vehicle.

U.D.D.S
FEDERAL TEST PROCEDURE - DRIVING PATTERN

This mode is designated "LA No.4" because it simulates the actual vehicle driving pattern encountered on a certain stretch of U.S. Highway 4 running through Los Angeles County, California.

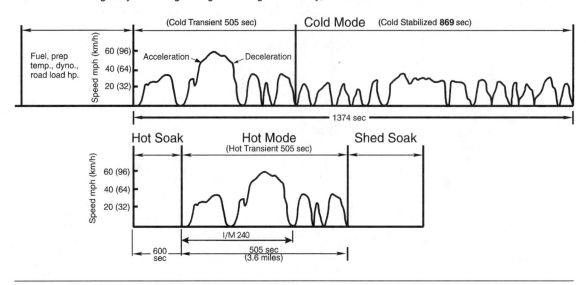

Figure 5.8 Federal Test Procedure *(Courtesy NCVESCS, Colorado State University)*

Electrical inertia simulation (or eddy current) units are also becoming popular as a testing method. This procedure uses a power absorption unit (PAU) to simulate the drag forces working against the vehicle as it is being driven.

The test begins with key-on and continues through a driving cycle that would be similar to driving to work or running errands. It consists of a series of starts, stops, accelerations, and decelerations. The cycle was developed from a series of case studies done in the late 1960s. This particular driving cycle is currently under review and may be changed. However, it does provide consistency for testing across the country.

Phase 1 of the cycle is the *cold transient phase* and lasts 505 seconds (Figure 5.8). Most vehicle emissions are produced during this phase.

Phase 2 continues immediately after phase 1 and is called the *cold stabilized phase*. Portions of this phase simulate highway or freeway driving. This phase lasts 869 seconds. The total for phases 1 and 2 is 1,374 seconds.

At the end of phase 2, the vehicle is shut off and allowed to sit for 10 minutes. This simulates the vehicle being parked in a parking lot (a stop at a grocery store) and is called *hot soak*. At the end of the hot soak the vehicle starts phase 3 of the driving cycle. Phase 3 lasts 505 seconds and is called the *hot transient phase,* or the *hot 505*. This phase is used extensively by research and development people when they need some indication of how the vehicle in question is reducing emissions.

Phases 1, 2, and 3 take a total of 31 minutes, 19 seconds to complete. This part of the FTP is called the *Urban Dynamometer Driving Schedule,* or UDDS.

During the UDDS the vehicle's total exhaust flow is being collected by the constant volume sampling (CVS) system. A sample of the exhaust from each driving phase is collected into "tedlar bags" and held until analysis begins. The bag samples are labeled "Bag 1" for phase 1, "Bag 2" for phase 2, and "Bag 3" for phase 3. Background air is also drawn into the bags to dilute, very precisely, the exhaust gas sample.

Analysis of the bag samples is done with very costly and elaborate equipment. The end result of the analysis is to determine the amount of THC, CO, NO_x, and CO_2 by gram weight and then, by using the distance information gathered from the dyno, make the determination of grams per mile (gpm) for each pollutant.

At the end of the UDDS, the vehicle is immediately put into the evaporative enclosure and sealed (similar to parking in a closed garage). This is the second part of the evaporative determination and lasts one hour. The current standard for both phases of the evaporative emissions determination is 2 grams per test.

The I/M 240 test procedure is similar to the FTP in that it incorporates a driving cycle and the results are in grams per mile. Although the driving schedule for the I/M 240 is related to the 505 second portion of the UDDS, the similarity ends there. There is no drain and refill of the fuel, no cold soak or hot soak, and a different evaporative determination is used. The I/M 240 test procedure is also designed to include purge and pressure testing of the fuel storage and evaporative emissions control system (Figure 5.9).

The I/M 240 was designed to replace current I/M idle testing in nonattainment areas where enhanced I/M is required. The test is capable of identifying more true emissions failures than current 4-gas emissions "short" tests.

The test is 240 seconds long, during which a modal analysis (real time, dilute, continuous) integration is performed (Figure 5.10). Extensive

The I/M 240 Test Procedure

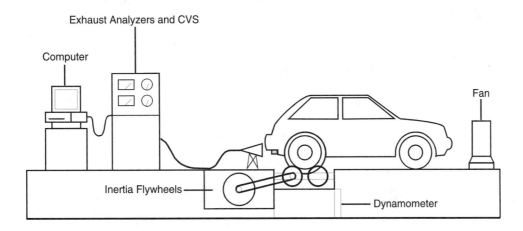

Figure 5.9 I/M 240 chassis dynamometer layout *(Courtesy NCVESCS, Colorado State University)*

I/M 240 Driving Trace

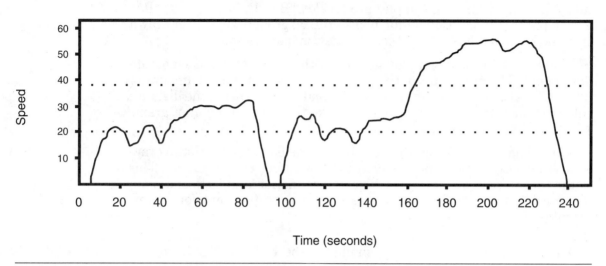

Figure 5.10 I/M 240 driving cycle *(Courtesy NCVESCS, Colorado State University)*

designing and testing of the driving cycle of this test have shown that it correlates extremely well with the FTP (minus the evaporative test).

It appears that this test will become the industry standard and will be used for emission testing on all fuels.

Steady-State Testing

Most NGV conversion system manufacturers require technicians to set up and adjust the fuel system using steady-state testing. Steady-state testing is a setup technique utilizing a power dyno without inertia weights and a 4-gas analyzer. The vehicle is driven on the dyno in a loaded cruise mode which allows the NGV technician to fine-tune the fuel system for maximum efficiency. While this may be practical for the cruise operation, it does not allow the technician to adjust power settings for accelerations. Power enrichment adjustment is unique to each manufacturer and must be done with care following that manufacturer's procedures.

Conversion system manufacturers using steady-state testing as a setup process may ask the technician to adjust the system to a predetermined CO level. This will ensure good driveability of the vehicle, but it also places the system in a fuel-rich mode of operation. Therefore, the NGV technician must not exceed the upper limits of the specification and should make every attempt to keep the CO level at a minimum to ensure low mass emission rates of CO, as would be identified with FTP testing.

EMISSIONS, ENGINE DIAGNOSIS, AND TUNING

UNDERSTANDING EMISSIONS TEST RESULTS/READINGS

Until the late 1980s, NG fuel systems were mechanically operated and controlled. The systems were not capable of self-adjustment during use, since there was no feedback mechanism in place. Therefore, they required a periodic adjustment by the technician. This type of fuel-management technology is often referred to as *open loop* technology.

With the passage of the Alternative Motor Fuels Act of 1988 and the Clean Fuel Fleet program requirement in the Clean Air Act Amendments of 1990, the demand for NGVs has increased dramatically and so has the demand for lower emitting vehicles. In order for NGVs to be low emitters, while still providing good performance and driveability, it has been necessary to adopt the oxygen sensor-based *closed loop* technology pioneered by the automakers in the early 1980s.

The NGV technician is faced with a bit of a dilemma. Closed loop technology conversion systems are experiencing a technical evolution that is moving at a very rapid speed. Closed loop systems are currently in two forms. One is a stand alone system where the system manufacturer supplies a system control computer that utilizes some of the original engine sensors to control the fuel flow to the engine. The other is an integrated system that interfaces with the original engine control module (ECM) to accomplish the same task. Both work well when set up properly. However, both can present their own unique set of problems that can cause some headaches for technicians. It remains to be seen which control technology will emerge as the preferred system.

SYSTEMATIC APPROACH TO DIAGNOSIS, REPAIR, AND ADJUSTMENTS TO ACHIEVE EMISSIONS COMPLIANCE

The importance of achieving a good balance between driveability and low emissions on an NGV cannot be overstated. Since even the best converted NGV will be slightly less powerful than its gasoline counterpart (due to volumetric and mechanical effectiveness), the technician must carefully install and adjust the system so that there is no hesitation or stumble to aggravate the vehicle's owner and, at the same time, still achieve a low level of tailpipe emissions.

Most conversion system manufacturers will require the technician to adjust the system, using a 4-gas analyzer, to specified CO percentages at idle and high idle or cruise (Figure 5.11). These percentages will range from 0.2 percent to 1.5 percent, depending on the application. The technician

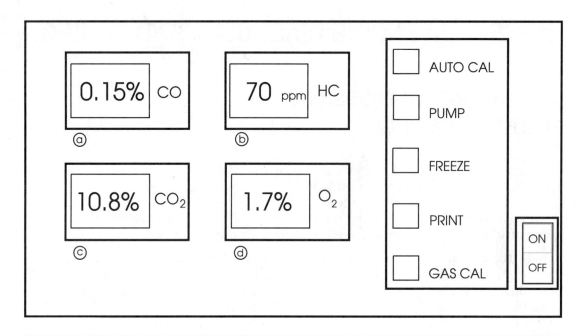

Figure 5.11 Typical 4-gas analyzer readout

must remember that the presence of high levels of CO in the exhaust stream indicates a fuel-rich air/fuel mixture. The small percentages (.1 percent to .4 percent) indicate that the engine is running close to stoichiometric; the low CO being a product of good combustion.

Placing a load on the engine is also required by some manufacturers. This can best be accomplished by using a power dyno which will allow the vehicle to be driven under load. An alternate method on automatic transmission equipped vehicles is to set the parking brake, check the wheels, and place the vehicle in gear while adjusting the system. This latter method does pose some safety problems, and careful attention must be paid by the technician. This, of course, cannot be done on manual transmission vehicles.

As an alternative to the CO method of adjustment, the NGV technician is encouraged to look at the *CO_2 balance method* of adjustment as a way to achieve maximum combustion efficiency, low emissions, and good driveability.

In the CO_2 balance method, the technician must understand that as the air/fuel ratio moves from a fuel-rich condition to a lean condition, the CO_2 in the exhaust stream will increase to a peak and then fall off. The peak CO_2 indicates the point of maximum combustion efficiency and lowest emissions (Figure 5.12).

Note: The air injection system must be disabled before attempting this adjustment. This can be easily accomplished by clamping off the air injection line to the exhaust stream.

Using the CO_2 in the exhaust stream as a reference, and beginning with a fuel-rich air/fuel mixture, the technician carefully leans the mixture until it reaches the CO_2 peak. Care must be taken not to exceed the

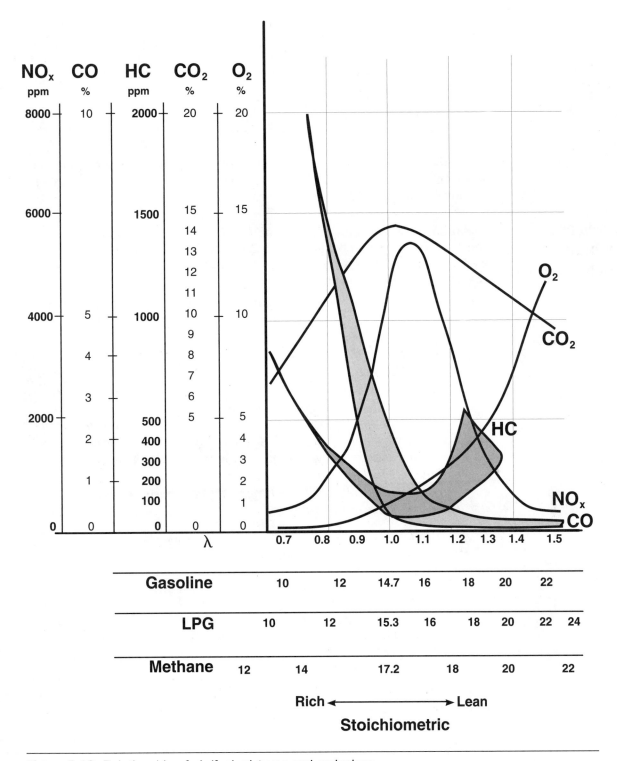

Figure 5.12 Relationship of air/fuel mixtures and emissions

peak and consequently lean the air/fuel ratio too much. The technician must identify the peak, securing the adjustment just before the peak is reached. This should produce very low emissions and still maintain driveability.

Proper air/fuel mixture is important for proper engine operation. Ideally, the mixture should be such that all the oxygen and fuel are consumed during combustion to form carbon dioxide and water. This ideal point is used to describe the air/fuel ratio. This concept is represented by the following equation:

$$\text{lambda } (\lambda) = \frac{\text{air/fuel (actual)}}{\text{air/fuel (stoichiometric)}}$$

Lambda is equal to one at stoichiometric operation, is less than one when the mixture is fuel rich, and is greater than one when the mixture is lean. Lambda is also referred to as *excess air ratio*.

Diagnosis and Repair of NGV Emissions Failures

Similar problems or symptoms among the various conversion systems tend to have the same basic causes. Once the technician has gained experience with one or two conversion systems, then a generic troubleshooting approach can be used.

Note: Since the use of conversion systems generally implies that the vehicle will be a bi-fuel vehicle, it is doubly important that the technician isolate the problem to either the OEM gasoline system or the NG system. If the problem occurs when the vehicle is operated on both fuels, then it is highly probable that the fault is with parts common to both systems. It is highly recommended that the condition of the OEM fuel system components not common to both fuel systems (fuel pump, injectors, cold start valves, etc.), the emissions control system, and the engine mechanical condition be confirmed first and, if necessary, repaired before proceeding with a diagnosis of the NG fuel system. The technician who fails to follow this process may waste valuable time chasing "ghosts" before finding the real cause of the problem.

WARNING! Tampering (including any adjustments outside the manufacturer's recommended limits) with the emission control system (ECS) by anyone for any reason is *illegal* and punishable by very stiff fines (Section 203 (a) (3) of the Clean Air Act Amendments). The EPA has further clarified this issue in their Memorandum 1A which defines tampering in detail. Tampering with the ECS will adversely affect the performance of the vehicle and will cause emissions to rise.

There are five major emissions problems that occur with any fuel system. These problems and their potential causes in an NG fuel system are shown below. The causes are listed in order of their probability of occurrence (most likely to occur to least likely to occur).

1. High CO at idle on NG:

   • idle mixture circuit misadjusted

   • mixing of fuels from both fuel systems

   • restricted or dirty air intake system

   • engine coolant temperature too low

- AIS failure
- OEM or NG system computer failure
- inoperative catalytic converter

2. High CO at loaded cruise speed on NG:
   - power enrichment circuit misadjusted
   - idle mixture circuit misadjusted
   - mixing of fuels from both fuel systems
   - restricted or dirty air intake system
   - engine coolant temperature too low
   - AIS failure
   - OEM or NG system computer failure
   - inoperative catalytic converter

3. High HC at Idle on NG:
   - ignition timing incorrect
   - idle mixture circuit misadjusted
   - ignition system failure
   - vacuum leakage
   - EGR malfunction
   - OEM or NG system computer failure
   - AIS failure
   - inoperative catalytic converter
   - regulator pressure(s) not properly adjusted

4. High HC at loaded cruise speed on NG:
   - dual curve ignition module failure
   - OEM ignition system failure
   - vacuum leakage
   - OEM or NG system computer failure
   - AIS failure
   - inoperative catalytic converter
   - regulator pressure(s) not properly adjusted

5. High NO_x at loaded cruise speed on NG:
   - power enrichment circuit misadjusted
   - dual curve ignition module failure
   - OEM ignition system failure
   - EGR system failure
   - combustion chamber temperature too high
   - engine coolant temperature too high
   - OEM or NG system computer failure
   - inoperative catalytic converter

It should be noted here that NG air/fuel mixtures require a significant amount of ignition energy (spark) to ignite, much more than that required by gasoline air/fuel mixtures. Insufficient ignition system energy can result in driveability or emissions problems that may not occur when the vehicle is operated on gasoline. Therefore, the condition and strength of the ignition system must be maintained at peak levels and verified by a scope check diagnostic routine.

Road Tests and Driveability

A road test of the vehicle while running on natural gas is a must following natural gas fuel systems adjustments or any engine and performance related repairs. Free-revving checks, snap idles, and even chassis dyno checks cannot detect all potential driveability problems. A road test under varied conditions is recommended as a final check-out. The road test should include urban stop-and-go driving, hill climbing, full-throttle accelerations, and a highway run at the legal speed limit.

Driveability Terms

Driveability is a subjective term and is, therefore, subject to individual evaluation. Nevertheless, attempts have been made to categorize specific driveability issues. Driveability terms that are inherited from gasoline-fueled vehicle complaints include:

- *Tip-in sag*—a momentary loss of power as the throttle is opened during an attempted acceleration from a complete stop or while moving.

- *Stumble*—a quick "jerk-like" reaction to a throttle opening. It is similar to a momentary ignition misfire due to a faulty spark plug.

- *Hesitation*—a brief interruption of power or a momentary lack of response to a throttle opening, for the purpose of acceleration, either from a complete stop or while moving.

SUMMARY

- The three major air pollutants from automobiles are: oxides of nitrogen (NO_x), unburned hydrocarbons (HC), and carbon monoxide (CO).

- Natural gas is made of 80–95 percent methane and therefore creates mostly methane hydrocarbons (CH_4).

- Reactive hydrocarbons (nonmethane hydrocarbons) contribute to the formation of ozone and atmospheric smog.

- Nonreactive hydrocarbons (methane hydrocarbons) do not contribute to smog formation.

- Carbon monoxide emissions are created by too little oxygen in the combustion process.

- Carbon monoxide emissions are colorless, odorless, and can be deadly.

- Carbon monoxide emissions have the potential to be lower while using CNG because the mixing of two gases (O_2 + NG) results in better combustion than the mixing of a gas with a liquid.

- Oxides of nitrogen (NO_x) are a number of compounds grouped together for measurement purposes, consisting of NO, NO_2, NO_3, and others.

- Oxides of nitrogen can create difficulty seeing and breathing. NO_x compounds can also damage plants and react in the atmosphere to form photochemical smog and acid rain.

- Oxides of nitrogen emissions are created during "rapid combustion" phases before combustion chamber temperatures are highest.

- Oxides of nitrogen emissions need to be monitored on an NGV because of its lean running characteristics.

- A lean mixture creates higher combustion chamber temperature and therefore the possibility of forming NO_x.

- Evaporative emissions are created when hydrocarbons are allowed to evaporate into the atmosphere.

- Gasoline-fueled vehicles create evaporative emissions every time they are refueled; however, a properly maintained NGV will have no evaporative emissions.

- The concentration of emitted carbon dioxide (CO_2) is lower while operating on CNG (approximately 11%) than while operating on gasoline (approximately 15.5%).

- Catalytic converters can play a major role in reducing harmful tailpipe emissions as long as an ideal air/fuel ratio (stoichiometric) is maintained.

- The two basic methods used to introduce NG into the vehicle's engine are: (1) mixer systems and (2) gaseous fuel injection systems.

- Mixer systems are less expensive and less complex than gaseous fuel injection systems.

- Gaseous fuel injection systems are more precise and have the potential to reduce emissions more than mixer systems.

- The Clean Air Act of 1963 was the first significant piece of federal legislation for controlling vehicle emissions.

- Urban areas with populations above 200,000 were targeted for improved air quality through the establishment of the National Ambient Air Quality Standards (NAAQS).

- The Clean Fuel Vehicle (CFV) program, established by the Clean Air Act of 1990, requires the use of CFVs in the government sector and encourages their use in the private sector.

- The 96% reduction in vehicle emissions over the past 23 years has been offset by the increase in the number of vehicles and vehicle miles traveled (VMT).

- Tier I standards for light-duty vehicles are: .25 gpm of NMHC, 3.4 gpm of CO, and 0.4 gpm of NO_x.

- Tier II standards will be put into effect in the year 2004, if needed for attainment, and consist of a 50 percent reduction of all pollutants from the Tier I standards.

- NGV3.1, standards for construction and performance of NGV components, was recently adopted and includes the following components: (1) check valves, (2) cylinder valves, (3) manual valves, (4) gas/air mixers, (5) pressure measurement devices, (6) pressure regulators, (7) automatic valves, and (8) engine rotation sensors.

- Mass emissions measurement is a type of measurement in which pollutants are measured by their weight instead of by their concentration and is therefore a more effective means in which to determine the amount of pollutants a vehicle actually emits.

- The Federal Test Procedure (FTP) is a two-part test that includes a driving cycle and an evaporative emissions measurement.

- The FTP measures the weight of each pollutant produced during the test and divides by the number of miles traveled to indicate the grams per mile of each pollutant.

- The Inspection/Maintenance 204 (I/M 240) test is similar to the FTP because they both have a driving cycle and both determine the total weight of pollutants in grams per mile.

- The I/M 240 test varies from the FTP in that the driving cycle is shorter, the fuel is not drained, there are no hot or cold soak phases, and the I/M 240 uses a different evaporative determination.

- Steady-state dynamometer testing is a setup technique utilizing a power dyno without inertia weights and a 4-gas analyzer.

- Steady-state dynamometer testing is required by most NGV conversion manufacturers to ensure proper setup for acceptable driveability and reduced emissions.

- The two most common methods of adjusting an NGV conversion are the CO method and the CO_2 balance method.

- The five major emissions problems that occur with any NG fuel system are: (1) high CO at idle, (2) high CO at loaded cruise, (3) high HC at idle, (4) high HC at loaded cruise, and (5) high NO_x at loaded cruise.

REVIEW QUESTIONS

1. List the emissions of concern and identify the impact of each pollutant on the environment and human health.

2. Explain the difference between reactive and nonreactive hydrocarbons.

3. Explain how NGVs are beneficial in terms of emissions.

4. List the advantages and disadvantages of both NG fuel systems—NG mixers and gaseous fuel injection.

5. Describe the current federal emissions standards and relate them to Tier I and Tier II standards.

6. Explain the difference between mass emissions measurement and concentration measurement.

7. Describe how the I/M 240 test procedure compares with the Federal Test Procedure.

8. Describe the two adjusting techniques that can be used while performing steady-state testing.

9. Define lambda (λ) and explain how it relates to increases or decreases in emissions.

10. List the five major emissions problems and give at least three possible causes for each problem.

CHAPTER 6

NGV Operation and Fueling Stations

OBJECTIVES

- Identify the procedure that should be followed to properly refuel an NGV.
- Identify the areas of common concern while operating an NGV.
- Explain the procedure that should be followed if an NGV is involved in an accident.
- Determine the procedure that should be followed to switch fuel while operating a bi-fuel vehicle.
- Explain the difference between fast fill and timed fill.
- Identify the components need to perform a fast fill.
- Identify the components needed to perform a timed fill.
- Identify any necessary modifications to the shop including: air circulation and exchange devices, gas detectors, alarms, and fire extinguishers.

KEY TERMS

NGV-1

Timed fill

Fast fill

Cascade

Priority panel

Sequential panel

Uniform Building Code

DRIVER ORIENTATION

An NGV is very similar in operation to a gasoline-powered vehicle. Almost all preventative maintenance procedures and safety considerations remain the same. However, there are a few different procedures that should be addressed. The most noticeable difference is the method of fueling.

FUELING

Fueling an NGV is a very simple procedure (Figure 6.1). The greatest problem may occur from not having the same type of fuel connector as that provided with the fuel dispenser. Soon this will not be an issue as

Figure 6.1 Filling vehicle

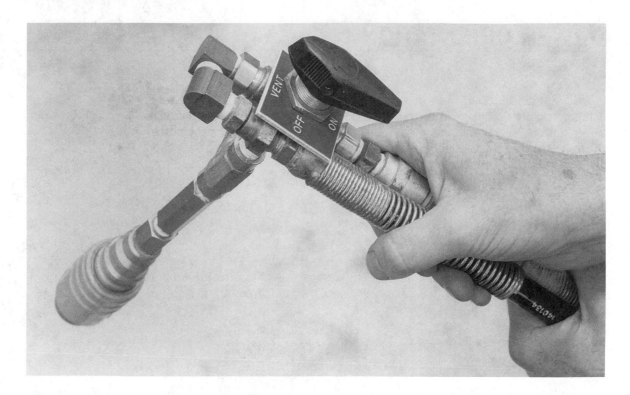

Figure 6.2 NGV-1 coupling—female

the NGV-1 fuel receptacle is accepted for general use (Figures 6.2 and 6.3). However, if you travel, it is possible that you may encounter various types of older fueling connectors. There are three common fuel connectors used (as described previously). It is recommended that additional fueling adapters be stored in the vehicle for use when needed.

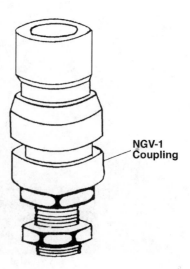

NGV-1
Coupling

Figure 6.3 NGV-1 coupling—male

Figure 6.4 Turning on the dispenser

Follow the steps below to fill an NGV:

1. Remove the dust cap from the fill valve.

2. Connect the fill dispenser hose to the fill valve on the vehicle and turn the valve to the FILL position.

3. Turn the dispenser to the ON or FILL position (Figure 6.4). (You may hear a whistling sound as you fill the vehicle.)

4. When the vehicle is filled to its desired level, turn the fuel dispenser back to the OFF position.

5. After five seconds, turn the fill valve on the vehicle to OFF or VENT and remove the hose from the vehicle.

6. Replace the dust plug.

OPERATION AND MAINTENANCE

The operation and maintenance of an NGV is similar to other vehicles. A visual check of the engine components and the fuel delivery system prior to fueling is always a good idea. Normally, however, no special attention is required to ensure the safe operation of an NGV. As with gasoline-powered vehicles, if a problem does occur, the vehicle should be serviced immediately by an NGV specialist. The following is a list of common concerns on NGV operation.

The Manual Shutoff Valve

The manual shutoff valve is a safety device that should be used only when it is necessary to prevent natural gas from reaching the engine compartment. This situation may occur in the event of an accident where fuel lines or NGV components have been damaged, when the vehicle's fuel system is being serviced, or when a vehicle is to be parked for an extended period of time. The manual shutoff valve should not be used on a daily basis. It must be clearly labeled and located where it can be quickly and easily reached by the driver in the event of an emergency. Therefore, the valve is most commonly placed under the driver's side door.

Check Regularly for Natural Gas Leaks

The vehicle should be checked for gas leaks at least once a year. It is a good idea to use a methane detector to check for gas leaks occasionally after a conversion has been completed or the fuel system serviced. However, once it is established that the vehicle is functioning properly, it is not necessary to check for leaks more than once a year, as long as the distinctive natural gas smell is not detected.

Starting an NGV

Starting an NGV is identical to starting a gasoline-powered vehicle. If the vehicle is bi-fuel, then switch fuels while the vehicle is running. This may be done without interruption while the vehicle is in operation. In some early applications this may require the vehicle to be traveling over 25 mph.

Preventative Maintenance

Whatever preventative maintenance needs to be done to a gasoline-powered vehicle should be done to a vehicle powered by natural gas. Some primary regulators require seat block rotation periodically. No other special maintenance is suggested. However, it is highly recommended that the vehicle be thoroughly inspected once a year to identify and replace worn-out components.

In Case of an Accident

In the event of an accident with an NGV, the operator should keep three things in mind:

1. Turn off the manual shutoff valve, if you can.

2. Don't touch any other component on the vehicle and stay clear of the accident.

3. Notify all emergency personnel that the vehicle operates on compressed natural gas.

Switching Between NG and Gasoline in a Bi-Fuel Vehicle

When the natural gas fuel cylinders are nearing empty, the vehicle's performance will start to decrease. On modern conversion systems, you can switch from natural gas to gasoline in a bi-fuel vehicle when starting the vehicle, when the vehicle is running, or when the vehicle is not running.

On older systems with carburetors, both fuel systems are shut off for a period while the float bowl is emptied. Then the vehicle can be switched to natural gas. In these systems, leave the switch in the middle until the vehicle's motor starts to die, then select natural gas.

COMPRESSED NATURAL GAS VEHICLE FUELING STATIONS AND FUEL SUPPLY

FUELING NGV VEHICLES

The fueling of NGVs starts with an infrastructure of over 2.1 million miles of natural gas transmission lines (Figure 6.5).

Compressed natural gas fueling stations are designed in three basic configurations: fast fill, timed fill, and combination fill. The fast fill method takes from two minutes to five minutes to fuel a vehicle, which is comparable to a gasoline fueling station. The timed fill method may take between 8 and 12 hours for complete fueling. The timed fill method, sometimes referred to as *time fill*, is suitable for NGVs operated by private individuals or fleet owners who can fuel their vehicles overnight. The fast fill method is suitable for public filling stations or high volume fleets (Figures 6.6 and 6.7). The most common fueling station is the combination fill, which includes both fast fill and timed fill methods. This type of station is used when some vehicles return to a central location for fueling and others need to be fueled on the go.

Components of the Fast Fill Station

The fast fill station, although time efficient, requires a large investment. A fast fill station designed to accommodate 20 vehicles may cost between $30,000 and $350,000, depending on size and location. The

Figure 6.5 Map showing concentration of natural gas transmission lines in the United States

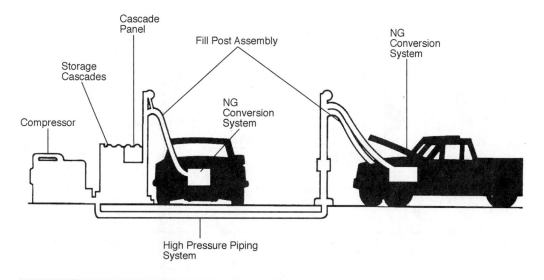

Figure 6.6 Typical fast fill and timed fill station

primary components of the fast fill station include:

- natural gas pipeline

- compressor

- high pressure bulk storage system (commonly referred to as a *cascade*)

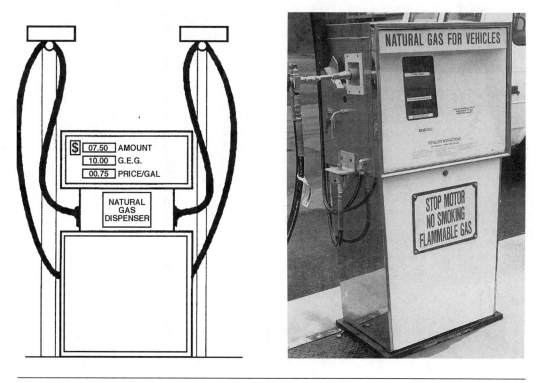

Figure 6.7 Natural gas dispenser. *Photo:* NG dispenser

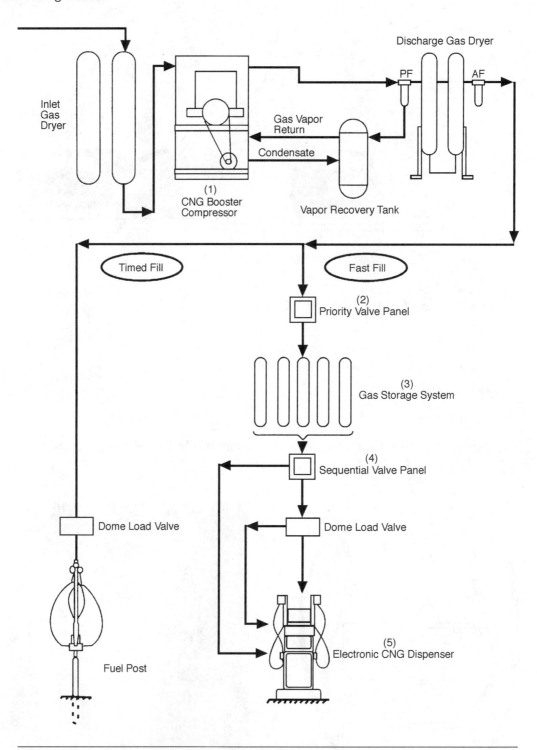

Figure 6.8 Components of filling station (fast and timed fill) *(Courtesy Xebec, Inc.)*

- sequential valves panel (used to manage dispensing)
- priority valves panel (used to manage refilling the cascade)
- fuel dispenser(s)

Figure 6.8 shows the components of a fast fill station. Natural gas travels through a network of natural gas pipelines to the fueling station. The compressor (1) compresses the gas to a preset pressure for storage in the priority panel (2). The priority panel controls the natural gas supplied to the cascade as supply diminishes. The high pressure bulk storage system (3) consists of a series of steel cylinders or pressure vessels. The sequential panel (4) controls the sequence of natural gas leaving the storage system. Natural gas enters the fuel dispenser (5) which is a hose containing a fill valve on the end for attaching to the vehicle. Finally, the gas enters the vehicle's fuel cylinders while the fuel dispenser meters the flow of fuel. Figure 6.9 shows a variation of a fast fill station.

The timed fill method is much slower than the fast fill but has the advantage of dramatically reduced costs. The major cost of the timed fill method is the compressor which can cost between $3,000 and $10,000, depending on the size. The primary components of the timed fill method include:

Components of the Timed Fill Station

- natural gas transmission lines

- compressor (Figure 6.10)

- fuel dispenser(s)

Gas flows through the pipeline directly to the compressor which compresses the gas. Natural gas then flows through a hose to the dispenser which delivers it to the vehicle's fuel cylinders. There is no need for a priority panel, sequential panel, or high pressure storage.

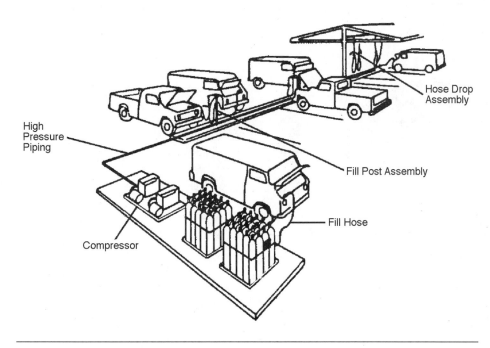

Figure 6.9 Typical filling station

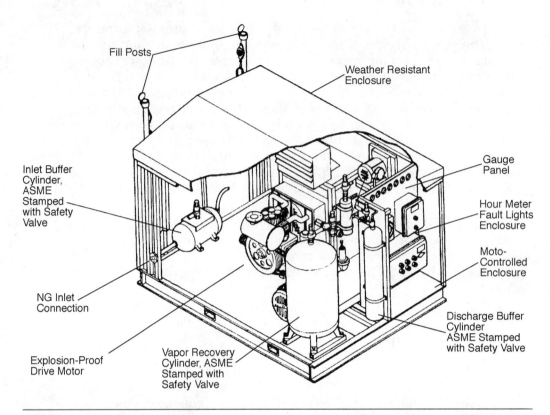

Fill Posts

Weather Resistant
Enclosure

Inlet Buffer
Cylinder,
ASME
Stamped
with Safety
Valve

Gauge
Panel

Hour Meter
Fault Lights
Enclosure

Moto-
Controlled
Enclosure

NG Inlet
Connection

Discharge Buffer
Cylinder
ASME Stamped
with Safety Valve

Explosion-Proof
Drive Motor

Vapor Recovery
Cylinder, ASME
Stamped with
Safety Valve

Figure 6.10 All-weather natural gas refueling compressor *(Courtesy Bauer Compressors, Inc.)*

SAFETY SUMMARY

SAFETY ISSUES AND REGULATIONS

There are many safety regulations that should be followed for constructing, operating, and maintaining an NGV fueling facility. The National Fire Protection Association (NFPA) has developed standards for compressed natural gas vehicle fuel systems. A detailed description of all regulations concerning fueling facilities should be obtained from the NFPA prior to designing a station. These regulations are designed to ensure the safety of the operators, customers, and the environment.

Because natural gas is a flammable gas stored at a high pressure, leaks are the greatest concern for fueling station managers and mechanics. Mechanics working on a vehicle should have hand-held natural gas leak detectors if possible. Smoking, welding, and other activities that could cause the gas to ignite should be restricted near gas lines and fuel cylinders. Also, safety fluorescent lights should replace shop extension lights that contain bulbs that may explode when dropped. Portable fire extinguishers of 20-B:C or higher should be available at the fueling station.

The quality and condition of the filling station equipment is also important for creating a safe environment. Natural gas approved hoses, pipes, valves, gauges, and cylinders should be used. All hoses used for natural gas must be corrosion resistant. Only fueling station equipment in good operating condition should be used in order to avoid introducing foreign contaminants and debris into the vehicle fuel system. To ensure quality, all equipment should be inspected and maintained regularly according to manufacturers' recommendations. Control devices designed to protect equipment from icing or hydrate formation should also be installed.

To create a safer environment, outdoor fueling is recommended wherever practical. An outdoor station diminishes the chance of an explosion due to leaking gas. Even though the fueling station may be indoors, charged natural gas fuel storage containers not connected for filling should be stored outdoors. All storage of natural gas should be above ground to eliminate the chance of underground contamination. When fueling equipment is operated unattended, it must be equipped with a high discharge and low suction pressure automatic shutdown control. Another recommendation is to enclose the facility or any equipment located outdoors to minimize vandalism.

Indoor fueling facilities should be limited to 10,000 cubic feet of natural gas storage capacity. This does not include the vehicle storage cylinder. The building should be designed exclusively for NGV fueling and servicing if possible. Only noncombustible materials should be used in the construction of the building. Explosion venting should also be built into the design in case of a natural gas leak. This will require a continuous mechanical ventilation system containing methane detectors which will sound a warning alarm when a 1 percent methane level is detected. A 5 percent methane level creates a combustible environment. The ventilation system may also automatically shut down compression equipment, open garage doors, and turn on the fans.

NGV FUELING STATIONS

Most fleets that convert to operate on natural gas construct their own fueling stations and are not dependent on public facilities. However, many public NGV fueling stations are being developed near industrial parks where fleets flourish. Many cities have public NGV fueling stations. New stations are opening nationwide at the rate of one per business day. Public fueling stations will help the NGV market develop more rapidly while providing greater versatility and range for NGV fleets.

Facility Specifications

There are no regulations in the 1992 NFPA 52 Standard for Compressed Natural Gas Vehicle Fuel Systems specifically addressing the repair and maintenance of NGV vehicles in buildings. Standards from NFPA 52 related to NGV repair indoors are addressed but are not complete. However, there are other standards, e.g., NFPA 70, NFPA 88, and NFPA 88B Standard for Repair Garages (1985), that offer more information on this topic.

Rooms within or attached to other buildings should be constructed of noncombustible or limited-combustible materials. Interior walls or partitions should be continuous from floor to ceiling, be securely anchored, and have a fire resistance rating of at least two hours. At least one wall should be an exterior wall. Windows and doors should be located so they are readily accessible in case of emergency.

Access doors should have warning signs with the words "WARNING! NO SMOKING: FLAMMABLE GAS." Such wording should be in plainly legible, bright red letters on a white background with letters not less than one inch high.

Indoor locations should be ventilated using air supply inlets and exhaust outlets (Figure 6.11) arranged to provide air movement as uniformly as practical.

Ventilation should be provided by a continuous mechanical ventilation system or by a mechanical ventilation system activated by a continuous monitoring natural gas detection system.

Note: A gas detection system should be equipped to sound an alarm when a maximum of 1 percent natural gas is in the air. Activation of the ventilation system should be based on a gas concentration of not more than 1 percent natural gas in the air.

Air supply inlets should be uniformly arranged on exterior walls near floor level. Outlets should be located at the high point of the room in exterior walls or the roof. The ventilation rate should be at least 1 cubic foot per minute per 12 cubic feet of room volume. This is equivalent to five air changes per hour. A ventilation system for a room within or attached to another building should be separate from any ventilation systems for the other building. In addition, each person working in a natural gas facility should know the operation of the ventilation system for

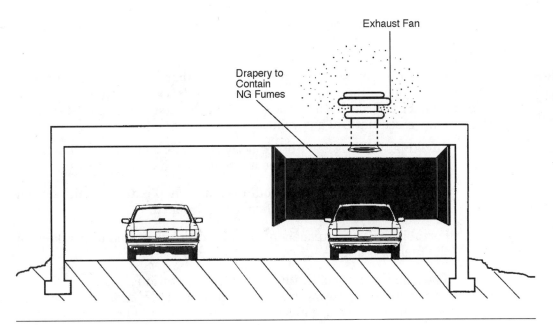

Figure 6.11 Section of a typical NGV shop

that area. Training and education programs should be a regular and continuing activity.

Use fluorescent lights as trouble lights to reduce the likelihood of sparks in the case of an accidentally broken bulb. Hand-held gas detectors are available and are a wise investment for the natural gas vehicle technician. If a smoker is working on natural gas vehicles, smoke away from the work and never carry a single acting (Bic style) lighter. Open flames are prohibited in oxidant or flammable gas cylinder storage areas.

NFPA 52 states that storage of natural gas should be limited to 10,000 cubic feet of natural gas in each building or room with the exception of natural gas stored in the vehicle's mounted fuel supply cylinders. All federal, state, and local regulations regarding fuel storage and use of compressed natural gas cylinders should be referenced.

Make sure a written emergency evacuation plan has been established and communicated to all associated personnel. This plan should include procedures for evacuating the building and performing a head count. It should be posted in several easily seen places on each floor of the building. It must be posted in a way that will make accidental or deliberate removal difficult.

Telephone numbers for emergency squads, the fire department, and safety offices should be posted at all telephones. Instructions on how to obtain an outside line should also be posted. Large signs specifying that safety glasses or other safety equipment are required for entry into certain rooms should be posted. Location of exits and signs for eyewash stations, first aid systems, fire equipment, and other safety related materials must be posted clearly. An adequate supply of water should be available for first aid, fire actions, or dilution of corrosive material in the event of a spill. Limited access areas should be posted with appropriate warning signs.

In an emergency, evacuate the building by activating the fire alarm, and call the proper authorities.

Safety Summary for NGV Fueling Facilities

There are many safety regulations that should be followed for constructing, operating, and maintaining an NGV fueling facility. The National Fire Protection Association (NFPA) has developed standards for compressed natural gas vehicle fuel systems.

- Smoking, welding, and other activities that could cause the gas to ignite should be restricted near gas lines and fuel cylinders.

- Safety fluorescent lights should replace shop extension lights that contain bulbs that may explode when dropped.

- Portable fire extinguishers of 20-B:C or higher should be available at the fueling station.

- The quality and condition of the filling station equipment is also important for creating a safer environment. Natural gas approved hoses, pipes, valves, gauges, and cylinders should be used.

- To create a safer environment, outdoor fueling is recommended wherever practical. Enclose the facility or any equipment located outdoors to minimize vandalism.

- Indoor fueling facilities should be limited to 10,000 cu. ft. of natural gas storage capacity. The building should be designed exclusively for NGV fueling and servicing. This will require a continuous mechanical ventilation system containing methane detectors which will sound a warning alarm when a 1 percent methane level is detected.

In addition to NFPA 52, the Uniform Fire Code Article 52 and the Uniform Fire Code Standard No. 52-1 will impact how CNG fueling stations are installed and operated in jurisdictions that have adopted the Uniform Fire Code. Currently, states that have adopted the Uniform Fire Code include California, Oregon, Washington, Arizona, Wyoming, Minnesota, Utah, and most municipalities of Colorado. The Uniform Fire Code and the Uniform Fire Code Standards are a model fire code that provides minimum design requirements for building and site fire protection, the safe storage and use of hazardous materials, general fire and life safety requirements, and maintenance requirements for the fire safety and fire protection designs of the Uniform Building Code. The code and standards are published every three years with the latest version published in 1994.

Overall, the standards and regulations for NGV fueling facilities outlined in NFPA 52 and the Uniform Fire Code and the Uniform Fire Code Standards correlate. However, revisions were made by the International Fire Code Institute that are not contained in the NFPA regulations. These significant revisions are summarized:

- All primary fueling equipment (compressed NG dispensers, dispenser nozzles, flexible hoses, methane gas detection equipment, and electrical components used for fuel storage and dispensing systems) must be certified by a third-party testing laboratory such as the American Gas Association's Certification Laboratories.

- Overall, the Uniform Building Code's requirements for explosion control are more restrictive than are NFPA 52's. For example, dispensing of compressed NG inside of buildings will require an automatic sprinkler system to be installed throughout the building. Also, the building structure must have a method of explosion control.

- Local fire departments must establish areas where compressed NG can be stored and dispensed. This will ensure there is a physical barrier between the general public and a potentially hazardous material.

- The Uniform Fire Code has prohibited the installation of vehicle and residential fueling appliances; specifically, timed fill compressors designed for overnight fueling.

SUMMARY

- To safely refuel an NGV, there are six basic steps that should be followed.

- Operation and maintenance of an NGV is similar to other vehicles.

- The areas of concern while operating an NGV are: (1) proper use of the manual shutoff valve, (2) periodic checks for gas leaks, (3) proper starting procedures, (4) proper procedures after being involved in an accident, and (5) proper procedures for switching between fuels.

- The fast fill method is more convenient than the timed fill method but requires a larger initial investment.

- The primary components of a fast fill station are: (1) natural gas pipeline, (2) compressor, (3) high pressure bulk storage system, (4) sequential/priority panels, and (5) fuel dispensers.

- The primary components of a timed fill station are: (1) natural gas pipeline, (2) compressor, and (3) fuel dispensers.

- The NFPA has established minimum standards for the design, construction, and operation of refueling facilities.

- The major safety points for fueling stations include: use of hand-held NG leak detectors, limiting activities that could cause gas to ignite, use of safety fluorescent lights, having necessary safety equipment accessible, and the use of make-up air exchangers with methane detectors.

REVIEW QUESTIONS

1. List the specific areas of instruction each driver should be aware of before operating an NGV.

2. List the proper procedure for refueling an NGV.

3. List the procedures that should be followed in case of an accident involving an NGV.

4. Explain the procedure that should be followed to switch operating fuels on a bi-fuel vehicle.

5. List the major components of a fast fill station and describe how the station operates.

6. List the major components of a timed fill station and describe how the station operates.

7. List any safety equipment needed specifically for service or refueling of NGVs.

8. List any restrictions that must be followed in designing an indoor refueling facility.

9. Summarize the revisions by the International Fire Code Institute that are not contained in the NFPA regulations.

10. Compare the safety characteristics of CNG versus gasoline.

CHAPTER **7**

Diagnostic Methods and Troubleshooting

OBJECTIVES

- Understand the general approach that helps technicians learn vital troubleshooting skills.
- Understand the four main elements involved in the critical thinking process.
- Identify the five-step procedure for basic troubleshooting.
- Identify proper troubleshooting procedures for some common NGV symptoms.
- Identify a relationship between diagnostic theory and practice.
- Understand the importance of critical thinking when analyzing a schematic.
- Recognize that becoming a successful troubleshooter is a talent that is learned and not an art.

KEY TERMS

Critical thinking
Analytical
Schematic

Flow chart
Supersonic
Systematic

AUTOMOTIVE SKILLS AND TRAINING

SYSTEMS APPROACH TO PROBLEM SOLVING

Most vehicle problems are rather complex, since a number of factors are involved simultaneously. Generally, these factors are grouped into subsystems that can be checked or verified by asking, "What works?"

When a problem occurs with a vehicle, a systematic approach is often needed for its solution. It may not be a simple mechanical, resource, or troubleshooting problem, but rather some combination of the three. In other words, a whole set of symptoms may be involved. However, it is the critical thinking skills of a troubleshooting expert that are central to approaching a problem. The steps taken by an expert include identifying the problem, analyzing alternatives, and proposing a solution. The systems approach allows the troubleshooter not only to repair problems, but also to teach others how to develop this ability.

Critical thinking helps to break the mindset which has been forced upon the technician by automation. Build on what is known and exploit your talent to see the problem in a new light. Look at problems critically.

It is not easy to accept another person's definition of a problem. It may be difficult to accept and offer a solution to someone else's analysis of a problem. Acting in haste can create serious problems for an expert responsible for the diagnosis and troubleshooting of problems in a vehicle. For example, unnecessary costs may result from the following:

1. Unneeded equipment mistakenly purchased.

2. Time and manpower wasted on fixing the wrong problem.

3. In the replacement of parts that are not broken, good parts are damaged.

4. While fixing an apparent mechanical problem the *true* mechanical problem may be revealed. This can result in the creation of a multidimensional problem since the symptoms may not be matched with the underlying problem.

What examples can you come up with from your past experiences?

Automotive diagnostic experts, skilled in troubleshooting and critical thinking skills, resist accepting a solution until they are sure they have identified the problem. To properly handle a problem and prevent more problems from arising, the troubleshooter must gain a clear understanding of the problem. Most repairs do not have alternatives. They may be hard to find, but they have only one fix. A good rule of thumb to follow is, "Fix it right the first time."

Experience has shown that many of the failures involving NGV engines can be traced to a general engine fault rather than to the NG

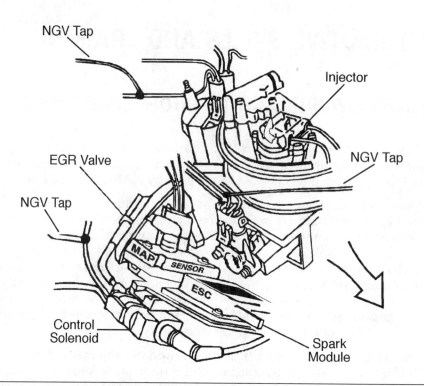

Figure 7.1 Overview of NGV wiring (possible loose connections abound in systems) *(Courtesy Alternative Fuels Technology Corp.)*

equipment itself. Therefore, normal engine diagnosis should be followed to ensure that the problem is related to the NG system (Figure 7.1).

TECHNICIAN KNOWLEDGE, SKILLS, AND ABILITIES AND TROUBLESHOOTING SKILLS TRAINING

NGV technicians have skills that have been refined through their past experience. This factor influences their training in troubleshooting skills. It is difficult for an individual technician to take all characteristics into account. However, some general approaches will help technicians learn vital troubleshooting skills. These approaches, illustrated in Figure 7.2, require the technician to do the following:

1. Develop a certain proficiency level.

2. Develop troubleshooting skills.

3. Actively participate in troubleshooting skills training.

Technician Proficiency Level

Proficiency is the ability of the technician to use troubleshooting skills effectively, and typically involves a combination of knowledge, skills, and abilities. In most technician training experiences, the actual level of

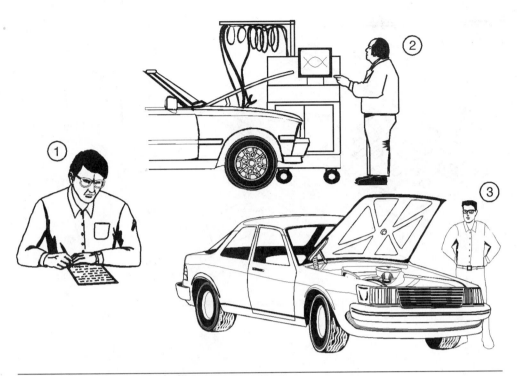

Figure 7.2 Master Technician instructing technicians how to best use troubleshooting skills when diagnosing NGV engine performance

performance reflects the individual's level of proficiency as well as the influence of other participants and/or the trainer.

Some insight into the technician's existing abilities and deficiencies is very useful. Awareness of the discrepancy between abilities and desired level of proficiency can motivate the technician to take part in training activities to enhance knowledge, skills, and abilities in troubleshooting NGVs.

Troubleshooting Skill Development

Technicians differ in how they approach and use training sessions. The preferred ways in which they learn are known as their *learning styles*. How can trainers help in developing their styles? Intelligence, personality, age, formal education, and previous specialized experience all contribute to a technician's way of learning new skills. It is important for technicians to know how they will best learn these new skills in a training environment. Training also requires learners to acquire information (Figure 7.3). This information may be relayed through speech, active participation, role playing, repetition, and nonverbal clues designed to facilitate learning.

Personal learning styles differ. They range from people who do not pay attention to details to people who have the potential to be problem solvers. By being aware of personal learning styles, technicians can improve their ability to see issues from many perspectives. Visual learning is one style that can be developed. Another type of learner is the one who talks and does not listen yet can focus and identify underlying

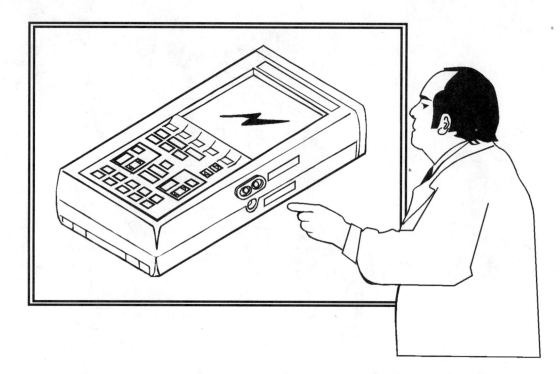

Figure 7.3 Modern electronic instruction

issues. These differing learning styles can be helpful. Troubleshooters can become experts in the diagnosis of problematic situations by adopting more favorable traits or habits.

The specific problem-solving skills that technicians must acquire have common dimensions: (1) they must learn to be analytical, (2) they must concentrate on the problem at hand, (3) they must ponder several alternative causes before deciding on an answer, (4) they must recognize impulsiveness, and (5) they must be able to come to a logical, clear conclusion.

Progress in learning these vital problem-solving skills depends greatly on a technician's understanding of how these skills relate to the job and, more specifically, how they relate to the goals and objectives of finding the cause of an NGV problem and devising a clear plan to correct the problem.

Active Participation

Technicians must actively participate in troubleshooting in order to understand the purpose of the new skills and to master them. Trying to learn skills can be confusing. The trainer should use activities to help the technicians relate previous experiences to new concepts (Figure 7.4).

The outcome of troubleshooting skills training is influenced by expectations of a technician's employer (the technician will stay current with knowledge of troubleshooting and fixing an NGV), and by individual aspirations (desire to know about NGV conversion in order to become a master technician).

Figure 7.4 Master Technician training a technician in troubleshooting skills

It has been noted by experts that a fine line separates the technician from the diagnostician. Diagnosticians have developed the ability of higher order thinking. They go beyond the knowledge, comprehension, and application of methods to the analysis, synthesis, and evaluation of the system. These terms are nothing more than labels placed on specific aspects of troubleshooting. In the next section, we will examine how these aspects relate the troubleshooting experience to critical thinking.

CRITICAL THINKING AND PROBLEM SOLVING

CRITICAL THINKING SKILLS

Critical thinking skills are vital to all NGV experts responsible for diagnosing problems in NGVs (Figure 7.5). Defined according to the focus of this manual, critical thinking involves the expert's sustained suspension of judgment of a problem situation. It is important to remember that following a pattern of decision making for a specific problem will not guarantee a correct solution every time.

Basic skill development helps to remove a technician's limitations. Technicians develop higher order thinking by approaching a problem in stages. The phrase "Do = Think = Feel" represents the stages of skill development, which consist of the following hierarchy:

Analysis
Synthesis
Evaluation

⬆

Critical | Thinking

Knowledge
Comprehension
Application

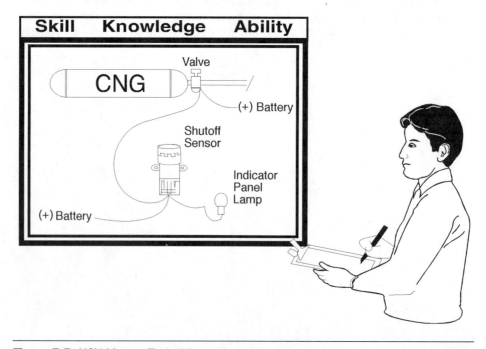

Figure 7.5 NGV Master Technician using critical thinking skills in troubleshooting a problem

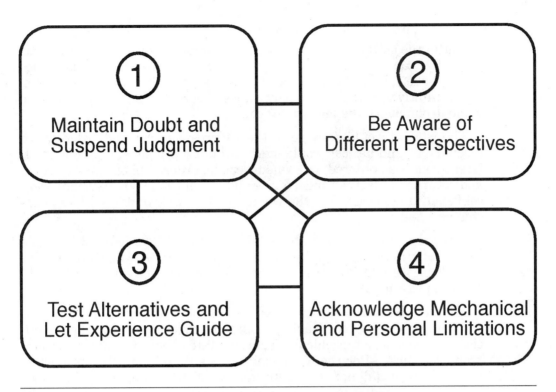

Figure 7.6 The four main elements of the critical thinking process

Knowledge, comprehension, and application are basic skill developments. The higher order thinking abilities are analysis, synthesis, and evaluation. Getting to the higher order involves critical thinking.

The best knowledge that an NGV technician can have is the recognition of the fact that there are alternative methods to gathering evidence. Critical thinking involves four main elements (Figure 7.6):

1. maintaining doubt and suspending judgment;

2. being aware of different patterns and perspectives;

3. testing alternatives and letting positive experience guide; and

4. being aware of mechanical, equipment, and personal limitations.

Maintaining Doubt and Suspending Judgment

The most frequent error in problem solving is when the technician arrives prematurely at a judgment about the nature of a problem. A skilled NGV troubleshooter examines the problem and refuses to rush to a conclusion. By doing this, the technician creates the mental attitude needed to take a fresh, original look at the problem(s) and is therefore better able to identify the problem, analyze the situation, isolate the cause, and offer a solution without unnecessary waste of material or time.

The importance of critical thinking skills to an NGV technician when troubleshooting a problem are illustrated in the following problem scenarios.

Scenarios Involving Doubt and Judgment

One of the better stories comes from a complaint by a woman in Texas about her car that would not start. "My car does not like pistachio ice cream," she said to the Texas automotive shops. Studying the problem, representatives of the automotive shops observed the following routine while driving with the lady in her car.

The woman would daily go to the ice cream parlor and order an ice cream cone, and her car would start without a problem. Each day a different cone was ordered, but whenever she ordered pistachio ice cream and returned to her car, indeed it would not start. The technicians were confused. It appeared that the woman had a car that did not like pistachio ice cream.

Before reading on, think about this situation. The answer will be discussed later in this section. Remember to suspend your judgment (Figure 7.7). These were trained troubleshooters who were convinced her car did not like pistachio ice cream.

Another scenario involves an NGV's engine that cranks but does not start on gasoline or NG. Having rebuilt the mixer assembly, the technician responsible for problem diagnosis states that the mixer valve is probably stuck. After the technician spends time fixing the "problem," the vehicle still will not start. Assuming that the mixer must be a faulty piece of equipment, the technician purchases and installs a new one. The result—the NGV still does not start.

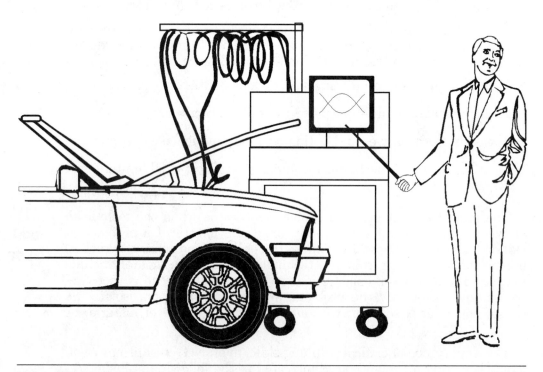

Figure 7.7 Master Technician instructing other technicians on how best to use troubleshooting skills when diagnosing NGV engine performance

Doubt and Judgment—Troubleshooting Error

The previous sample problem illustrates how wasteful it is to prematurely arrive at a solution without a clear understanding of the problem.

How could maintaining doubt and suspending judgment have been helpful in examining the problem? The technician, having rebuilt the mixer, may have been able to recall what general experience with NGVs has shown. Many failures can be traced to a general engine fault rather than the NGV equipment itself.

Remember the pistachio ice cream cone that prevented the woman from Texas from starting her car? It turns out that after months of investigation the dealers did discover the problem. Pistachio ice cream cones take longer to pack than chocolate or vanilla ice cream cones. Whenever she ordered a pistachio ice cream cone, the car would sit for a longer time in the parking lot in the Texas heat, and vapor lock would occur.

Being Aware of Different Perspectives

It is important to recognize that an NGV problem can be viewed from different diagnostic perspectives. Emphasis is placed on the critical thinking and analytical skills of the troubleshooting expert:

- Mechanical perspective emphasis is placed on specific vehicle parts (Figure 7.8).

- Resource perspective emphasis is placed on specific resources such as information, tools, or equipment available (Figure 7.9).

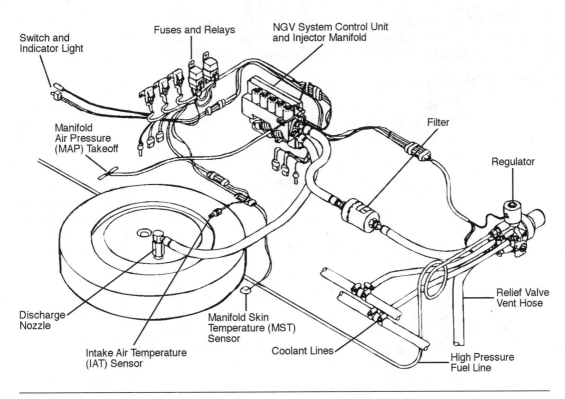

Figure 7.8 NGV system *(note components involved in the delivery of natural gas)*

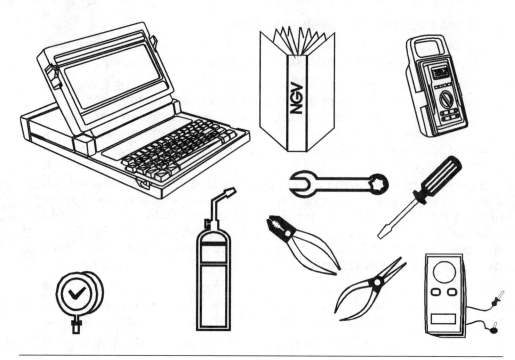

Figure 7.9 Various tools available to mechanics

The following critical question is the ultimate test for determining which perspective is most useful in problem solving: Will approaching a problem from one specific angle tell you something more about the problem than you would have known had you approached it from a different angle? Look for other perspectives that tell you more about the problem. The next sample problem is an example of the way perspective can be applied to an NGV problem diagnosis.

Scenario Involving Perspectives

An NGV is running roughly and the vehicle must be analyzed to determine why. This car has a problem. The technician can look at it from a mechanical, resource, or a diagnostic point of view. It makes sense to approach it first from a mechanical point of view; i.e., look at the parts and pieces and see what is going on. The technician must start troubleshooting somewhere. Resources such as readily available manuals or tools can be used. However, it would not make sense for the technician to look at the situation from a resource point of view. How can the technician fix the car if only, for example, a hammer and a screwdriver are available? The car could not be fixed, so the technician would look for more resources.

Perspectives—Troubleshooting Error

Does examining the problem from only the resource perspective tell you anything new about the current situation to help you solve the problem? No. Therefore, the technician examines the situation from other perspectives. The situation must be carefully analyzed from all possible perspectives. By identifying new information about the problem it will be easier to determine an effective solution.

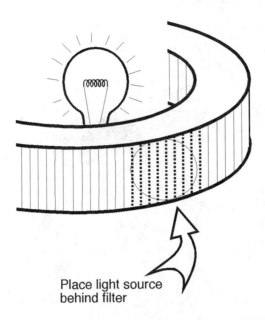

Place light source
behind filter

Figure 7.10 Typical analysis procedure to check the condition of an air filter

What critical thinking perspective would have been most helpful in examining the problem? Careful analysis will show that a mechanical point of view is one way to isolate and identify the primary problem in the situation. The problem was that the vehicle was running poorly because of a dirty air filter (Figure 7.10). Given this information, would it be safe to assume that the vehicle also gets poor mileage when running on gasoline?

As you can see, the critical thinking required in troubleshooting can be simple or complex because of the many different perspectives that must be considered. Inability to analyze a problem from different perspectives may prevent a technician from identifying and fixing problems.

Customers also realize this. The perspectives that technicians are open or closed to have been studied and written about. The perception that male mechanics tend to undervalue the female customer's perspective is a volatile subject that has been brought to the attention of female customers in books and other publications, such as *What the Mechanic Doesn't Want You to Know*.

Not all aspects of a problem can be known in advance. Often, it is necessary to test possible causes and to use knowledge and experience to further clarify and isolate the cause of the problem (Figure 7.11). This critical thinking skill is vital to diagnostics because the thinking process is the technician's best tool for examining and understanding the exact cause of the problem. The process of analysis—separating symptoms from causes—depends upon the technician's critical thinking ability.

If the technician cannot examine the situation critically by testing alternatives, several things may occur:

• the problem will not be clearly understood

**Testing
Alternatives and
Letting Experience
Be the Guide**

Figure 7.11 Thinking process

- symptoms will continue to confuse technicians by appearing as causes

- the problem will never be isolated

- the problem will not be fixed

The troubleshooting procedure will often fail because the technician is unable to think critically. Thinking critically involves examining alternatives as part of a process in order to isolate the cause of the problem.

Scenario Involving Alternatives and Experiences

A bi-fuel NGV's engine cranks but will not start on gasoline or compressed natural gas. The technician examines the situation and knows that there could be several reasons why it will not start. The technician also knows to examine other possible alternative causes. Because the vehicle will run on either gasoline or natural gas, the technician centers all analysis on the alternatives related to parts unique to NGVs. Possible alternative causes are:

1. the fuel selector switch is damaged (Figure 7.12)

2. a fuse is blown on the selector switch circuit (Figure 7.13)

3. there is a fault on the dual curve ignition device (Figure 7.14)

The technician examines these causes but does not find any of them to be the problem. The technician is confused as there appears to be no

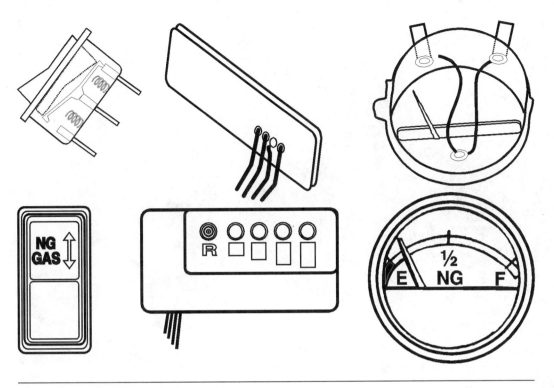

Figure 7.12 NGV fuel selector switch and gauges

cause for the problem. Why wasn't the cause found if all the alternatives were carefully examined?

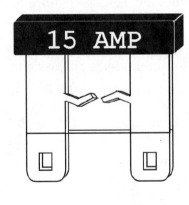

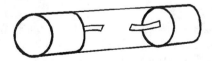

Figure 7.13 Blown fuses

Figure 7.14 Dual curve ignition device *(Courtesy Alternative Fuels Technologies Corp.)*

Alternatives and Experience—Troubleshooting Error

The technician examined possible causes; that is, the possible alternatives for those parts unique to an NGV vehicle. Often, NGV technicians take for granted those parts that are basic to the function of the vehicle itself; i.e., those that are similar in both gasoline-powered vehicles and NGVs. Examination of the alternatives would have eliminated the possibility of the battery having low voltage. Failure to recognize low battery voltage is possible because different symptoms also would have been evident. For example, the engine would not turn with a voltage so low that it would also cause an ignition problem. The diagnosis of low battery voltage would thereby be eliminated as a possibility.

An examination of alternative possibilities would have included both those parts unique to an NGV system (fuel selector switch, mixer, etc.) as well as those basic to the operation of a vehicle (battery, ignition system, etc.), regardless of the type of fuel used.

A thorough analysis would have also taken into consideration the following possible causes of the problem:

1. defective crank sensor

2. fault in the ignition system

3. defective coolant sensor

The crank sensor as well as the coolant sensor, however, have been designed as integral parts of the onboard computer system (Figure 7.15). Their failure would allow the symptoms described to occur in this scenario.

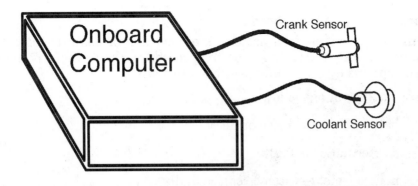

Figure 7.15 Integral parts to the proper operation of the OBC

It is important to remember that not all problems with NGVs are related to parts unique to the NG fuel system (Figure 7.16). Several basic vehicle parts can affect the overall operation of the vehicle as well. As you can see, if the technician does not examine all possible alternative causes of a problem, the actual cause may never be determined and the problem will not be fixed.

There is clearly a difference between what technicians *should* do and what they *can* do. Certain solutions may be beyond the expertise of the technician. Being aware of the feasibility of solutions (whether they actually are possible) will help a technician choose the right solution to a problem. It will also save time and money by avoiding situations that are beyond the customer's financial resources or the service technician's expertise.

Being Aware of Mechanical and Personal Limitations

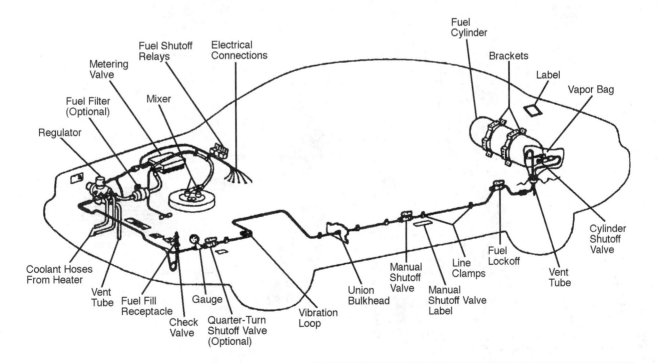

Figure 7.16 Schematic of NGV fuel system *(Courtesy GFI Control Systems, Inc.)*

Scenario Involving Limitations

An NGV's engine does not crank on gasoline or compressed natural gas. In following the troubleshooting procedure, the technician analyzes the symptoms by examining possible alternatives.

1. battery voltage is low

2. battery clamp is loose or dirty

3. starter motor is faulty

4. neutral safety-switch circuit is faulty

The first three possible sources of potential problems or causes were eliminated. The technician decided that the problem was isolated—the neutral safety-switch circuit had a fault. The technician, also experienced in NGV conversions and maintenance, decided to try to fix the circuit. After spending much time on the repair, the technician found that: (1) the vehicle's engine still would not turn on gasoline or compressed natural gas and (2) the neutral safety-switch circuit now had several wires cut and exposed. To the technician, the circuit appeared to be destroyed. An "expert" in NGV systems, however, would likely have the electrical training to deal with the circuit (Figure 7.17).

Limitations—Troubleshooting Error

In the above scenario, the technician successfully identified the problem. He just could not fix the problem. A skilled technician not familiar with the system would not take it on as a task. Technicians are aware of

Figure 7.17 Mechanical abilities

the consequences of causing further damage to vehicle systems. The forging of new ground is not typical of any technician. New problems created by a technician cost additional time and money to repair.

How would being aware of personal and mechanical limitations have been helpful in this problem? Are mechanical and personal limitations considerations that technicians should make when troubleshooting or are they considerations that technicians should take into account after the problem is identified? Does management get involved by putting the best person on the job? What would you have done?

PROCEDURAL DIAGNOSTICS

FIVE-STEP TROUBLESHOOTING PROCEDURE

The troubleshooting process begins by verifying the problem. The technician then looks for causes of the symptoms of the problem by analyzing the system for possible indications of the fault. This suggested procedure is one of many available through training programs around the world. It has been chosen for its comprehensiveness. The application of critical thinking is applied to this model procedure, just as it may be applied to another model. The technician is required to supply the brainpower and critical thinking skills necessary for the troubleshooting process. As a class, you may want to discuss your own procedure prior to continuing in the manual. Ask yourself the following questions about your own procedure: Why do you use it? How do you use it? When did you start using it? Is it effective? What can be done to improve it?

Procedures can be applied to a problem to help the technician to isolate a problem. The symptoms will also help isolate possible causes of the problem. The possible causes of the problem are further analyzed and tested until the primary cause of the problem is isolated. Only when the cause is isolated can the problem be corrected and checked. These indications are discovered by isolating the symptoms. The symptoms will help isolate possible causes of the problem.

The "Five-Step Troubleshooting Procedure" has been developed to assist you in the development of the critical troubleshooting thought process. This process can be summarized in a simple five-step procedure (Figure 7.18): (1) *verify* the complaint, (2) *analyze* the symptoms, (3) *isolate* the trouble, (4) *correct* or *repair* the problem, and (5) *check* for proper operation.

Step 1—Verify the Complaint

Technicians must identify and organize the facts surrounding the complaint. Technicians must ask questions in order to gain the information advantage over a problem. Besides knowing the vehicle make and model so they can locate the proper repair manual for reference, they need to know what the complaint or problem is.

Technicians need to have the complaint verified. If the customer is available, try to ascertain the status of the vehicle when the problem occurs. Is the NGV going uphill, around town, or cruising on the expressway? Does the problem occur only when it rains, when it is foggy, in the drizzle, snow, heat, or humidity? What is the climate like when the vehicle is being operated? Under what drive cycle is the problem observed? Is it only during start-up, or while hot, cold, at idle, under load, or cruising? How old is the vehicle? What is the mileage on the NGV? When did the problem first occur? Is there a pattern to the problem? Does it happen once in a while, constantly, periodically, or intermittently? How many times has the problem occurred? Is the problem getting worse, getting better, or staying the same?

1. VERIFY the complaint.

2. ANALYZE the symptoms.

3. ISOLATE the trouble.

4. CORRECT or REPAIR the problem.

5. CHECK for proper operation.

Figure 7.18 Five-step troubleshooting procedure

These questions all deal with what *is* observed or reported by the driver. But, what about that which is *not* observed or reported by the driver? What *does* work?

This step simply involves estimating the dimensions of the problem. The most important question at this point is, "What is the problem?" Technicians must first experience the symptoms. The technician must have a clear statement of the problem so that he or she knows there is a problem and has a clear understanding of what it is.

Problems that could confront an NGV technician may include:

- "The vehicle's engine idles very rough when fueled by compressed NG."

- "The engine backfires during acceleration when running on NG."

- "The engine starts on gasoline but not on NG."

- "It hesitates when switched between fuels."

Step 2—Analyze the Symptoms

What is the cause of the problem? Why is there a problem? Why was the problem not solved during routine maintenance checks? These are some of the questions the technician must ask in analyzing the situation. Finding the answer will involve some detailed detective work while fact gathering. Facts must be gathered through personal interviews with the people who operate the NGV, those technicians familiar with the mechanics of the NGV, and the person or persons who identified the problem. Generally, the more information the technician collects on the problem, the better understanding he or she will have of the situation.

Figure 7.19 Master Technician confirming a problem through computerized vehicle analysis *(Courtesy HEX Industries Cryoquip, Inc.)*

Step 3—Isolate the Trouble

Using the information gathered in the analysis step, the technician must now isolate the cause of the problem. The problem, given the result of the analysis, must be carefully investigated by the technician in order to determine the exact cause (Figure 7.19). Critical thinking skills are very important in the process of separating possible causes.

Step 4—Correct the Problem

After a technician isolates a problem and its cause, and has a clear understanding of the problem, it is possible for the technician to make decisions about (1) what *should* be done and (2) what *can* be done about the problem. These two aspects of the decision-making process should remain separate because they are quite different.

After the cause of a problem on an NGV has been isolated, there is usually a clear procedure of how to fix the vehicle. For example, if an electronic circuit board is malfunctioning, there are ways to correct the problem in the board. It can either be fixed (by manual repair, soldering, replacing a faulty chip, or reprogramming) or replaced. However, NGV technicians may lack the skill to fix an electronic circuit board. It is such a specialized problem that the cost of the labor involved in fixing the real problem may exceed the value of the onboard computer unit.

It is the job of NGV technicians to know what their specific goals and responsibilities are at their place of employment. In addition, the available resources (information and equipment) vary among organizations so there is no universal rule that all problems will be solved the same way in all shops.

People may think that the problem solving process is over once a decision is made to pursue a given option and an NGV is fixed. Actually, there is one last step that is one of the most important in the NGV problem solving process. The vehicle must be checked to ensure that everything is operating properly. Checking the NGV for proper operation is the only way to determine that the solution was the correct one and that other problems do not exist. To make sure the problem was solved, recreate the situation in which the symptom was first experienced.

Wise troubleshooters wait until as much data as possible are gathered and checked before making a decision as to what the correct solution may be. Even then, they carefully observe the initial problem correction process to see if they were right. These problem recognition and critical thinking skills are vital for technicians who are responsible for diagnosing and troubleshooting problems in gasoline- or diesel-powered automobiles as well as NGVs.

Step 5—Check for Proper Operation

NGV FIVE-STEP TROUBLESHOOTING PROCEDURE

The troubleshooting required for a converted NGV vehicle is similar to the troubleshooting procedures for an unconverted vehicle. Experience has shown that most of the problems involving engines using natural gas as a fuel can usually be traced to general engine faults. They are similar to unconverted vehicle faults (electrical fault, dirty air cleaner, etc.) and are not necessarily attributable to the specific NGV equipment (Figure 7.20).

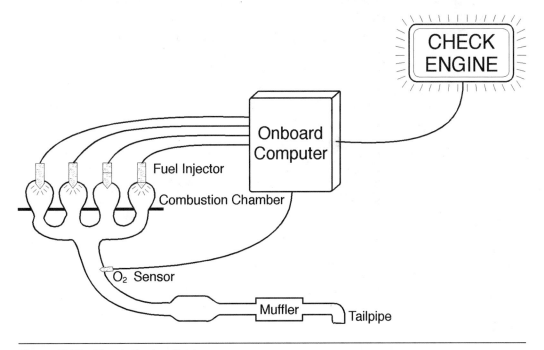

Figure 7.20 Check Engine light on

Many of the problems with the NGV system are a direct result of poor installation (e.g., bad wire connection, loose mixers, etc.). Care must be taken to ensure that every conversion is carried out according to the guidelines in the manufacturer's installation manual.

It is therefore recommended that in the event of a problem arising in NGV operation, normal engine troubleshooting procedures should be carried out to ensure that the problem is from the NGV system and is not just a basic engine fault. Internal combustion engines require an ignition source, fuel, mechanical compression, and air to operate. NGVs are no different.

In addition to the electrical connections that have been mentioned already, crimp-type connectors can be the cause of intermittent driveability problems on both gasoline- and natural gas-powered vehicles. When called for, the technician should inspect the connections under the hood for poor solder joints (on older systems) and corrosion resulting from a lack of water sealant. Any corroded, loose, or improper connections should be repaired to eliminate them as causes of the problem (or problem symptom).

To make troubleshooting easier, the technician should be familiar with the three distinct fuel subsystems of natural gas vehicles (these subsystems are similar to gasoline systems): (1) the natural gas storage components, (2) the transfer components, and (3) the fuel regulation and delivery. Figure 7.21 gives a general indication of the three distinct fuel subsystems that are separated by the physical components of the vehicle.

ELECTRICAL AND ELECTRONIC DIAGNOSIS

In order to perform an effective diagnosis of the electrical and electronic systems of the NGV, technicians should follow the same logical steps outlined for overall system diagnostics:

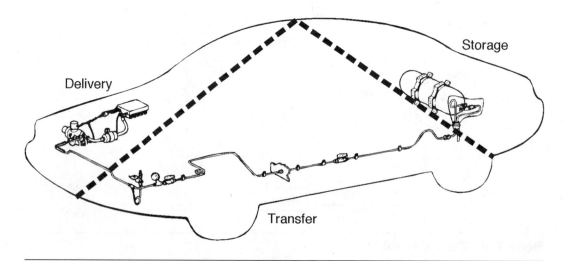

Figure 7.21 The three aspects of an NGV fuel system *(Courtesy GFI Control Systems, Inc.)*

1. Verify the problem, performing operational checks and determining related symptoms.

2. Analyze all symptoms.

3. Isolate the dimensions of the problem.

4. Correct the problem.

5. Check for proper operation.

Verifying the Problem

The electrical circuit's schematic should always be rechecked so that technicians have a clear understanding of the operation of the circuit. Reviewing the circuit's schematic diagram will allow for easier tracing of the circuit. In order to determine how symptoms relate to the diagnosed problem, it is necessary to perform operational checks on all circuits that are in any way connected to the faulty circuit. Operational checks are done without the aid of diagnostic equipment. These operational checks are based on tracing the schematic to find any common points and devices that are connected to the faulty circuit. Those devices must be tested for proper operation.

Analyzing Symptoms

Symptoms of electrical and electronic circuit failures in an NGV are usually caused by such problems as an open circuit or a short circuit. An open circuit has infinite resistance, which stops the flow of current. Open circuits can be caused by faulty parts, loose connections, broken or frayed wires, or dirty contacts. Another characteristic of an open circuit is that the circuit functions correctly part of the time and is faulty at other times. Faulty connections can be the result of loose connectors, which can be caused by weather or vibration. A short circuit, which has no resistance, can cause an excessive flow of current through a circuit. A short circuit can also be intermittent if it has a frayed or otherwise damaged wire that touches another. This is usually caused by vibrations.

To test for an open or short circuit, the following equipment is commonly used:

• *test light*—for checking continuity and/or the presence of voltage

• *self-powered test light*—for checking continuity between two points with no voltage applied

• *voltmeter*—for measuring wide ranges of voltages

• *ammeter*—for measuring the amount of current in a circuit

• *ohmmeter*—for measuring resistance

• *jumper wires*—for bypassing part of a circuit for testing

Isolating the Problem

Troubleshooting for a given circuit should be thought out in advance in order to quickly and efficiently solve the problem. After the technician performs operational checks, other malfunctioning devices connected to the faulty circuit should be located. The problem within the circuit should always be located between a working circuit (device) and a non-working circuit (device). When the trouble spot has been determined, it is then necessary to develop a plan for troubleshooting. There should be a method of testing parts that wear out first, the parts that are easiest to reach, or parts that have been serviced previously. It is also best to split the test area in half in order to complete the troubleshooting. An organized method of testing and eliminating parts of the circuit will quickly isolate the problem area of the circuit.

Correcting and Checking for Proper Operation

Solving the problem simply consists of replacing, repairing, or adjusting the faulty device as specified by the manufacturer. After repairs have been made, it is necessary to make sure that the problem has been resolved and that no new problems have been created.

NGV Troubleshooting—Electronics/ Electrical Related Problems

The chart in Figure 7.22 indicates typical problems that can be caused by the malfunctioning or misadjustment of NGV electronic and electrical components. Note the importance of timing to these systems. The chart indicates that timing be checked (or verified) under both gasoline and NGV systems.

PROBLEM	GASOLINE	NATURAL GAS
Not Starting	• Check system fuse • Check ignition output state • Bypass dual curve ignition module • Check fuel lockoff solenoid (carbureted) • Check changeover controls and relays (fuel injected)	• Check system fuse • Check ignition output state • Bypass dual curve ignition module
Stalling	• Check for trouble codes (fuel injected) • Verify ignition timing • Bypass dual curve ignition module • Check changeover controls and relays	• Engage dual curve at idle to verify gasoline idle specifications and set natural gas idle • Bypass dual curve ignition module
Hesitating	• Check for trouble codes (fuel injected) • Verify OEM ignition timing and timing curves (carbureted) • Verify onboard computer timing • Check ignition output state • Bypass dual curve ignition module • Check changeover controls and wiring	• Bypass dual curve module
Missing	• Check for trouble codes (fuel injected) • Check ignition system • Bypass dual curve ignition module • Inspect changeover controls, relays, and wiring	• Check ignition system • Bypass dual curve ignition module • Inspect changeover controls, relays, and wiring
Poor Cold Performance	• Check for trouble codes (fuel injected) • Check ignition system • Bypass dual curve ignition module • Check changeover controls and wiring • Check coolant temperature sensor (fuel injected)	• Check ignition system • Check for excessive ignition timing (fuel injected)
Poor Hot Performance	• Check for trouble codes • Check ignition systems • Bypass dual curve ignition module • Check changeover control, wiring, and reference voltages	• Check ignition components • Verify proper natural gas timing • Bypass dual curve ignition module • Check voltage references for electronic controls
Poor Fuel Economy	• Check for trouble codes	• Verify timing • Check for trouble codes
High CO at Idle	• Check for faulty onboard computer controls	• Check for faulty onboard computer controls • Readjust idle circuit or sensitivity screw • Check functions on injector interface relay • Check temperature control sensor
High CO at Loaded Mode	• Check for faulty onboard computer controls	• Check for faulty onboard computer controls • Readjust idle circuit • Check temperature control system
High HC at Idle	• Check ignition timing • Check ignition system plugs, wire, distributor • Check for faulty onboard computer controls	• Check ignition timing • Check ignition system plugs, wire, distributor • Check for faulty onboard computer controls
High HC at Loaded Mode	• Check ignition load, high-tension wires, spark plugs, distributor cap, and ignition coil • Check for faulty onboard computer controls	• Check ignition load, high-tension wires, spark plugs, distributor cap, and ignition coil • Check ignition timing • Check for faulty onboard computer controls
High NO$_x$ at Loaded Mode	• Check control solenoid, back-pressure transducer, and base temperature sensing switch • Check coolant temperature switch • Check knock sensor • Check O$_2$ sensor	• Check control solenoid, back-pressure transducer, and base temperature sensing switch • Check coolant temperature switch • Check knock sensor • Check O$_2$ sensor • Check dual curve ignition timing • Check OEM timing

Figure 7.22 NGV electronics troubleshooting chart

SYSTEM AND SUBSYSTEM APPLICATIONS

NGV SYSTEM TROUBLESHOOTING

Troubleshooting an NGV system is easier when the technician views all the systems of the vehicle as interrelated systems. The technician should see the relationship as a dynamic technical system that exists, for example, among subsystems A, B, and C. If something happens to A (which may represent the fuel injector), it will have a direct impact on how the related system components B (the oxygen sensor) and C (the Check Engine light) interact. Each of these components are part of a system. The result of a malfunctioning injector has become evident in a complaint the technician receives of a Check Engine light. Let us go through a typical procedure for troubleshooting a problem.

Symptom: "Check Engine" Light

A technician received a symptom report that a computerized bi-fuel natural gas vehicle had a Check Engine light on. The technician checked for the symptom after his operational check and verified the complaint. He verified that the Check Engine light was illuminated. After analyzing the vehicle status through gauges on the dashboard and from the trouble codes from the onboard computer, he was able to isolate the problem to the injectors. In this case, the injector had an internal failure. The technician purchased a replacement injector and installed it in the vehicle, thereby correcting the problem with an appropriate repair. After resetting the trouble code, the technician checked to ensure the Check Engine light did not illuminate (Figure 7.23).

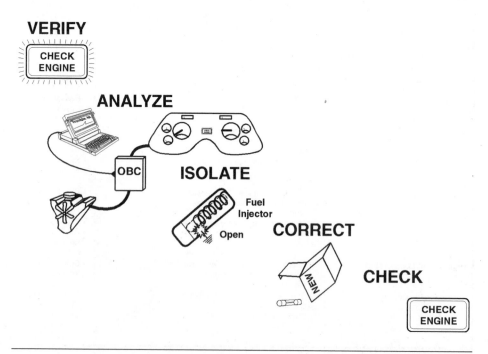

Figure 7.23 Application of the process for checking the Check Engine light

The technician should be familiar with the normal conditions of the system being worked on. The NGV normally does not emit any raw natural gas odors. Symptoms that deal with smell usually indicate an escape of gas. The technician receives a report that indicates there is a distinct odor of natural gas around the vehicle's storage system.

Verify that all sources of ignition are extinguished and the source of the odor located. NG odors that are confined to a smaller area can be detected by an odor detector. Fueling system components are designed to withstand the high pressures associated with the delivery and transfer of natural gas. Odor will generally lead the technician to a section of the vehicle. In this situation, leaks may be heard, thus narrowing the area for further inspection. Think about safety when pinpointing leaks. Also, use a fan to dispense vapors.

Analyze the fueling, vapor, and transfer area for all possible sources of natural gas leakage. The unique smell of natural gas is caused by the added odorant, mercaptan.

The technician should follow the procedure below to isolate the leak:

1. Isolate the source of the leak by using sensors designed for this purpose.

2. Look for obvious defects in workmanship, missing parts, poor connections, or damage to fuel lines, tanks, and valves in the system.

3. Once a specific area is located, soapy water can be used to pinpoint the leak.

Repair of the NG system (cylinder area), the NG transfer system (high-psi shutoff and lines), or the NG vaporizing system (engine area) can be accomplished once the leak is isolated to the appropriate system.

Check to ensure there are no natural gas odors emanating from the other systems. Once all sources of leakage have been repaired, the technician performs an operational check of the vehicle.

The technician should be familiar with the normal conditions of the fill system (Figure 7.24). The NGV normally emits a sound when being fueled with natural gas. The sound comes from the rushing of compressed gas through throttle or choke points in the fuel lines.

The symptom of slow filling can be caused by filling a system with a partially closed valve or by improper compressor pressure. The technician should complete the five-step diagnostic procedure.

First, verify the symptom by recognizing the sound coming from the filling procedure as being normal or as indicating a possible restriction or expansion in the system. The temperature of the line will drop where a choke-point occurs.

Here, supersonic gas flow may play a part. Once the supersonic flow is achieved, Boyle's law no longer applies to the gas. A larger transfer of volume-per-time can be achieved through the use of larger tubing, as long as the flow can be maintained below supersonic. Once the flow rate achieves supersonic, flow rate (fill time) cannot be estimated.

Symptom: Gas Smell

Symptom: Slow Filling

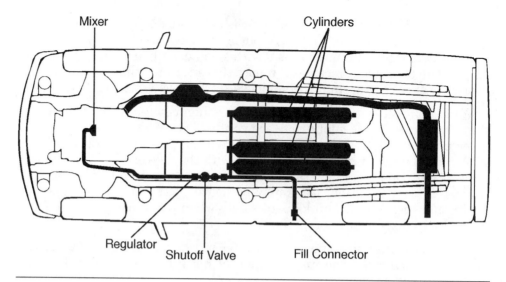

Figure 7.24 Primary component view of an NGV *(Courtesy General Motors Corp.)*

Next, analyze the components in the system for proper operation and pressure ratings. Does the valve turn freely? Are the fittings made of stainless steel, copper, brass, or aluminum?

Then isolate defective valves, fittings, and pinched or crimped lines in the system.

Repair of the NG system can be accomplished only after the natural gas pressure is relieved from the system.

Finally, check to ensure the component that caused the hissing sound does not continue to emit the sound when being fueled (Figure 7.25). It takes less time to fill the first 3/4-tank because of the pressure differential that exists between the supply and the tank being filled. The final 1/4-tank takes more time because there is less pressure differential.

Figure 7.25 Fueling an NGV

NGV SUBSYSTEM TROUBLESHOOTING

All the devices that make up a vehicle are designed with a purpose. It is the technician's responsibility to know what a component does so he or she will know when it is not operating properly. This is a key feature of successful troubleshooting. A checklist aid has been developed to help the technician apply thinking skills to common problems. The checklists contain a number of problems. We will start with the "Not Starting" checklist (Figure 7.26). The checklist has been developed to be used in conjunction with this manual. The checklist contains information relevant to each system. Inspecting the cards will help you become familiar with some of the basic relationships among components. Other relationships will not be quite so obvious. Take the time to review the checklists and become familiar with the effect each component has on the overall system.

A symptom of "not starting" is a common symptom. Verify the vehicle being worked on to see if it is NG dedicated or bi-fuel. If the vehicle is bi-fuel, it should go without saying that the technician has verified that the identical trouble does not occur with gasoline. The technician should have isolated the problem to the NG system. If so, he or she will have narrowed down the options considerably. Once the technician is certain the problem is in the NG system, the chances of repairing the vehicle rapidly increase.

Symptom: Not Starting

Analyze the vehicle to see if the valves are open (even the manual shutoff valve, which may have been struck by a foreign object or forgotten by a technician). Also, the technician should analyze the sequence of events that normally occur when starting the vehicle. This may be as simple as listening for the clicks of solenoids or the engaging of the flywheel.

Isolate the fuel system components that may be causing the problem from those that are used on both fuels in a bi-fuel vehicle. The condition of the fuel system, electrical system, and air delivery system on the dedicated fuel vehicle must be checked thoroughly. The technician then isolates any events that were supposed to occur but did not during the starting sequence, and notes anything that occurred which was not supposed to happen. It is these observations that allow the troubleshooter to diagnose the common problem underlying the symptoms.

Repair can take place only after the symptoms and the possible cause are isolated.

Check the symptom of not starting by following the starting procedure once again.

Technicians can successfully perform NGV emission diagnostics. Their knowledge of the impact of emissions on vehicle performance and driveability is assumed to have been acquired through training on gasoline vehicles. Excessive carbon monoxide on NGVs is commonly related to equipment settings and faulty components. These can be checked using the standard troubleshooting practices common to emissions on gasoline vehicles (Figure 7.27). Reference the checklists in Figures 7.28A and 7.28B regarding high carbon monoxide.

Symptom: High Carbon Monoxide (CO)

Verify	Analyze	Isolate	Repair	Check
fuel contents	amount of fuel pressure	low or no fuel pressure	fill cylinder to full reading	✔
power to system	current being provided to system	faulty system fuse, corroded connections	replace with OEM stated fuse rating	✔
system components	dual curve ignition	bypass dual curve ignition	faulty dual curve ignition module	✔
ignition components	ignition output state	low or no ignition output	faulty ignition component and/or adjust to OEM	✔
changeover controls	ease of movement	switch and/or connections	repair/ replace to OEM	✔
choke valve (carburated) or fuel pressure at injectors (EFI)	the fuel (pressure) supplied to engine combustion chamber	low or improper mixture settings, overpriming, or overfueling	manually prime NGV system, set to OEM	✔
air valve and mixture position	component fastening	security, cracks	repair/ replace to OEM	✔

Figure 7.26 Not Starting troubleshooting matrix

A symptom of excessive carbon monoxide (CO) emissions is created by too little oxygen in the combustion process. This can be a rich mixture of fuel or a restriction of the available air. In a perfect world, if the chemical

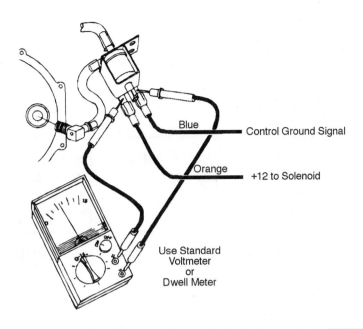

Blue — Control Ground Signal

Orange — +12 to Solenoid

Use Standard
Voltmeter
or
Dwell Meter

Figure 7.27 Natural gas interface equipment *(Courtesy Alternative Fuels Technologies Corp.)*

reaction started by the ignition of the air/fuel mixture were complete and the mixture were stoichiometric, then the only carbon/oxygen compound emitted from the tailpipe of a vehicle would be carbon dioxide (CO_2). However, real situations involve incomplete combustion of the air/fuel mixture and the result is the formation of CO. Incomplete combustion is caused by the poor mixing of the air and fuel in the combustion chamber or the lack of air in the air/fuel mixture. This can be attributed to high altitude operation or misadjustment/failure of the fuel metering circuitry.

Verify the carbon monoxide level using a four- or five-gas analyzer. The reading can be observed through the operating temperature range of the engine. The technician starts with a cold vehicle at idle and operates the vehicle to the high temperature range, recording readings at 1,500 rpm, 2,500 rpm, and, if possible, under simulated load conditions.

Analyze the readings with the data supplied by the manufacturer if the stoichiometric chart is not available. The data supplied by the manufacturer should be consulted when analyzing any reported performance problems.

Isolate the problem to the appropriate vehicle system. The fuel system components are the devices that normally affect the vehicle's emissions. However, such devices as the automatic timing advance and choke valves also have a role to play. The technician ensures that emissions is causing the problem being reported and not the perceived difference of NG operation, which generally produces a reduced emissions reading.

Repair of the system normally will occur with the adjustment of the vehicle components according to the manufacturer's recommended settings. Emissions are adjusted as close to stoichiometric as possible.

Verify	Analyze	Isolate	Repair	Check
catalyst	ability to catalyze the mixture	inefficient operation	replace to OEM	✔
air injection system	ability to time and inject proper amounts	failure of the system	repair or replace to OEM	✔
closed loop computer controls	ability to read and send proper information	faulty controls	replace to OEM	✔
regulator idle circuit	setting of idle circuit or sensitivity screw	misadjusted setting	adjust idle circuit or sensitivity screw	✔
power valve and idle circuit	settings appropriate for proper operation	misadjusted power valve setting	readjust power valve and idle circuit to OEM	✔
dual fuel mixing	ability of fuel solenoid to prevent fuel flow	improper solenoid lockoff on nonselected fuel	replace or adjust to OEM	✔
natural gas regulator operation	ability to prevent flow when not in use	leakage past third stage during gasoline operation	replace or adjust to OEM	✔

Figure 7.28A Carbon Monoxide troubleshooting matrix

Check the vehicle's operation by testing the vehicle in the range of operating temperatures similar to those during the reported occurrence of high levels of carbon monoxide emissions. If the problem persists, the steps are reapplied and the emissions data analyzed for stoichiometric proximity.

Verify	Analyze	Isolate	Repair	Check
canister purge solenoid operation	solenoid operation	improperly functioning solenoid	repair or replace to OEM	✔
fuel injector operation	ability to prevent fuel dribble	fuel injector leak down	repair or replace to OEM	✔
air cleaner or intake operation	ability to allow air flow	dirty air cleaner or restricted air intake	repair or replace to OEM	✔
choke valve operation	ability to adjust to various settings	a sticking or stuck choke valve binding	repair or replace to OEM	✔
choke thermostat operation	ability to adjust to various temperatures	lack of heat to unit or inability to adjust	heat source replace thermostat	✔
low engine temperature	ability of thermostat to adjust to various temperatures	malfunctioning thermostat	replace to OEM	✔
electric fan temperature control sensor	ability to turn on fan at proper temperature	defective sensor	replace to OEM	✔

Figure 7.28B Carbon Monoxide troubleshooting matrix

Unburned hydrocarbons are hydrogen- and carbon-containing compounds that are not oxidized in the combustion process. They are the principal unburned components of today's motor vehicle fuels. The HC compounds come in many forms and are difficult to separate. They also result in quenching effects, whereby the burning flame front of combustion is extinguished by the relatively cool surfaces of the combustion chamber. Because the quench zone contains more HC, an excessively rich air/fuel mixture can also contribute to unburned hydrocarbons.

Symptom: High Hydrocarbons (HC)

Verify	Analyze	Isolate	Repair	Check
vacuum hose and hardware	ability to hold and deliver a vacuum	leaks in hoses, intake manifold, throttle body, EGR	replace faulty component	✔
power brake booster operating properly	ability to react to vacuum	vacuum leak in booster	repair/ replace to OEM	✔
mixer position	positioning and sealing ability	leaks or loose connections	tighten or replace to OEM	✔
mixer air gap (crown style)	the gap setting	misadjusted gap setting	readjust to OEM	✔
ignition system operation	ability to produce ignition sources in engine	malfunction of plugs, high-tension wires, distributor malfunctions	repair/ replace to OEM	✔
idle setting	possibility of producing lean or rich fuel mixture	setting of an improper adjustment	reset to OEM	✔
ignition timing	appropriate application of ignition energy	misadjusted ignition timing	reset to OEM	✔
choke valve/ choke break	ability for proper and appropriate operation	stuck, slow, or sticking valve	repair/replace or consult with supplier	✔

Figure 7.29A NGV High Hydrocarbons troubleshooting matrix

Symptoms of excessive hydrocarbons in NGVs are commonly related to equipment settings and improper components. These can be checked using the standard troubleshooting practices common to emissions testing on gasoline vehicles. The root of high hydrocarbon emissions is the air/fuel mixture containing an excessive amount of raw fuel (reference

Verify	Analyze	Isolate	Repair	Check
changeover controls	possibility of dual fuels being mixed	changeover controls, switch, wiring	repair/ replace to OEM	✔
2nd stage regulator	water circulation/ thermostat operation	low and no flow causes	repair/ replace the thermostat(s)/ regulator to OEM	✔
vacuum hoses and fittings	ability to transport a vacuum and seal hoses to equipment	seepage, leaks, cracks	tighten or replace hoses and/or fittings	✔
mixture position	possibility of improper position and fastening	improper position and fastening	repair/install to OEM	✔
dual curve ignition module	possibility of internal failure or breakdown at load	bypass dual curve ignition module	repair/ replace to OEM	✔
closed loop computer controls	ability to read and send proper information	faulty controls primarily O_2 sensor	replace to OEM	✔
regulator idle circuit	setting of idle circuit or sensitivity screw	misadjusted setting	adjust idle circuit or sensitivity screw	✔
air injection system	ability to time and inject proper amounts	failure of the system	repair or replace to OEM	✔

Figure 7.29B NGV High Hydrocarbons troubleshooting matrix

the checklists in Figures 7.29A and B, and Figure 7.30 regarding high hydrocarbons and hesitating).

Verify	Analyze	Isolate	Repair	Check
check air lift operation on carbureted engine	possibility of diaphragm not responding to air movement	diaphragm that is punctured, sticking	repair/ replace to OEM	✔
power valve and idle	stable and predictable readings	erratic/unstable readings	reset power valve and idle to OEM	✔
clean air filter	ability to pass air freely	light visible through the element	replace dirty air filter	✔
throttle valve open	ability of valve to allow air flow	stuck or sticking valve	repair/ replace to OEM	✔
EGR valve for testing	ability to recycle exhaust gases	stuck or sticking valve	repair/ replace or consult with supplier	✔
vacuum fittings	ability to seal hoses to equipment	seepage, leaks	tighten, replace	✔
dual curve ignition module	possibility of internal failure	bypass dual curve ignition module	repair/ replace to OEM	✔
2nd stage regulator	ability to reduce pressure	output pressure not set to OEM	set to OEM	✔
mixture position	mounting on the engine	security, cracks	repair/ replace to OEM	✔
changeover controls	possibility of dual fuels being mixed	changeover controls, switch, wiring	repair/ replace to OEM	✔
ram air effect	the possibility of ram air into system	position of duct	position hose to eliminate ram effect	✔

Figure 7.30 Hesitating troubleshooting matrix

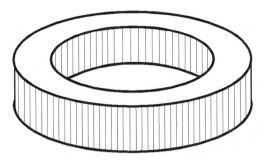

Figure 7.31 Air filter

Verify the excessive hydrocarbons using a four- or five-gas analyzer. The technician verifies that the identical trouble does not occur with gasoline in a bi-fuel vehicle.

Analyze data supplied by the manufacturer and compare it with the recommended stoichiometric setting.

Isolate the problem to the appropriate vehicle system. The fuel system components are the devices that normally affect the vehicle's emissions. However, such devices as automatic timing advance and choke valves also have a role to play, along with the electrical system. The technician checks the air cleaner because it commonly becomes clogged with particles during operation and acts as a choke on the NGV (Figure 7.31).

Repair of the system will normally occur with the adjustment of the vehicle components to the manufacturer's recommended settings. Emissions are adjusted as close to stoichiometric as possible.

Check the operation of the vehicle by testing the vehicle in the range of operating temperatures similar to the method used during the reported occurrence of the high hydrocarbons. If the problem persists, the technician reapplies the steps and analyzes the emissions data for stoichiometric proximity.

Excessive oxides of nitrogen in NGVs are also commonly related to equipment settings and faulty components. The root cause of high oxides of nitrogen emissions is the opposite of the causes of high carbon monoxide. It is not a low burning temperature of the air/fuel mixture but rather an excessive burning temperature. Throughout the troubleshooting procedure with a symptom of high NO_x, the technician should keep in mind the devices that can cause a higher than normal operating temperature of the engine.

Verify the high oxides of nitrogen emissions by using the five-gas analyzer. The reading can be observed through the operating temperature range of the engine. The technician starts with a cold vehicle at idle and operates the vehicle to the high temperature range, recording readings at 1,500 rpm, 2,500 rpm, and, if possible, at simulated load conditions (using a dynamometer, if possible).

Analyze the NO_x reading and compare it to the stoichiometric reading. The lambda is referenced and can be used as a starting point for further

Symptom: High Oxides of Nitrogen (NO_x)

Verify	Analyze	Isolate	Repair	Check
idle setting	smoothness of engine at idle	rpm range	set to OEM	✔
ignition timing	spark firing range	plugs firing out of range	set to OEM± TDC	✔
clean air filter	ability to pass air freely	light visible through the element	replace dirty air filter	✔
throttle valve open	ability of valve to allow air flow	stuck or sticking valve	repair/replace to OEM	✔
vacuum hose	ability to carry a vacuum	integrity, wear, leaks	repair/replace	✔
vacuum fittings	ability to seal hoses to equipment	seepage, leaks	tighten, replace	✔
fuel lock operation	ability to stop and/or allow flow	seepage, leaks, stuck, sticking	repair/replace to OEM	✔
2nd stage regulator	ability to reduce pressure	output pressure set to OEM	set to OEM	✔
mixture position	security of components, cracks, seals	security, cracks	repair/replace to OEM	✔
changeover controls	ease of movement	switch and/or connections	repair/replace to OEM	✔
ram air effect	the possibility of ram air into system	position of duct	position hose to eliminate ram effect	✔

Figure 7.32 NGV Stalling troubleshooting matrix

analysis (reference the checklists in Figures 7.32 and 7.33 regarding stalling and missing).

Verify	Analyze	Isolate	Repair	Check
ignition system operation	ability to produce ignition sources in engine	lack of spark production, bad wires, connection	repair/ replace to OEM	✔
power valve and idle	possibility of a rich setting	a rich fuel mixture	reset to OEM	✔
ignition timing	appropriate ignition energy	misadjusted ignition timing	reset to OEM	✔
changeover controls	possibility of dual fuels being mixed	changeover controls, switch, wiring	repair/ replace to OEM	✔
2nd stage regulator	water circulation/ thermostat operation	low and no flow causes	repair/ replace the thermostat(s)/ regulator to OEM	✔
vacuum hoses and fittings	ability to transport a vacuum and appropriate seal	seepage, leaks, cracks to hoses or equipment	tighten or replace hoses and/or fittings	✔
mixture position	possibility of improper position and fastening	improper position and fastening	repair/install to OEM	✔
dual curve ignition	module possibility of internal failure	bypass dual curve ignition module	repair/ replace to OEM	✔

Figure 7.33 "Missing" troubleshooting matrix

Isolate the problem to the appropriate vehicle system. Such devices as automatic timing advance and spark plugs, as well as the cooling system and chamber deposits, may also have a role to play. Less commonly explored is the ignition system and the voltage produced for the spark plug.

Repair or correction occurs when the components are adjusted to the manufacturer's recommended settings. Emissions are adjusted as close to a stoichiometric reading as possible.

Check the vehicle's operation by testing the vehicle in the range of operating temperatures similar to those occurring during the report of high oxides of nitrogen. If the problem persists, the steps should be reapplied and the emissions data analyzed for stoichiometric proximity.

It should also be noted again that NG air/fuel mixtures require a significant amount of energy (spark) to ignite—much more energy than that required by gasoline/air mixtures. Insufficient ignition system energy (spark) can result in driveability or emissions problems that may occur when the vehicle is operated on NG. Therefore, the condition and strength of the ignition system must be maintained at peak levels and verified by a scope check diagnostic routine.

INTEGRATION SUMMARY

PUTTING IT ALL TOGETHER

A thorough knowledge of systemic interactions and the ability to reconstruct the relationships of the components mentally will allow the troubleshooter to successfully attain the proficiency he or she desires.

As diagnosticians, we must rearrange what we know in order to find out what we don't know. To do this, we must become detectives and investigate the facts presented to us by the customers and discern their portrayal of the problem (usually explained with quick judgments) from the underlying actual cause. To do this, we ask, "What works?" The shortcuts to determine "what works" are commonly taught in basic automotive courses. A testing device connected to a point in the system allows the technician to verify the system operation. This block analysis of system integration produces functionality checks.

Diagnostics build on what is known about a problem. The unknown, or what does not work, permits the technician to see the problem in a new light. The symptom or reported problems then serve as tools, as information, and as resources that allow the technician the opportunity to sharpen his or her observation of what is known.

These relationships can be seen in the system's block diagram where each subsystem works together with the others (Figure 7.34). When we

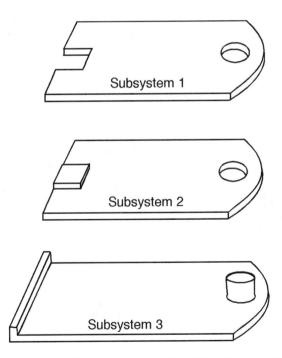

Figure 7.34 Frequently, a number of systems interact yet are independent of one another, thereby increasing the difficulty of diagnosing problems

look at the picture we don't ask, "What is wrong with it?"; rather we look at it and assume it will work. Will the pieces fit together or did you jump to a conclusion without analyzing the facts, the shapes of the forms, the size of the holes, the diameter of the projection?

Electrical Schematic

This guide is not meant to replace a manufacturer's manual of the components and systems. Rather it is a general view of troubleshooting of all systems. The names of components have been included for the sake of clarity and to illustrate the interdependence of all components. The troubleshooter also recognizes that when one subsystem goes bad, the system's integrity will suffer. Electrical systems are intricate computers and, as such, manufacturer's suggested repairs are encouraged for your protection, the vehicle warranty, and for the protection of the customer's rights.

One of the skills a good troubleshooter needs is the ability to read and interpret a schematic as it relates to an electrical system. The relationships among the components are basic and simple to comprehend. The relationships among the components in Figure 7.35 (battery, wire, and bulb) form a complete loop. If one of these components were missing (simulating an actual fault), then the system would not work.

Reading a Schematic Critically

Simply following a schematic can be good practice in understanding the components' relationships. A battery is not a source of energy that fills the lamp with energy. There must be a "passing through" in a

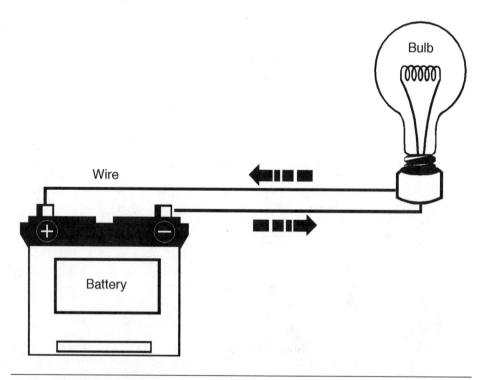

Figure 7.35 A typical electrical diagram showing the dependency among the components in a system

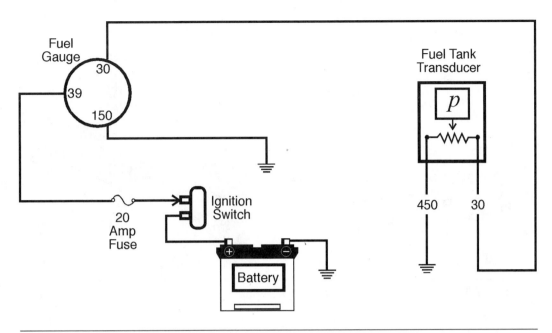

Figure 7.36 Components of the natural gas system fuel level electrical system. Where is the source of power coming from? The transducer, the gauge, or both? *(Courtesy General Motors Corp.)*

circuit. Current does not flow into a lamp, nor does it flow out of a lamp. Current flows through a lamp, just as it does anywhere else in a circuit, including the battery itself. If the technician has a thorough knowledge of the system and recognizes which paths must be completed for a component to operate, then he or she may start diagnosis at the component. If the technician is not familiar with a system, then he or she will normally start with power in the vehicle—the battery—and work through the electrical system (Figure 7.36).

Optional Schematic Views

The ability to read and interpret a schematic as it relates to other systems is overlooked in diagnostics. Although skill in the following of vacuum line routing may have been acquired in basic automotive training, not all routing charts are the same. One of the simplest is the drawing of vacuum lines to individual components that can be recognized according to their general location in the engine compartment.

This concept is applied to an NGV fuel system in a similar fashion (Figure 7.37). The method remains the same. The source of flow in the air (NG) system is expanded to include the source of air (NG) and its pressure, not electricity. The knowledgeable, systems-aware technician has an advantage in recognizing the order in which paths are completed and which of the paths remain open in a normally operating system. The technician may apply the method used in the electrical system to the air system, vacuum lines, etc.

Flow charts will help the learner visually comprehend the basic design used in the troubleshooting process. The process is represented in Figure

Flow Charts

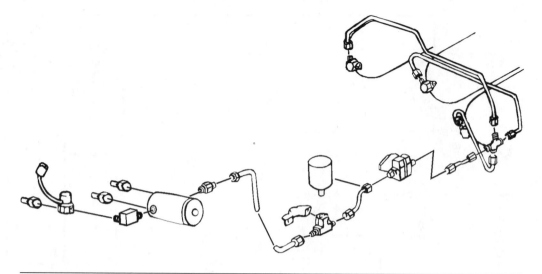

Figure 7.37 Hardware component analysis—fuel control system *(Courtesy General Motors Corp.)*

7.38, showing terminology. Symbols represent the various distinctions seen in systems. The flow chart presented here represents the theoretical approach of critical thinking in systematic troubleshooting.

The symptom reported to a technician is processed as input into the troubleshooting process. The technician then verifies the symptom's input and immediately begins to analyze the associated dimensions of the problem. The technician recognizes short-term symptoms and then has to determine if the symptom has occurred in the past or is part of a long-term problem. This analysis of the dimensions of the problem is

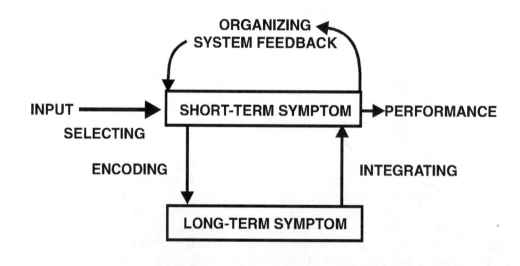

Figure 7.38 Flow chart relationship in troubleshooting

then compared to the normal performance of the system. Vehicle performance (or lack of performance) is what helps the technician to isolate the problem.

The systems approach is once again applied as the driver is directly involved in analyzing the symptoms. The driver is represented as an integral part of the system since the manner in which he or she operates the vehicle is important. Poor drivers need to be informed of this fact. A recent article in *USA Today* found that 80% of American drivers state they are "above average drivers." Someone has to break the news to them.

The driver's input into the operation of the vehicle is essential. If there is a problem with the way the driver operates the vehicle, then the vehicle will not function properly. The performance of the vehicle will then suffer and a tow-truck driver may grumble one rainy night after receiving a late service call.

The driver of the vehicle in this scenario reported a symptom input to the troubleshooter that the vehicle would not start. The troubleshooter then had to determine if the problem was repetitive, a short-term problem, or a long-term symptom. Being familiar with the company vehicle, the troubleshooter easily decoded the symptom and integrated the history of the vehicle into his analysis of the symptom. Organizing system feedback occurred when the troubleshooter analyzed the expected performance of the vehicle with the expected driver inputs (rainy night, new car, driver in a hurry). Perhaps, if the driver was more familiar with his own driving habits, that service person would have saved a trip. The discrepancy was apparent and the troubleshooter solved the problem by putting the vehicle shift lever in park so it would start.

Decision-Making System

The technician often has to follow an instruction manual provided by an equipment manufacturer in order to diagnose problems in the supplied system. Although there are many types of flow charts, they all have one thing in common: They provide the technician a visual representation of the decision-making process.

Fresh Perspectives

The technician who maintains a fresh outlook on new problems will have a sought-after skill. This technician will be appreciated by an employer and receive great job satisfaction. The diagnostician, like the detective, gains immense satisfaction from being able to solve problems that no one else can. This troubleshooter views each problem as new and mysterious. He or she can sit back and analyze the facts and components as if each were a piece of a puzzle. The puzzle, like a vehicle, does not function when an improper fit between its mechanical devices is apparent.

Analytical Training

The ability to visualize the interior workings of a system and their interconnections is important for the troubleshooter. A technician familiar with the system can become a diagnostician. In diagnosing a problem, the technician who has no knowledge of a system's interrelationships is at a huge disadvantage. Therefore, it is important for the technician to

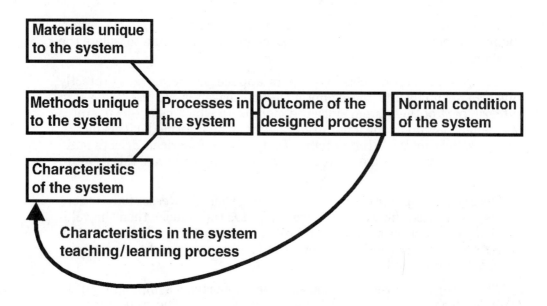

Figure 7.39 The outcome is the result of the materials, methods, and characteristics of the system

understand the systems he or she will deal with. Ongoing training is suggested if one desires to excel in the ability to analyze the internal relationships involved in the operating systems of the natural gas vehicle.

Through familiarization training, the technician develops skills as a troubleshooter in both old and new designs. New training programs bring updated information on new NGV systems. With the new information in hand, the technician can look at the "old system" from a new reference point. He or she can see how it worked before and understand how it works now. Ongoing training provides a fresh look at an old system; knowledge that the old system will still come in with the same "old" problems until it is updated. Only the informed technician can look, understand, and describe the problem to others in a new fashion.

The troubleshooting process is a system itself. The entire process begins with a symptom or problem and ends with the solution or repair. Between these two conditions, a technician can develop a way of critically viewing systems by looking for the facts that exist. It is this thinking process that allows the technician to become either a great troubleshooter or one that just passes the buck to the next shift worker.

This process as it applies to troubleshooting (Figure 7.39) involves the systems process of how each of those subsystems interacts with other subsystems. The outcome of the subsystem design will then help the learner understand the underlying factors that affected the normal condition of the system and how the changes have improved the system.

The Art

Remember that successful troubleshooting is not a mysterious art practiced only by professional mechanics. It is simply the result of knowledge combined with critical thinking applied in an intelligent, systematic approach to a problem.

Technicians want to be professional. The word *professionalism* is so much a part of our world that it influences how we see problems that challenge us.

Diagnosing problems is a talent. It is a talent often exploited to make money. The diagnostician is not to be considered gifted; he is talented. He learned his talent just as others, like you, have learned their talents. Successful diagnosticians do not approach a problem with the attitude, "If at first you don't succeed, quit."

Can you imagine what would have happened to you if you had quit? Imagine a reading class where a teacher brought out books and waited to see which students were the natural readers. The absurdity of the situation is obvious to everyone. But what is missed when it comes to the skill of critical thinking is that people take for granted that you can either do it or you can't. Everyone has a mind; therefore, everyone has the ability to think.

After you complete this course, try the process at work. You can always go back. Use your own process with the simplest solution and work to the most complex (compare your method to this one). Never overlook the obvious. Anyone can run the gas tank dry or leave the lights on overnight, so don't assume that we are exempt from such oversights.

Prevention

Finally, always establish a clear idea of why a problem has occurred and take steps to ensure that the cause has been corrected. If the electrical system fails because of a poor connection, then a check of all the other connections in the area may prevent future failure as well. If a particular fuse continues to blow, find the underlying cause. The failure of a small component can often be indicative of a major potential failure or the incorrect functioning of a more important component or system.

Most of you may remember a fictitious character named Mother Goose. For those who are not familiar with her, she was a character that had very good reasoning ability. She helped people to see the logical connectors in life. A famous saying deals with problem solving. It involves separating problems into two categories, those you can do something about and those you can do nothing about. If someone comes to you with an impossible problem, you can reply, "Indeed it is a problem." To which they may reply, "You should fix it." Then, you may state, "Indeed I should not because there is nothing I can do about the problem. I'm going to work on the problems that I *can* do something about." This is good thinking and good reasoning.

Mother Goose left it up to the person to think about the saying:

> *"For every problem under the sun;*
> *There is a solution, or there is none;*
> *If there be one, seek till you find it;*
> *If there be none, then never mind it."*

SUMMARY

- A systematic approach is often needed to find a solution when a problem occurs with a vehicle.

- A general approach to learning vital troubleshooting skills includes: (1) developing a certain level of proficiency, (2) developing troubleshooting skills, and (3) actively participating in troubleshooting skills training.

- The four main elements involved in the critical thinking process are: (1) maintaining doubt and suspending judgment, (2) being aware of different patterns and perspectives, (3) testing alternatives and letting experience guide, and (4) acknowledging mechanical and personal limitations.

- The five steps of basic troubleshooting are: (1) verify the complaint, (2) analyze the symptoms, (3) isolate the trouble, (4) correct or repair the problem, and (5) check for proper operation.

- Many failures involving NGV engines can be traced to a general engine fault rather than to a component specific to the NGV system.

- An NGV conversion system can be divided into three subsystems for diagnostic purposes: (1) CNG storage, (2) CNG transfer, and (3) CNG delivery.

- Common symptoms of problems associated with NGVs include: (1) Check Engine light, (2) gas smell, (3) slow filling, (4) not starting, (5) high carbon monoxide emissions, (6) high hydrocarbon emissions, and (7) high oxides of nitrogen emissions.

- An NG/air mixture requires more energy (spark) to ignite than a mixture of gasoline and air.

- The ability to read and interpret a schematic as it relates to other systems is commonly overlooked.

- Successful troubleshooting is simply the result of knowledge combined with critical thinking applied in an intelligent manner with a systematic approach to the problem.

REVIEW QUESTIONS

1. List the main elements involved in the critical thinking process.
2. List the steps involved in the basic troubleshooting procedure.
3. List the three basic subsystems of a CNG conversion system.
4. List the basic components of each of the three basic subsystems.
5. Explain the process used to isolate a Check Engine light on an NGV.
6. Explain the process used to isolate a gas smell on an NGV.
7. Explain the process used to diagnose a not starting condition on an NGV.

8. Explain the process used to diagnose high CO on an NGV.

9. Explain the process used to diagnose high HC on an NGV.

10. Explain the process used to diagnose high NO_x on an NGV.

Appendix

CONTENTS

RESOURCE CONTACTS—NATIONAL

American Gas Association
NGV Market Development
1515 Wilson Blvd.
Arlington, VA 22209
Phone: (703) 841-8574

Canadian Gas Association
950 Burnhamthorpe Road West
Mississauga, Ontario
Canada L5C 3B4
Phone: (416) 897-1690

Canadian Gas Research Institute
55 Scarsdale Road
Don Mills, Ontario,
Canada M3B 2R3
Phone: (416) 447-6465

Chrysler Corporation
(FFVs & NGVs)
800 Chrysler Drive East
Auburn Hills, MI 48326-2757
Phone: (313) 576-4991

Ford Motor Company
Alternative Fuels Division
14310 Hamilton Avenue
Highland Park, MI 48203
Phone: (800) 258-3835

Gas Research Institute
8600 Bryan Mawr Avenue
Chicago, IL 60631
Phone: (312) 399-8170

General Motors Corporation
Alternative Fuels Division
30500 Mound Road ARMB 336
Warren, MI 48090
Phone: (313) 986-5719
Phone: (313) 986-5715

Institute of Gas Technology
3424 S. State Street
Chicago, IL 60616-3896
Phone: (312) 567-3877

National Alternative Fuels Hotline for
  Transportation Technologies
P.O. Box 70879
Washington, D.C. 20024
Phone: (202) 554-5047
Phone: (800) 423-1DOE

National Fire Protection Association
  Gas Standards
One Batterymarch Park
P.O. Box 9101
Quincy, MA 02269-9191
Phone: (617) 984-7407

National Renewable Energy
  Laboratory
1617 Cole Boulevard
Golden, CO 80401-3393
Phone: (303) 231-1288

Natural Gas Vehicle Coalition
1515 Wilson Boulevard
Arlington, VA 22209
Phone: (703) 527-3022

Society of Automotive Engineers (SAE)
400 Commonwealth Drive
Warrendale, PA 15095-0001
Phone: (412) 772-7159

U.S. Department of Energy
Office of Domestic and Energy Policy
Mail Stop EP (PE-50)
1000 Independence Avenue, S.W.
Washington, D.C. 25085
Phone: (202) 586-4456

U.S. Environmental Protection Agency
National Vehicle & Fuel Emissions
  Laboratory
2565 Plymouth Road
Ann Arbor, MI 48105
Phone: (313) 668-4275

RESOURCE CONTACTS—STATE AND U.S. TERRITORY

Alabama
Alabama Department of Economic and
 Community Affairs
P.O. Box 5690
Montgomery, AL 36103-5690
Phone: (205) 242-5292

Alaska
Alaska Housing Finance Corp.
520 E. 84th Avenue
Anchorage, AK 99503
Phone: (907) 561-1900

American Samoa
Territorial Energy Office
American Samoa Govt.
Pago Pago, AS 96799
Phone: (684) 699-1101

Arizona
Arizona Department of Commerce
Energy Office
3800 North Central, Suite 1200
Phoenix, AZ 85012

Arkansas
Arkansas Energy Office
One State Capitol Mall
Suite 4B/215
Little Rock, AR 72201
Phone: (501) 682-7815

California
California Energy Commission
1516 9th Street, MS-31
Sacramento, CA 95814
Phone: (916) 654-5000

Colorado
Colorado Office of Energy Conservation
1675 Broadway, Suite 1300
Denver, CO 80202
Phone: (303) 620-4292

Connecticut
Policy Development and Planning
Office of Policy and Management
80 Washington Street
Hartford, CT 06106
Phone: (203) 566-4298

Delaware
Division of Facilities Management
Energy Office
P.O. Box 1401
Dover, DE 19903
Phone: (302) 739-5644

District of Columbia
District of Columbia Energy Office
613 G Street, N.W., 5th Floor
Washington, DC 20001
Phone: (202) 727-9700

Florida
Florida Energy Office
Dept. of Community Affairs
2740 Center View Drive
Tallahassee, FL 32399-2100
Phone: (904) 488-6764

Georgia
Office of Energy Resources
254 Washington Street, S.W.
Suite 401
Atlanta, GA 30334
Phone: (404) 656-5176

Guam
Guam Energy Office
P.O. Box 2950
Agana, GU 96910
Phone: (671) 472-8711

Hawaii
Energy Program
Administrator, Economic Dev. and
 Tourism
335 Merchant Street, Room 110
Honolulu, HI 96813
Phone: (808) 587-3812

Idaho
Department of Water Resources
Energy Division
1301 North Orchard
Boise, ID 83706
Phone: (208) 327-7900

Resource Contacts—State and U.S. Territory *(cont.)*

Illinois
Department of Energy and Natural
  Resources
325 W. Adams Street, Room 300
Springfield, IL 62704
Phone: (217) 785-2002

Indiana
Department of Commerce
Office of Energy Policy
1 North Capitol, Suite 700
Indianapolis, IN 46204-2288
Phone: (317) 232-8940

Iowa
Iowa Energy Bureau
Iowa Dept. of Natural Resources
Wallace State Office Building
Des Moines, IA 50319
Phone: (515) 281-8681

Kansas
Kansas Corporation Commission
Energy Programs Section
1500 S.W. Arrowhead Road
Topeka, KS 66604
Phone: (913) 271-3100

Kentucky
Kentucky Division of Energy
691 Teton Trail
Frankfort, KY 40601
Phone: (502) 564-7192

Louisiana
Louisiana Department of Natural
  Resources
Energy Division
P.O. Box 44156
Baton Rouge, LA 70804
Phone: (504) 342-2133

Maine
Department of Economic and
  Community Development
State House Station #59
Augusta, ME 04333
Phone: (207) 289-6800

Maryland
Maryland Energy Administration
45 Calvert Street, 4th Floor
Annapolis, MD 21401
Phone: (301) 974-3755

Massachusetts
Massachusetts Division of Energy
  Resources
Leverett Saltonstall Building
Room 1500, 100 Cambridge Street
Boston, MA 02202
Phone: (617) 727-4732

Michigan
Michigan Public Service Commission
P.O. Box 30221
6545 Mercantile Way
Lansing, MI 48909
Phone: (517) 334-6270

Minnesota
Minnesota Dept. of Public Service
900 American Center Building
150 East Kellog Boulevard
St. Paul, MN 55101
Phone: (612) 296-6025

Mississippi
Mississippi Dept. of Economic &
  Community Development
Energy Division
510 George Street, Suite 101
Jackson, MS 39202-3006
Phone: (601) 359-6600

Missouri
Missouri Dept. of Natural Resources
Division of Energy
P.O. Box 176
Jefferson City, MO 65102
Phone: (314) 751-4000

Montana
Department of Natural Resources and
  Conservation
Energy Division
1520 East Sixth Avenue
Helena, MT 59620-2301
Phone: (406) 444-6697

Resource Contacts—State and U.S. Territory *(cont.)*

Nebraska
Nebraska Energy Office
P.O. Box 95085
110 The Atrium
Lincoln, NE 68509
Phone: (402) 471-2867

Nevada
Nevada Office of Community Services
Capitol Complex
Carson City, NV 89701
Phone: (702) 687-4990

New Hampshire
Governor's Office of Energy and
  Community Services
57 Regional Drive
Concord, NH 03301-8506
Phone: (603) 271-2611

New Jersey
Department of Environmental
  Protection and Energy
401 E. State Street
Trenton, NJ 08625
Phone: (609) 292-2885

New York
New York State Energy Office
2 Rockefeller Plaza
Albany, NY 12223
Phone: (518) 473-4376

North Carolina
North Carolina Dept. of Commerce
Energy Division
430 N. Salisbury St.
Raleigh, NC 27611
Phone: (919) 733-2230

North Dakota
Office of Intergovernmental Assistance
State Capitol Building
Bismarck, ND 58505
Phone: (701) 224-2094

Northern Mariana Islands
Commonwealth Energy Office
P.O. Box 340
Saipan, CM 96950
Phone: (670) 322-9229

Ohio
Ohio Dept. of Development
Community Dev. Division
Office of Energy Efficiency
77 S. High Street, 25th Floor
Columbus, OH 43266-0413
Phone: (614) 466-3465

Oklahoma
Oklahoma Dept. of Commerce
Div. of Community Affairs and Dev.
P.O. Box 26980
Oklahoma City, OK 73126-0980

Oregon
Oregon Department of Energy
625 Marion Street, N.E.
Salem, OR 97310-0831
Phone: (503) 378-6063

Pennsylvania
Pennsylvania Energy Office
116 Pine Street
Harrisburg, PA 17101-1227
Phone: (717) 783-9981

Puerto Rico
Dept. of Consumer Affairs
P.O. Box 41059, Minillas Station
San Juan, PR 00902-1059
Phone: (809) 721-0809

Republic of Palau
Bureau of Public Works
P.O. Box 100
Koror, Palau, RP 96940
Phone: (608) 486-2508

Rhode Island
Governor's Office of Housing, Energy
  and Intergovernmental Relations
State House Room 111
Providence, RI 02903-5872
Phone: (401) 277-2850

South Carolina
Office of the Governor
Div. of Finance and Administration
Office of Energy Programs
1205 Pendleton St., 3rd Floor
Columbia, SC 29201
Phone: (803) 734-0440

Resource Contacts—State and U.S. Territory *(cont.)*

South Dakota
Governor's Office of Energy Policy
217 1/2 West Missouri
Pierre, SD 57501
Phone: (605) 773-3603

Tennessee
Tennessee Dept. of Economic &
 Community Development
Energy Division
320 6th Avenue North, 6th Floor
Nashville, TN 37219-5308

Texas
Governor's Energy Office
Capitol Station, P.O. Box 12428
Austin, TX 78711
Phone: (512) 463-1931

Utah
Governor's Energy Office
355 West North Temple
3 Triad Center, Suite 450
Salt Lake City, UT 84180-1204
Phone: (801) 538-5428

Vermont
Department of Public Services
Energy Efficiency Division
120 State Street
Montpelier, VT 05620
Phone: (802) 828-2393

Virgin Islands
Virgin Islands Energy Office
81 Castle Coakley, Christiansted
St. Croix, VI 00820
Phone: (809) 772-2616

Virginia
Department of Mines, Minerals and
 Energy
2201 West Broad Street
Richmond, VA 23220
Phone: (804) 867-0979

Washington
Washington State Energy Office
P.O. Box 43165
Olympia, WA 98504-3165
Phone: (206) 956-2001

West Virginia
West Virginia Development of Fuel and
 Energy Office
State Capitol Complex
Building 6, Room 558
Charleston, WV 25305
Phone: (304) 558-4010

Wisconsin
Wisconsin Division of Energy and
 Intergovernmental Relations
101 E. Wilson St.
P.O. Box 7865
Madison, WI 53707-7868
Phone: (608) 266-8234

Wyoming
Division of Economic and Community
 Development
Energy Division
Barrett Building
Cheyenne, WY 82002
Phone: (307) 777-7284

INTERNATIONAL APPROVAL SERVICES "NGV LIST"— MARCH 1995

NGV Conversion Kit
- Automotive Natural Gas, Inc. (ANGI)
- CNG Company dba Tri-Fuels
- Combustion Labs, Inc.
- GFI Control Systems, Inc.
- MESA International
- Metropane, Inc.
- NESC Williams, Inc.
- Propane Equipment Co.
- SLP Engineering, Inc.
- Synchro-Start Products, Inc.

Cylinders
- EDO Canada, Ltd.
- Lincoln Composites

Regulators
- GFI Control Systems, Inc.
- Landi Renzo S.P.A.
- Tescom Corporation
- Vialle, B.V.

Refueling Applications
- FuelMaker Corporation
- Williamson

Hoses
- Furon, Synflex Division
- Swagelok

Fueling Connectors
- Sherex Industries
- Hansen
- Parker Hannifin Corp.— Quick Coupling Div.
- STAUBLI Corporation
- Snap-Tite
- WEH GmbH

Fuel Filter
- Balston Inc.

Manual Valves
- GFI Controls
- Whitey
- Parker Hannifin Corp.— Instrumentation Valve Div.

Solenoid Valves
- Landi Renzo
- Advanced Fuel Components

Cylinder Valves
- GFI Control Systems, Inc.
- Superior Valve Company

Check Valves
- Parker Hannifin Corp.— Instrumentation Valve Div.
- Nupro Company
- Sherex/OPW, Inc.
- Snap-Tite
- Superior Products, Inc.

Injector
- Synchro-Start Products, Inc.— DAI Controls Division

Metering Valve
- GFI Controls

Single Mount Brackets
- Brunswick Composites
- COMDYNE I., Inc.
- CNG Cylinder Company

Regs., Valves, Mixers
- IMPCO

Solenoid Valve, Reg.
- Hercules Engines, Inc.

Fuel Filter
- Parker Hannifin Corp.— Racor Div.

Valves, Fittings
- Hoke

Pressure Sender
- TSE, Inc.

Fittings, Connectors
- Bilok Ihara Corporation
- Crawford Fitting Company
- Parker Hannifin Corp.— Tube Fittings Div. Instrumentation Connectors Div.

Fittings
- Cajon, Inc.

Electronic Fuel Monitoring and Selection Systems
- Energy Kinetics

NGV CONVERSION SYSTEM MANUFACTURERS

The following is a list of manufacturers of NGV conversion systems components compiled by the International Approval Services, which is a joint venture of AGA Laboratories and CGA Approvals, Inc. The list is current as of March 1995.

Advanced Fuel Components, Inc.
P.O. Box 168
300 Woolley Drive
Marshall, MI
Phone: (616) 781-1111
Fax: (616) 781-4377

Automotive Natural Gas, Inc. (ANGI)
265 North Janesville St.
Milton, WI 53563
Phone: (608) 868-4626
Fax: (608) 868-2723

Balston, Inc.
260 Neck Road
Haverville, MA 01835
Phone: (508) 374-7400
Fax: (508) 374-7070

Bilok Ihara Corporation
R.D. #2, Box 613 Mosiertown Road
Meadville, PA 16335
Phone: (814) 337-0380
Fax: (814) 337-0229

Brunswick Composites
4300 Industrial Avenue
Lincoln, NE 68504
Phone: (402) 464-8211
Fax: (402) 464-2247

Cajon, Inc
9760 Sherpard Road
Macedonia, OH 44056
Phone: (216) 467-0200
Fax: (216) 467-5000

CNG Cylinder Company of North
  America
2250 Cherry Industrial Circle
Long Beach, CA 90805
Phone: (310) 630-5768
Fax: (310) 630-1382

Combustion Labs, Inc
6275 Highway 85
Riverdale, GA 30274
Phone: (404) 997-0425
Fax: (404) 997-0171

COMDYNE I., Inc.
6800 County Road 189
West Liberty, OH 43357
Phone: (513) 465-8615
Fax: (513) 465-1225

Crawford Fitting Company (Swagelok)
29500 Solon Road
Solon, OH 44139
Phone: (216) 248-4600
Fax: (216) 349-5970

EDO Corporation
14-04 11th Street
College Point, NY 11356
Phone: (718) 321-4000
Fax: (718) 321-4194

EDO Canada Ltd.
1940 Centre Avenue N.E.
Calgary, Alberta, Canada T2E 0A7
Phone: (800) 361-8262
Fax: (403) 569-5499

Energy Kinetics, Inc.
184 East Shuman Blvd., Suite 200
Naperville, IL 60640
Phone: (708) 357-3370
Fax: (708) 357-3819

FuelMaker Corporation
70 Worcester Road
Rexdale, Ontario, Canada M9W 5X2
Phone: (416) 674-3034
Fax: (416) 674-3042

NGV Conversion System Manufacturers *(cont.)*

FuelMaker Corporation
4745 Amelia Earhart Dr., Suite 470
Salt Lake City, UT 84116
Phone: (801) 328-0607
Fax: (801) 328-0671

Furon, Synflex Division
10585 Main Street
Mantua, OH 44255
Phone: (216) 274-5170
Fax: (216) 274-0473

GFI Control Systems, Inc.
100 Hollinger Crescent
Kitchener, Ontario, Canada N2K 2Z3
Phone: (519) 576-4270
Fax: (519) 576-4010

Hansen Coupling Division/Tuthill
   Corporation
1000 West Bagley Road
Berea, OH 44017
Phone: (216) 826-1115
Fax: (216) 826-1105

Hercules Engines, Inc.
101 Eleventh Street, S.E.
Canton, OH 44707-3802
Phone: (216) 438-1345
Fax: (216) 438-1321

Hoke International
One Tenakill Park
Cresskill, NY 07626
Phone: (201) 833-6501
Fax: (201) 568-5913

IMPCO Technology, Inc.
16804 Gridley Place
Cerritos, CA 90701-1792
Phone: (310) 860-6666
Fax: (310) 809-1240

Landi Renzo S.P.A.
Via F. III Cervi 75/2
42100 Reggio Emilia
Italy
Phone: 0522/382678
Fax: 0522/77373

MESA International
3125 West Bolt St.
Ft. Worth, TX 76110
Phone: (817) 924-2353
Fax: (817) 924-8017

Metropane, Inc.
2772 Sawbury Blvd.
Columbus, OH 43235
Phone: (614) 792-7606
Fax: (614) 792-8187

NESC Williams, Inc.
P.O. Box 31
18 Harrison St.
Zanesville, OH 43702-0031
Phone: (614) 453-0375
Fax: (614) 453-5640

Nupro, A Swagelok Company
4800 East 345th St.
Willoughby, OH 44094
Phone: (216) 951-7100
Fax: (216) 951-4872

Parker Fluid Connectors
9400 Memorial Parkway South
Huntsville, AL 35802
Phone: (205) 881-2040
Fax: (205) 881-5730

Parker Hannifin Corporation
2651 Alabama Highway 21 North
Jacksonville, AL 36283-0069
Contact: Frank Bryan
Phone: (205) 435-2130
Fax: (205) 435-7718

Propane Equipment Corp.
11 Apple St.
Tinton Falls, NJ 07724
Contact: Ron Cassell
Phone: (908) 747-3795
Fax: (908) 291-0161

Racor (Parker Hannifin Corporation)
3400 Finch Road
Modesto, CA 95353
Contact: Bill Decarlo
Phone: (209) 575-7443
Fax: (209) 529-3278

NGV Conversion System Manufacturers *(cont.)*

Sherex Industries
1400 Commerce Parkway
Lancaster, NY 14086
Phone: (716) 681-6250
Fax: (716) 681-0270

Sherex/OPW, Inc.
4180 Morris Drive
Burlington, Ontario, Canada L7L 5L6
Phone: (905) 639-7701
Fax: (905) 639-9537

Snap-Tite, Inc.
201 Titusville Road
Union City, PA 16438-8699
Phone: (814) 438-3821
Fax: (814) 438-3069

STAUBLI Corporation
P.O. Box 189
Duncan, SC 29334
Phone: (803) 433-1980
Fax: (803) 433-1988

Superior Products, Inc.
3786 Ridge Road
Cleveland, OH 44144
Phone: (216) 651-9400
Fax: (216) 651-4071

Superior Valve Company
2200 North Main Street
Washington, PA 15301
Phone: (412) 225-8000
Fax: (412) 225-6188

Swagelok Quick-Connect Company
5171 Hudson Drive
Hudson, OH 44236-3799
Contact: Jake Boland
Phone: (216) 656-3700
Fax: (216) 656-1036

Synchro-Start Products, Inc.
DAI Controls Division
5100 Academy Drive
Lisle, IL 60532
Contact: Chuck Cornell
Phone: (708) 971-2442
Fax: (708) 971-2642

TSE, Inc.
540 N. Commercial Street, Unit #5
Manchester, NH 03101
Contact: Steve Dakoulas
Phone: (603) 641-5707
Fax: (603) 666-4377

Tescom Corporation
12616 Industrial Boulevard
Elk River, MN 55330-2491
Phone: (612) 441-6330
Fax: (612) 241-3224

Tri-Fuels, The CNG Company
1015 Waterwood Pkwy., Ste. H2
Edmond, OK 73034
Phone: (405) 359-6485
Fax: (405) 359-6486

Vialle, B.V.
Ekkersrijt 4106
Psotbus 150
5690 AD SON, The Netherlands
Phone: 04990-89911
Fax: 04990-77288

Whitey Company, A Swagelok Company
316 Bishop Road
Highland Heights, OH 44143
Phone: (216) 473-1050
Fax: (216) 473-0402

Williamson NGV Fleet Systems, Inc.
102 Armstrong Ave.
Georgetown, Ontario, Canada L7G 4S2
Phone: (905) 873-2272
Fax: (905) 877-0362

CYLINDER RETEST CENTERS

Company	Address	Phone No.	Comments
Arizona			
Phoenix Fire & Safety	1605 West Latham St. Phoenix, AZ 85007	(602) 253-3404	Jacket Size 20" x 84"
California			
Acurex Environmental Corp.	555 Clyde Ave. Mountain View, CA 94043	(415) 961-5700	Can test 13" O.D.
C. Bellone Enterprises MAK-3B-24	No. Hollywood, CA 91601	(818) 980-2332	Can test 13" O.D.
Certified Testing Labs Gary or Dan Moore	2648 E. 28th St. Signal Hill, CA 90806	(310) 424-9992	
Puritan, Margarot Div. MAK-3B-18	El Segundo, CA	(213) 772-1421	Can test 13" O.D.
Master Protection Ent.	Richmond, CA 94804	(510) 232-8080	
Matheson Gas MAK-3B-18	8800 Utica Ave. Rancho Cucamonga, CA 91730	(602) 894-1387	Can test 13" O.D.
Walter Kidde MAK-3B-18	Signal Hill, CA	(310) 896-2411	Can test 13" O.D.
H.R. Textron MAK-4B-12/24	10445 Glenoaks Blvd. Pacoima, CA 91331	(818) 896-2411	Can test 13" O.D.
Colorado			
Flight Safety	10184 W. Belleview Ave. Littleton, CO 80127	(303) 932-3680	Can test 13" O.D.
Florida			
Liquid Air CKC-4B-18 Conversion	Tampa, FL	(813) 626-4163	Can test 13" O.D.
Illinois			
Midwest Welding Supply	5318 S. Kedzie Ave. Chicago, IL 60632	(312) 737-6404	Can test 13" O.D.

Cylinder Retest Centers *(cont.)*

Company	Address	Phone No.	Comments
Kansas			
Aero Electric, Inc.	3414 W. 29th St. S Wichita, KS 67217	(316) 943-6100	Jacket Size 24" x 36"
Louisiana			
Firemark Fire Equipment MAK-4B-18F	306 Engineers Road Bell Chase, LA 70037	(504) 392-1050	Can test 13" O.D.

Fire & Safety
  Equipment, Inc.
    Contact: Bill Curry
	218 Lancaster Drive
	Houma, LA 70360
		(504) 868-6060	Can test 13"
			O.D.

Maryland			
Sea Safety & Survival	4715 Rhode Island Ave. Hyattsville, MD 20781	(301) 277-6655	Up to 60"
Nebraska			
Van Waters & Rogers, Inc. MAK-3B-18	3002 F Street Omaha, NE 68107	(402) 733-3266	Can test 13" O.D.
New Jersey			

Delaware Valley Industrial
Gases
  MAK-6B-18
    Contact: Joseph DeRosa
	Atlantic Avenue
	Waterford Works, NJ
	08089
		(609) 766-3781	

Kaplan Industries
  GKC-6B-18
    Contact: Roy Osterberg
	State Hwy 73 (Morris Ave)
	Maple Shade, NJ
	08052
		(609) 779-8181	Can test 13"
			O.D.

Unitor Ships Services
  MAK-6B-24
    Contact: Casey Matthews
	310 Port Jersey Blvd.
	Jersey City, NJ 07305
		(201) 433-9111	Can test 13"
			O.D.

New York			
S&S Fire Equipment, Inc. Contact: Charles Shaw	99 Industrial Drive	(716) 692-6800	Can test up to 17" x 72"
North Carolina			
National Safety Auditors Contact: Michael Wrenn	Durham, NC 27713	(919) 544-5544	

Cylinder Retest Centers *(cont.)*

Company	Address	Phone No.	Comments
North Carolina (cont.)			
National Welders Supply MAK-6H-18S	2503 E. Pettigrew St. Durham, NC 27703	(919) 596-0522	Can test 13" O.D.
Ohio			
ABCO Fire Protection, Inc. Contact: Ken May	913 N. Depot Street Sandusky, OH 44870	(419) 626-0012	
All Brite Welding MAK-44-18	Wooster, OH	(216) 264-2021	Can test 13" O.D.
Kidde MAK-6B-12/24 STDJC	Cleveland, OH	(216) 871-9900	
Pennsylvania			
Keystone Fire Equipment MAK-4B-DPF	Philadelphia, PA	(215) 288-9000	
Tennessee			
M.G. Burdett GKC-4-18	Chattanooga, TN	(312) 565-5000	Can test 13" O.D.
Texas			
City Machine & Welding, Inc. Contact: Reece Norwood	9200 W. Amarillo Blvd Amarillo, TX 79124	(806) 358-7293	
Firemaster GKC-4B-18	3301 E. John Carpenter Irving, TX 75062	(214) 445-0090	Can test 13" O.D.
Texas Fire & Safety	3301 Carpenter Fwy Irving, TX 75062	(214) 438-2808	Up to 17" O.D. Up to 61" length
Washington			
AAA Fire & Safety, Inc.	3013 3rd Ave. Seattle, WA 98109	(206) 284-1721	
Compressed Gas Western	4535 W. Marginal Way SW Seattle, WA 98106	(206) 935-5093	
Fire King of Seattle, Inc.	240 S. Holden St. Seattle, WA 98108	(206) 763-4177	

Cylinder Retest Centers *(cont.)*

Company	Address	Phone No.	Comments
Washington (cont.)			
Fireshield	Seattle, WA	(206) 763-4177	
Ohio Medical	Seattle, WA		
Smokey Fire	Burlington, WA	(206) 757-6162	
Sure Marine Service, Inc.	5320 28th Ave. NW Seattle, WA 98107	(206) 784-9903	
Wisconsin			
Amalopa Corp. MAK-6H-18	West Allis, WI	(414) 476-0500	Can test 13" O.D.
Automatic Fire Protection, Inc. MAK-4B-24	3265 N. 126th Street Brookfield, WI 53005	(414) 781-9665	
Pressed Steel Tank MAK-6B-18	Milwaukee, WI	(414) 476-0500	Can test 13" O.D.

(Courtesy CNG Cylinder Co.)

Glossary of Terms

Adaptive learning. An operational mode of a control computer that adjusts operation parameters according to various conditions.

Air-to-fuel ratio. The ratio of air volume to fuel volume. A specified ratio is necessary to achieve a desired character of combustion in a vehicle's engine.

All-composite cylinder. A cylinder with a plastic (nonmetallic) liner, reinforced with filament winding.

Alternating current (AC). Electrical current that changes direction between positive and negative.

Alternative fuel vehicles (AFVs). Vehicles with engines designed to run on a fuel other than gasoline or diesel.

Alternative transportation fuel. Fuels that can be substituted for traditional vehicular fuels such as gasoline or diesel.

Aluminum composite cylinder. Any cylinder with an aluminum liner that is reinforced with filament winding.

Ambient temperature. Temperature of the air surrounding an object.

American National Standards Institute (ANSI). The coordinating organization for the United States federated national standards system.

Amp (Ampere). A unit of measurement for the rate of current flow.

AND gate. A logic gate with at least two inputs and one output.

Asphyxiant. A gas or other noxious substance that interferes with normal breathing and may cause loss of consciousness or death.

Atm. Atmosphere.

Atmospheric pressure. The pressure attributable to the weight of the atmosphere (air and water vapor) on the earth's surface. Average atmospheric pressure at sea level (for scientific purposes) is defined as 14.696 pounds per square inch absolute.

Barometric pressure. A sensor or its signal circuit that sends a varying frequency signal to the processor relating actual barometric pressure.

Barrel (oil). A volumetric unit of measurement equivalent to 42 U.S. gallons. This is the unit of measurement commonly used to measure oil production and oil reserves within the U.S.

Base. The center layer of a bipolar transistor.

Bi-fuel natural gas vehicle. A vehicle with an engine capable of running on either natural gas or some other fuel (usually gasoline).

Binary code. A series of numbers represented by 1s and 0s or offs and ons.

Bit. A binary digit.

Boiling point. The degree of temperature where a liquid turns to a gas.

Boyle's law. A basic law of gases that expresses the relationship among gas volume, temperature, and pressure. The law states that the volume of a fixed amount of gas at a constant temperature is inversely proportional to the gas pressure.

British thermal unit (Btu). The quantity of heat necessary to raise the temperature of one pound of water one degree Fahrenheit.

Butane (C_4H_{10}). A low-boiling-point paraffin hydrocarbon that results from natural gas production as well as from a process used in petroleum refining.

Byte. A string of eight binary digits (bits).

CAFE standards. Law requiring auto makers to not only manufacture clean-burning engines but also to equip vehicles with engines that burn gasoline efficiently.

California Air Resources Board (CARB). The California regulatory agency responsible for air quality in that state. Several other states are also adopting CARB guidelines.

Capacitor. A device for holding and storing a surge of current.

Carbon (C). A nonmetallic element found as a constituent of coal, petroleum, asphalt, and other organic compounds.

Carbon monoxide (CO). A colorless, odorless, poisonous, combustible gas formed by incomplete combustion of carbon or reduction of carbon dioxide. CO is a criteria air pollutant that is emitted primarily through tailpipe emissions of a vehicle equipped with a spark-ignited engine.

Carbureted engine. An engine that uses a carburetor to control the mixture of air and fuel.

Carcinogen. A cancer-causing substance or agent.

Cardlock station. A fueling station that uses a card (similar to a credit card or a card with a magnetic strip) to access the dispenser and allow fuel to flow into the vehicle's fuel-storage cylinder(s).

Catalyst. A compound or substance that can speed up or slow down the reaction of other substances without being consumed itself. In an automatic catalytic converter, special metals are used to promote more complete combustion of unburned hydrocarbons and a reduction of carbon monoxide.

Caustic. A corrosive substance.

Check valve. A gate or valve that allows passage of gas or fluid in one direction only.

Clean Air Act Amendments (CAAA) of 1990. Federal legislation passed in 1990 designed to establish automotive emissions standards.

Closed loop. A conversion system that uses a feedback system to monitor and adjust engine performance.

Collector. The portion of a bipolar transistor that receives the majority of current carriers.

Compressed natural gas (CNG). Natural gas that is highly compressed (though not to the point of liquefaction) and stored in high pressure surface containers. Compressed natural gas is used extensively as a transportation fuel for automobiles, trucks, and buses.

Compression ratio. The ratio of the volume in the cylinder above the piston when the piston is at bottom dead center to the volume in the cylinder above the piston when the piston is at top dead center.

Compressor. A mechanical device used to increase the pressure of a gas.

Conductor. A device or material that readily allows for current flow.

Continuous injection system. A system that uses fuel under pressure to modulate or change the fuel injection area.

Controller. A term commonly used for an electronic control unit or module.

Corrosivity. The characteristic of a material that enables it to dissolve metals and other materials or burn the skin.

Crimp. The use of pressure to force a thin holding part to clamp to, or conform to the shape of, a part so it can't move.

Criteria air pollutant. An air pollutant for which acceptable levels of exposure can be determined and an ambient air-quality standard has been set. Examples include: ozone, carbon monoxide, nitrogen dioxide, sulfur dioxide, and PM-10.

Cryogenic. Involving very low or freezing temperatures.

Current. The number of electrons flowing past a given point in a given amount of time.

CVS. Constant volume sampling.

Dedicated natural gas vehicle. A vehicle that operates only on natural gas. Such a vehicle is incapable of running on any other fuel.

Detonation. Uncontrolled, rapid burning of the fuel charge that results in spark knock.

Diode. A simple semiconductor device that permits flow of electricity in one direction but not in the opposite direction.

Direct current (DC). Electrical current that flows in one direction.

Disable. A type of microcomputer decision that results in an automotive system being deactivated and not permitted to operate.

DOT. Department of Transportation.

Dual-fuel vehicle. A vehicle that runs on either diesel fuel only, or diesel fuel and natural gas simultaneously. In a dual-fuel vehicle, the combustion of the diesel fuel serves to ignite the natural gas.

Duty cycle. The percentage of on time to total cycle time.

Dwell time. The degree of crankshaft rotation during which the primary circuit is on.

Dynamometer. A device used to measure force or the mechanical power of an engine.

ECU. Electronic control unit.

Eddy current. A small circular current produced inside a metal core in the armature of a starter motor.

Electromagnetism. A form of magnetism that occurs when current flows through a conductor.

Electromechanical. Refers to a device that incorporates both electronic and mechanical principles in its operation.

Electron. A negative-charged particle of an atom.

Emissions. Pollutants discharged from a polluting source, such as vehicles.

Emitter. The outer layer of the transistor, which supplies the majority of current carriers.

Energy Policy Act (EPACT) of 1992. Federal legislation passed in 1992 designed to reduce America's dependence on foreign oil.

Environmental Protection Agency (EPA). The United States agency charged with setting policy and guidelines for the protection of national interests in environmental resources.

Ethane (C_2H_6). A colorless hydrocarbon gas of slight odor having a gross heating value of 1,773 Btus per cubic foot. It is a normal constituent of natural gas.

Ethanol (C_2H_4OH). An alcohol fuel made primarily from agricultural products, typically corn.

Feedback. Normally refers to the process in which computer commands and the results of such are monitored by the computer.

FMS. Fuel management system.

Foot-pound. A unit of measurement for torque. One foot-pound (ft.-lb.) is the torque obtained by a force of 1 pound applied to a wrench handle 12 inches long.

Fuel injection system. A system in a vehicle that allows fuel and air to be mixed in the engine.

Gas mixer. A device used to determine how much natural gas is mixed with air before entering the engine.

Gasoline gallon equivalent (GGE). A proposed unit for measuring compressed natural gas sold at public fueling stations.

Gross vehicle weight (GVW). Maximum weight of a vehicle, including payload.

Hall effect switch. A sensor that operates on the principle that if a current is allowed to flow through thin conducting material being exposed to a magnetic field, another voltage is produced.

Heavy-duty vehicle. According to the Environmental Protection Agency, a heavy-duty vehicle is any vehicle weighing 8,500 pounds Gross Vehicle Weight (GVW) or more. In California, vehicles weighing more than 14,000 pounds GVW are classified as heavy-duty vehicles.

Heptane. A standard reference fuel with an octane number of zero, meaning that it knocks severely in an engine.

Hexadecimal system. A numbering system using 16 as its base.

Hg (chemical symbol for mercury). A calibration material used as a standard for vacuum measurement.

High pressure fuel line. The fuel-piping system that travels from the onboard fuel-storage cylinder(s) to the regulator on a natural gas vehicle. Pressure in a high pressure fuel line may reach up to 3,600 psi.

High pressure storage tank. A container used to store compressed natural gas at a fueling station.

Hoop-wrapped cylinder. A metal-lined cylinder that is reinforced with circumferential filament winding in the straight side wall.

Hydrate. A chemical compound formed by the combination of a substance with water.

Hydrocarbon (HC). A chemical compound composed of carbon and hydrogen. Particles of gas combustion, present in the exhaust and in crankcase vapors, that have not been fully burned.

Hydrogen (H). A colorless, odorless, highly flammable gas used in hydrogenation of petroleum and to produce ammonia. Hydrogen is also an important constituent of manufactured gas.

Hydrostatic testing. A strength test used on equipment (cylinders). The cylinder is filled with liquid, subjected to suitable pressure and sealed, and pressure is monitored. This test is also used to determine whether a container is capable of holding a certain pressure.

IAT. Intake air temperature.

Ignitability. The characteristic of a solid that enables it to spontaneously ignite. Any liquid with a flash point below 140°F is also said to possess ignitability.

Individual fueling appliance. A natural gas fueling component that contains both compressor and fueling equipment. These appliances generally range in size from 1.75 cubic feet to 5 cubic feet per minute fueling capacity.

Indolene. The fuel used to certify gasoline vehicle emissions.

Induction. The process of producing electricity through magnetism rather than direct flow through a conductor.

Insulator. A material used to electrically isolate two conductive surfaces.

Integral. Made in one piece.

Integrated circuit. A large number of diodes, transistors, and other electronic components, all mounted on a single piece of semiconductor material and able to perform numerous functions.

Isooctane. A standard reference fuel with an octane number of 100, meaning that it does not knock in an engine.

Keep alive memory. A series of vehicle battery-powered memory locations in the microcomputer that allow the microcomputer to store information on input failure, identified in normal operations for use in diagnostic routines. Keep alive memory adopts some calibration parameters to compensate for changes in the vehicle system.

Lambda sensor. A type of oxygen sensor used on some European cars.

Lean. An air/fuel mixture that has more air than is required for a stoichiometric mixture.

Lean-burn combustion. Engine combustion optimized for a lean fuel-to-air mixture, usually with high turbulence to offset the low flame speed of such mixtures.

LEL. Lower explosive limit.

LEV. Low-emitting vehicle.

Light-duty vehicles. According to the Environmental Protection Agency, a light-duty vehicle is any vehicle weighing 8,500 pounds Gross Vehicle Weight (GVW) or less. In California, vehicles weighing less than 6,000 pounds GVW are classified as light-duty vehicles.

Liquefied natural gas (LNG). Natural gas that has been liquefied by reducing its temperature to -260 degrees Fahrenheit at atmospheric pressure. In volume at standard conditions, it occupies 1/600 that of natural gas as a vapor.

Liter (L). A metric measurement used to calculate the volume displacement of an engine. One liter is equal to 1,000 cubic centimeters or 61 cubic inches.

Load. The work an engine must do, under which it operates more slowly and less efficiently. The load could be that of driving up a hill or pulling extra weight.

Local distribution company (LDC). A company that obtains the major portion of its revenue from the operation of a retail natural gas distribution system.

Logic gates. Electronic circuits that act as gates to output voltage signals depending on different combinations of input signals.

Look-up tables. The part of a microcomputer's memory that indicates, in the form of calibrations and specifications, how an engine should perform.

LP gas. Liquefied petroleum gas, often referred to as *propane,* which burns clean in an engine and can be precisely controlled.

Manifold absolute pressure (MAP). A measure of the degree of vacuum or pressure within an intake manifold; used to measure air volume flow.

MAP sensor. The sensor that measures changes in the intake manifold pressure that result from changes in engine load and speed.

Methane (CH$_4$). The first of the paraffin series of hydrocarbons and the chief constituent of natural gas. Pure methane has a heating value of 1,012 Btus per cubic foot.

Methanol (CH$_2$OH). An alcohol fuel usually made from natural gas or coal.

Micron. One millionth (.000001) of a meter.

Microprocessor. The portion of a microcomputer that receives sensor input and handles all calculations.

MST. Manifold skin temperature.

National Ambient Air Quality Standards (NAAQS). Legal limits specifying the maximum level and time of exposure that can occur in the outside air for a given air pollutant, which are protective of human health and public welfare. NAAQS are standards that must be met in accordance with EPA requirements.

Natural gas. Any gas found in the earth, as opposed to gases that are manufactured.

Natural gas distribution system. This term generally applies to mains, services, and equipment that carry or control the supply of natural gas from the point of local supply, up to and including the sales meter.

Natural gas transmission system. Pipelines installed for the purpose of transmitting natural gas from a source or sources of supply to one or more distribution centers.

NFPA. National Fire Protection Association.

NGV-1. The NGV industry standard that pertains to natural gas fueling nozzle and receptacle certification, which was approved by ANSI.

NGV-2. An NGV industry standard that pertains to onboard fuel-storage cylinder certification. NGV-2 was approved by the American National Standards Institute (ANSI) on August 6, 1992. It is currently the only fuel-storage cylinder certification standard that applies specifically to vehicle fuel tank usage.

Nitrogen oxides (NO$_x$). A general term pertaining to compounds of nitrogen oxide (NO), nitrogen dioxide (NO$_2$), and other oxides of nitrogen. Nitrogen oxides are typically created during the combustion process and are major contributors to smog formation and acid deposition. NO$_2$ is a criteria air pollutant and may result in numerous adverse health effects.

NMHC. Nonmethane hydrocarbons.

Nonmethane organic gas (NMOG). Nonmethane hydrocarbons plus other organic species such as aldehydes and alcohols, which are not measured as hydrocarbons in current test procedures.

Nonroad vehicle (off-road vehicle). A vehicle that does not travel streets, roads, or highways. Such vehicles include construction vehicles, locomotives, forklifts, golf carts, etc.

Nozzle. The device on a natural gas fueling dispenser that connects to a receptacle on board the vehicle and allows fuel to flow into the onboard fuel-storage cylinder.

Octane rating. The anti-knock index number of a fuel.

Ohm. The unit of measure for electrical resistance.

Ohmmeter. A test meter used to measure resistance and continuity in a circuit.

Ohm's law. A basic law of electricity expressing the relationship among current, resistance, and voltage in any electrical circuit. It states that the voltage in circuit is equal to the current (in amperes) multiplied by the resistance (in ohms).

Onboard computer system. A computerized system on some vehicles that monitors and adjusts engine performance.

Onboard fuel-storage cylinder. Cylinders used for storing compressed natural gas on vehicles.

Onsite fuel-storage cylinder. Cylinders or other vessels used to store compressed natural gas at fueling station sites.

Open loop. An electronic control system in which sensors provide information, the microcomputer gives orders, and the output actuators obey the orders without feedback to the microcomputer.

Optimized NGV. A vehicle fitted with an engine designed to use natural gas.

Original equipment manufacturer (OEM). The original manufacturer of a vehicle or engine.

Oxidation. The combination of a substance with oxygen to produce an oxygen-containing compound. Also, the chemical breakdown of a substance or compound caused by its combination with oxygen.

Oxides of nitrogen (NO_x). Various compounds of oxygen and nitrogen that are formed in the cylinders during combustion and are part of the exhaust gas.

Ozone (O_3). An odorous, pale blue, reactive, toxic chemical gas consisting of three oxygen atoms. Ozone is a product of the photochemical process involving the sun's energy. Ozone exists in the upper atmosphere ozone layer, as well as at the earth's surface. Ozone at the earth's surface causes numerous adverse health effects and is a criteria air pollutant. It is a major component of smog.

Pintle. The center pin used to control a fluid passing through a hole; a small pin or pointed shaft used to open or close a passageway.

Pipeline-quality gas. A term used to designate the typical chemical composition of natural gas delivered through pipelines.

Pneumatic. Operated by compressed air.

Polarity. The particular state, either positive or negative, with reference to the two poles or to electrification.

Poppet valve. A valve consisting of a round head with a tapered face, an elongated stem that guides the valve, and a machined slot at the top of the stem for the valve spring retainer.

Portable fuel-delivery system. A system designed to deliver natural gas to fueling stations. Such systems are usually configured as tube trailers and mobile fueling systems. Fuel delivery usually occurs via over-the-road vehicles.

Potentiometer. A variable resistor that acts as a circuit divider to provide accurate voltage drop reading in response to the movement of an object.

Pounds per square inch (psi). An expression of pressure used to determine gas volume. Also **psia** (pounds per square inch, absolute) and **psig** (pounds per square inch, gauge).

Private fleet. A fleet of vehicles owned by a nongovernment entity.

Private fueling station. A fueling station that is built to serve a single fleet of vehicles.

PROM (programmable read only memory). Memory chip that contains specific data that pertains to the exact vehicle in which the computer is installed. This information may be used to inform the CPU of the accessories that are equipped on the vehicle.

Propane (C_3H_8). A gas whose molecules are composed of three carbon and eight hydrogen atoms. Propane is present in most natural gas in the U.S. and is the first product refined from crude petroleum. Propane contains approximately 2,500 Btus per cubic foot.

Public fueling station. Refers to a fueling station that is accessible to the general public.

Pulsewidth. The length of time in milliseconds that an actuator is energized.

Pulsewidth modulation. On/off cycling of a component. The period of time for each cycle does not change; only the amount of on time in each cycle changes.

Quick fill. Refers to the process of fueling a vehicle with natural gas in approximately the same time it would take to fuel the same vehicle with liquid fuels such as gasoline or diesel.

RAM (random access memory). Stores temporary information that can be read from or written to by the CPU.

Reactive hydrocarbons. Hydrocarbons that react with NO_x in the atmosphere to produce ozone. These are generally considered to include all hydrocarbons other than methane.

Receptacle. The device on board an NGV that allows natural gas to flow into the onboard fuel-storage cylinders.

Reference voltage. A voltage provided by a voltage regulator to operate potentiometers and other sensors at a constant level.

Reformulated gasoline. Gasoline that has been chemically formulated to reduce or eliminate one or more toxic substances as specified by the U.S. Environmental Protection Agency.

Regulator. The component in a conversion system that reduces the pressure of the fuel.

Relay. A device that uses low current to control a high-current circuit. Low current is used to energize the electromagnetic coil, while high current is able to pass over the relay contacts.

Resistance. Opposition to current flow.

Rich. An air/fuel mixture that has more fuel than is required for a stoichiometric mixture.

ROM (read only memory). Memory chip that stores permanent information. This information is used to instruct the computer on what to do in response to input data. The CPU reads the information contained in ROM, but cannot write to it or change it.

Sampling. The act of periodically collecting information, as from a sensor. A microcomputer samples input from various sensors in the process of controlling a system.

Scan tool. A microprocessor designed to communicate with a vehicle's onboard computer to perform diagnosis and troubleshooting.

Schematics. Wiring diagrams used to show how circuits are constructed.

Semiconductor. A material or device that can function as either a conductor or an insulator. Under certain conditions the semiconductor will conduct electricity; under other conditions it will not. Used in the production of solid-state devices.

Sensor. Any device that provides an input to the computer.

Servomotor. An electrical motor that produces rotation of less than a full turn. A feedback mechanism is used to position itself to the exact degree of rotation required.

Shutoff valve. A valve that is usually located between the onboard fuel-storage cylinders and the regulator. This valve usually has a manual shutoff feature.

Smog. Air pollution created by the reaction of nitrogen oxides to sunlight.

Solenoid. An electromagnetic device that uses movement of a plunger to exert a pulling or holding force.

Solenoid valve. A valve that controls the flow of natural gas in a natural gas vehicle.

Solid-state device. An electronic component constructed from semiconductor material that requires very little power to operate, is very reliable, and generates very little heat.

Specific gravity. The ratio of the weight of a given volume of gas to that of the same volume of air, both measured at the same temperature and pressure.

Splice. To join. Electrical wires can be joined by soldering or by using crimped connectors.

Steel-composite cylinder. Any steel-lined cylinder with filament winding which is always hoop wrapped.

Stoichiometric. Chemically correct. In automotive terminology, it refers to an air/fuel ratio in which all combustible materials are used with no deficiencies or excesses.

Tailpipe emissions. Emissions resulting from engine operation that exit through a vehicle's tailpipe system.

TDC (top dead center). When the piston is as high as it can travel in the cylinder.

Therm. A unit of heating value equivalent to 100,000 British thermal units (Btus).

Thermistor. A solid-state variable resistor made from semiconductor material that changes resistance in response to changes in temperature.

Thousand cubic feet (MCF). The quantity of natural gas occupying a volume of 1,000 cubic feet at a temperature of 60°F and at a pressure of 14–73/100 pounds per square inch, absolute.

Timed fill. A method of fueling a vehicle with natural gas over an extended period, usually four to six hours.

Toxic substance. A generic term referring to a harmful substance or group of substances. Typically, these substances are especially harmful to health.

Transducer. A device that converts energy from one system into another type of energy for another system. For example, onboard computer input sensors.

Transistor. A three-layer semiconductor used as a very fast switching device.

Transport Canada (TC). A Canadian regulatory agency that certifies onboard fuel-storage cylinders for use on vehicles operating in Canada.

Type A fire. A fire resulting from the burning of wood, paper, textiles, and clothing.

Type B fire. A fire resulting from the burning of gasoline, grease, oils, and other flammable liquids.

Type C fire. A fire resulting from the burning of electrical equipment, motors, and switches.

UEL. Upper explosive limit.

Vapor. A substance in a gaseous state. Liquid becomes vapor when brought above the boiling point.

Vapor density. Volumetric mass of the gaseous element.

Vaporization. The last stage of carburetion, in which a fine mist of fuel is created below the venturi in the bore.

Vapor lock. A condition wherein the fuel boils in the fuel system forming bubbles that retard or stop the flow of fuel to the carburetor.

Vehicle conversion. Retrofitting a vehicle engine to run on natural gas.

Venturi. An hourglass-shaped restriction placed in the barrel of a carburetor to speed up the flow of incoming air.

Viscosity. The tendency of a liquid to resist flow. A thicker liquid has a higher viscosity.

Volatility. The tendency for a fluid to evaporate rapidly or pass off in the form of vapor. For example, gasoline is more volatile than kerosene because it evaporates at a lower temperature.

Volt. A unit of measurement of electromotive force. One volt of electromotive force applied steadily to a conductor produces a current of one ampere.

Voltage. An electrical measurement of potential difference, electrical pressure, or electromotive force (EMF).

Volumetric efficiency. A measure of how well air flows in and out of an engine.

Working (operating) pressure. The varying pressure in a fuel supply container during normal vehicle operation.

ZEV. Zero-emitting vehicle.

* Glossary entries and abbreviations provided in part by the N.Y. Energy Office.

Job Aids

CONTENTS

NATURAL GAS VEHICLE INSPECTION REPORT
Pass   Fail

Inspection Date: _____ Inspector: _____

---

1. Customer Information:

_____
Name

_____
Address

_____
City   State   Zip

(___) _____   (___) _____
Telephone Number   Fax Number

---

2. Installer Information:

_____
Name

_____
Address

_____
City   State   Zip

(___) _____   (___) _____
Telephone Number   Fax Number

_____
Contact Person

_____
Installation Technician's Name

ASE Certified   Yes   No   (If yes, what are his or her areas of expertise?
                                    Attach a copy of the technician's certificate.)

The NGV Inspection Report certifies compliance with the items shown as "Pass" at the time of this inspection. No warranty of compliance with these standards applies after the vehicle leaves the facility. No warranty is implied as to the quality or durability of the parts installed unless specified on the Inspection Report, and no warranty is implied as to the safety or efficiency of the vehicle inspected.

3. Vehicle Information:

Owner _____

    Year _____ Make _____ Model _____

VIN# _____

License # _____ Vehicle Fleet #_____

    Fuel Injection   Bi-Fuel   Engine Displacement _____

    Carburetor   Dedicated

4. Conversion Equipment Information:

AGA Approved	Yes	No
Copy of Certificate Attached	Yes	No
Conversion Equipment Model	_____	
Serial Number	_____	
Mixer Model Number	_____	
Electronics Package	_____	
CARB Certified	Yes	No
Operator's Manual	Yes	No

Vehicle Weight (if applicable)   GVW _____   GVWR _____

Rated System Pressure (in psi) _____

5. Fueling Connection:

Pass   Fail

    A. NGV-I must be used.

    B. Dust cap is attached.

    C. Receptacle shall be securely mounted and working.

    D. Check receptacle with sample NGV-I.

    E. Manual 1/4-turn shutoff valve after fueling connection (optional).

6. Pressure Regulator:

Pass   Fail

A. Regulator is securely mounted.

B. Regulator oil drain plugs must be accessible and at the bottom.

C. Regulator has been checked for external leaks.

D. Venting of the first stage regulator's pressure relief satisfy the following requirements:

   1. Vent shall not exit into a wheel well, compartment, or near an exhaust system component.

   2. Seamless stainless steel line with 1/4-inch inside diameter vapor hose applicable to system pressure.

   3. Fuel-carrying components labeled: (manufacturer's name or trademark and design pressure).

   4. Vent line secured at the end and every 12 inches when exceeds 24 inches in length.

   5. Vent line will have cap or cover.

7. Natural Gas Cylinders:

Size: O.D. _____ L _____ Manufacturer _____ Water Volume _____
(gallons/liters)

        O.D. _____ L _____   _____   _____

        O.D. _____ L _____   _____   _____

        O.D. _____ L _____   _____   _____

Serial # _____   Retest Dates _____

_____   _____

_____   _____

_____   _____

• External Installation of Cylinders:

Applicable　　　　　Not Applicable

Pass　　Fail

1. Cylinders must be approved by DOT or NGV-2 for compressed natural gas.

2. Data markings must be fully visible and legible.

3. "CNG ONLY" is visible and in letters at least 1 inch high.

4. Cylinder(s) must not be in direct contact with the following:
   a. Frame members
   b. Suspension members
   c. Brake cables
   d. Exhaust components
   e. Any other items that could cause chafing

5. Use only approved installation brackets designed for the specific NGV cylinder(s). (For example, do not match an aluminum bracket with a steel cylinder.)

6. Each bracket has at least four securement points.

7. When the bolts pierce the body metal but not the frame, they reinforce both sides of each securement point with plates at least 1/8-inch thick within a 7-square-inch area.

8. Attaching bolts are not less than 7/16-inch diameter and grade #5 or better, including a 3-inch diameter heavy-duty washer. (Nylon lock nuts are not acceptable.)

9. Metal clamping bands and their supports (cradle) must be painted.

10. A resilient non-water-retaining gasket is used between the cylinder and metal clamp.

11. Cylinder mounting must not affect driving characteristic of vehicle.

12. Full composite NGV cylinder(s) must be grounded to prevent static charge.

13. Aluminum cylinders over 65 inches in length require a PRD at each end.

14. The cylinders must be shielded against direct heat if mounted less than 8 inches from the engine or the exhaust system.

• Undercarriage Installation of Cylinders:

		Applicable	Not Applicable

Pass   Fail

1. Cylinders must be approved by DOT or NGV-2 for natural gas.
2. Data markings must be fully visible and legible.
3. "CNG ONLY" is visible and in letters at least 1 inch high.
4. Cylinder(s) must not be in direct contact with the following:
   a. Frame members
   b. Suspension members
   c. Brake cables
   d. Exhaust components
   e. Any other items that could cause chafing
5. Use only approved installation brackets designed for the specific NGV cylinder(s). (For example, do not match an aluminum bracket with a steel cylinder.)
6. Each bracket has at least four securement points.
7. When the bolts pierce the body metal but not the frame, reinforce both sides of each securement point with plates at least 1/8-inch thick within a 7-square-inch area.
8. Attaching bolts are not less than 7/16-inch diameter and grade #5 or better, including a 3-inch diameter heavy-duty washer. (Nylon lock nuts are not acceptable.)
9. Metal clamping bands and their supports (cradle) must be painted.
10. A resilient non-water-retaining gasket is used between the cylinder and metal clamp.
11. Cylinder mounting must not affect driving characteristic of vehicle.
12. Full composite NGV cylinder(s) must be grounded to prevent a static charge.
13. Aluminum cylinders over 65 inches in length require a PRD valve at each end.
14. When the cylinders are mounted on the undercarriage, they must be between the front and rear axles and rear bumper, facing forward.
15. When the cylinders are mounted ahead of the front axle or the rear axle, they are installed transversely, where possible, or longitudinally with valve facing forward.
16. The cylinders must be shielded against direct heat if mounted less than 8 inches from the engine or the exhaust system.

17. If a cylinder is within 12 inches of the drive shaft, drive shaft safety loops are 6 inches back from the universal joints. This is optional except when required on specific vehicles such as:
    a. School buses
    b. Any other vehicles required as part of their specification

18. Minimum road clearance when loaded to GVW:
    a. 7 inches with a WB less or equal to 127 inches
    b. 9 inches with a WB greater than 127 inches

- ## Closed Compartment Installation of Cylinders:

		Applicable	Not Applicable
Pass	Fail		

1. Cylinders must be approved by DOT or NGV-2 for compressed natural gas.
2. Data markings must be fully visible and legible.
3. "CNG ONLY" is visible and in letters at least 1 inch high.
4. Cylinder(s) must not be in direct contact with the following:
   a. Frame members
   b. Suspension members
   c. Brake cables
   d. Exhaust components
   e. Any other items that could cause chafing
5. Use only approved installation brackets designed for the specific NGV cylinder(s). (For example, do not match an aluminum bracket with a steel cylinder.)
6. Each bracket has at least four securement points.
7. When the bolts pierce the body metal but not the frame, reinforce both sides of each securement point with plates at least 1/8-inch thick within a 7-square-inch area.
8. Attaching bolts are not less than 7/16-inch diameter and grade #5 or better, including a 3-inch diameter heavy-duty washer. (Nylon lock nuts are not acceptable.)
9. Metal clamping bands and their supports (cradle) must be painted.
10. A resilient non-water-retaining gasket is used between the cylinder and metal clamp.
11. Cylinder mounting must not affect driving characteristic of vehicle.
12. Aluminum cylinders over 65 inches in length require a PRD valve at each end.

13. All cylinders installed within a closed compartment with openings at either end must be bagged and vented.
14. When cylinder(s) are mounted in a closed compartment they require the following:
    a. PRD valve(s) on cylinder(s) vented to the outside and bagged
    b. Vent shall not exit into a wheel well, engine compartment, or near an exhaust system component
    c. Not less than a 3-square-inch opening
    d. Seamless stainless steel line with 1/2-inch inside diameter
    e. Vent line secured at the end and every 12 inches when line exceeds 24 inches in length
    f. Vent line(s) will have cap(s) or cover(s)

• Cylinder Valve Operations:

Pass   Fail

1. All valves must be accessible to vehicle user.
2. All valves must be protected from damage using vehicle structure valve protectors or suitable metal shield around valve and fittings.
3. Two PRDs are required when the cylinder(s) are over 65 inches in length.
4. PRD valve must match the specifications of the cylinder manufacturer.

System Service Pressure	Manufacturer	Testing of Cylinder**	Construction	Temperature	Pressure
	Press Steel Cylinder	3 years	Steel Composite	212°	5,000 psi
3,000 psi	CNG Cylinder Corporation	3 years	Aluminum Composite	217°	
	Brunswick Composite	NGV-2*	All Composite	Mirada 216°	
3,600 psi	Comdyne	3 years	Aluminum Fully Wrapped	Mirada 291°	5,400 + or - 300 psi
	EDO	NGV-2*	All Composite	217°	3,600 psi

*No testing required, except for a visual inspection every 3 years.

**Life span of 15 years on cylinder(s) in the U.S.

8. Piping:

Pass   Fail   N/A

The piping must satisfy the following requirements:

A. Seamless stainless steel only (suggested types are #304 or #316). If numbers are not visible on tubing, certification is required.

B. 2" I.D. expansion loop or pig tail:
   1. Between any two cylinders
   2. Cylinder(s) and vehicle
   3. Regulator to body to frame to cylinder valve

C. Securing clamps with insulated corrosion resistant metal straps.

D. Joint or connection is in an accessible location.

E. Supported within 4 inches of a fitting connection.

F. Supported every 24 inches.

G. Snugly-fitting grommets or bulkhead connector are used when passing through metal panels.

H. Protected when within 8 inches of the battery.

I. Piping shall not be located in a drive shaft tunnel.

J. Every connection is checked with a nonammonia soap solution or a leak detector.

9. Wiring and Connections:

Pass   Fail

A. All electrical connections will be compatible with the original equipment:
   1. Crimped or soldered
   2. Sealed with heat shrink tubing

B. Wiring and connections must be sized and fused, protected with the fuse adequate to the current draw.

C. All wiring must be secured and protected from abrasion and corrosion.

10. Decals:

Mark "pass" only when all boxes are checked.
(Exception: If both decals "A" and "B" below are located in one area, those decals can be combined into a single label.)

Pass   Fail

A. Engine compartment decal shows the following information:
   1. Manufacturer's name and address
   2. Model number
   3. Serial number
   4. Compressed natural gas fueled vehicle
   5. System service pressure
   6. Installer's name or company
   7. Container (cylinder retest dates or expiration date and the letters "DOT")
   8. Total container water volume in gallons/liters

B. Fueling connection receptacle decal shows the following information:
   1. Compressed natural gas fueled vehicle
   2. System working pressure
   3. Container retest date or expiration date

C. Lower right rear of the vehicle decal meets the following standards:
   1. Diamond shaped, silver or white reflective luminous material on a blue background; the inside will have the letters "CNG"
   2. Minimum of 4-3/4 inches long by 3-1/4 inches high
   3. Affixed to exterior vertical or near a vertical surface
   4. Compressed natural gas decals will not be placed on the bumper of any vehicle

D. 1/4-turn manual shutoff valve location decal states "Manual Shutoff Valve"

E. On the cylinders, the decal states:
   1. "CNG ONLY"
   2. The letters are at least 1 inch high
   3. Serial number of cylinder(s)
   4. Retest date
   5. Entire manufacturer's information label must be visible and legible after installation

F. Dashboard fuel gauge: Gasoline/Natural Gas

G. Fuel-carrying components labeled: (manufacturer's name or trademark and design pressure)
      Hose   Tubing

11. Tailpipe Emissions:

Completed

A. Vehicle started with engine temperature:

Cold _____ Hot _____

B. Sample taken after catalytic converter

C. Emission data recorded in customer file

D. Horsepower at the drive wheels:
   2,500 rpm loaded (dynomometer)

   Gasoline _____

   Natural Gas _____

   +_____%   -_____%
   (There must be no more than a 15% loss)

Pass   Fail

E. Curb idle: 2,500 rpm loaded (dynomometer)

Gasoline:

CO_2% _____% CO_2% _____%

O_2% _____% O_2% _____%

HC _____ppm   HC _____ppm

CO% _____%   CO% _____%

Natural Gas:

CO_2% _____% CO_2% _____%

O_2% _____% O_2% _____%

HC _____ppm   HC _____ppm

CO% _____%   CO% _____%

12. Fuel Line Safety Valve:

Pass   Fail

A. The body and handle of the manual shutoff valve are directional, and the arrow points toward the direction of flow.

B. The valve shall have no more than a 90-degree rotation, or a 1/4-turn, from the open to the closed position (optional after fueling connection).

C. The valve must be mounted on the exterior of the vehicle (not in the cabin, closed compartment, or under the hood) and it must be readily accessible for manual shutoff.

D. The safety valve must be securely mounted and shielded or in a protected location.

E. The valve must not be cast iron, aluminum, copper, or brass.

13. Proper Bi-Fuel Engine Operation: Gasoline

Pass   Fail

A. Fuel system securely installed

B. All hoses connected and secured

C. Air box dampers are operational

D. Vehicle's engine temperature: Cold _____ Hot _____

E. Base ignition timing correct for gasoline: _____

F. Driver's evaluation of vehicle performance during road test:

_____

G. Runs smooth on idle

H. Runs strong at road speeds

I. Driver's explanation of acceptance of gasoline throttle response:

_____

J. Fuel switchover is smooth with no stalling

K. Dashboard fuel gauge operates on either fuel

14. Proper Bi-Fuel Engine Operation: Natural Gas

Pass   Fail

     A. Fuel system securely installed

     B. All hoses connected and secured

     C. Vapor hose unobstructed

     D. Air box dampers are operational

     E. Vehicle's engine temperature: Cold _____ Hot _____

     F. Base ignition timing correct for natural gas: _____

     G. Driver's evaluation of vehicle performance during road test:

     _____

     H. Runs smooth on idle

     I. Runs strong at road speeds

     J. Driver's explanation of acceptance of natural gas throttle response:

     _____

     K. Fuel switchover is smooth with no stalling

     L. Dashboard fuel gauge operates on either gasoline or natural gas

     M. All appropriate valves are on during:
        1. Road test
        2. Leak check at system pressure

     N. System pressure (in psi): _____

15. Summary of Total Inspection:

VIN # _____

Pass   Fail

Final Inspection

If the vehicle failed inspection, explain what area(s) were deficient.

_____

_____

_____

_____

Road test mileage before inspection: _____

Road test mileage after inspection: _____

Inspector's Name: _____
(Print)

_____
(Signature)

Acknowledgements:

- AAA Mid-Atlantic

- PECO Energy Company

- Alternative Fuel Vehicle Program of West Virginia University

Additional Assistance:

- Pennsylvania Department of Transportation's Vehicle Equipment and Inspection Regulations

- National Fire Protection Association's NFPA 52 Standard for Compressed Natural Gas Vehicular Fuel System

- Recommendations from representatives in the natural gas industry

REFERENCE FIGURE #1

Typical 4-Gas Analyzer Scales

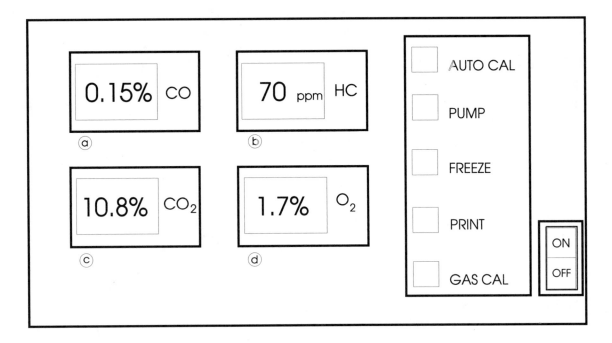

REFERENCE FIGURE #2

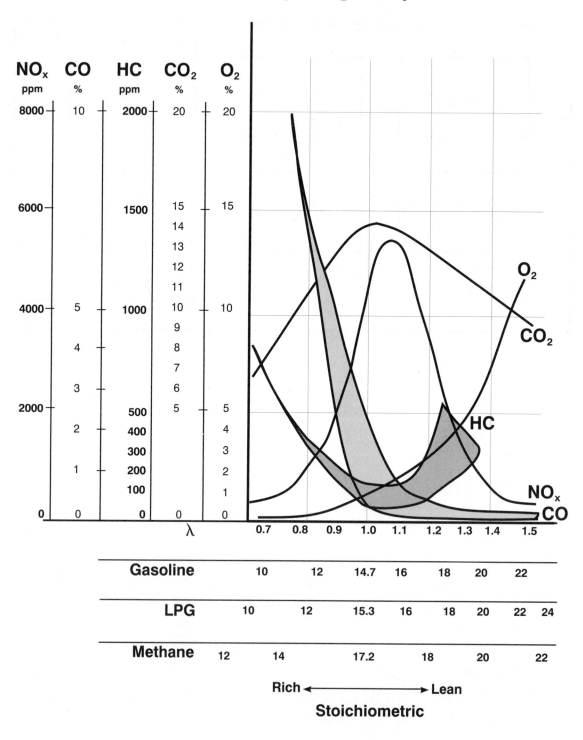

Emissions Readings on 4-gas Analyzer

REFERENCE CHART #1

Physical Properties of Five Fuel Types

	Methane	Propane	LNG	Gasoline	Diesel
Formula	CH_4	C_3H_8	C_4	C_8H_{16}	$C_{12}H_{26}$
Research Octane Number	130	112	130	91–98	NA
Motor Octane Number	130	97	130	83–90	NA
Cetane Number	-10	5–10	-10	8–14	40–47
Heat of Vaporization (Btu/lbm)	218	182	218	153	123
Stoichiometric A/F Ratio (mass)	17.3	15.7	17.3	14.7	15
Energy of Stoichiometric Mixture (Mj/m³)	3.58	3.79	3.58	3.91	
Lower Heat of Combustion (Mj/kg)	50	46.3	50	43.9	42.36
Lower Heating Value (LHV) (Btu/lbm)	21,459	19,879	21,459	18,341	18,574
Energy Content (Btu/gal)		84,486	75,535	114,264	126,000
Energy Density Ratio to Gasoline	26%	74%	66%	100%	110%
Energy Density Ratio to Diesel		67%	60%	91%	100%
Wobbe Number (Mj/m³)	48.2	74.7	48.2		
Density of Liquid at NTP (kg/L)	0.422	0.508	0.422	0.7	
Specific Gravity at NTP (kg/m³)	0.55	1.52	0.55	2–4	4–6
Density (lbm/gal)		4.25	3.52	6.23	6.75
Boiling Point (C)	-162	-42	-162	27–240	
Autoignition Temperature (C)	540	450	450	220	225
Reid Vapor Pressure (psi)	NA	NA		50–100	0.1–0.15
Peak Flame Temperature (C)	1,790	1,990	1,790	1,977	2,054
Diffusion Velocity in NTP Air (cm/s)	~0.51	~0.34	~0.51	~0.17	
Diffusion Coefficients in NTP Air (cm²/s)	0.16	0.1		0.05	
Quenching Gap in NTP Air (mm)	2.03	1.78	2.03	2	
Spark Ignition Energy (Mj)	0.29	0.25	0.29	0.24	0.24
Flammability Limits (vol%)	5–15	2.1–9.5		1.4–7.6	0.6–5.5
Detonation Limits (vol%)	6.3–13.5	3.4–35	6.3–13.5		
Max. Burning Velocity in NTP Air (cm/s)	37–45	43–52	37–45	37–43	
Flame Speed Rate (m/s)	NA	NA	NA	4–6	0.02–0.08
Flame Visibility, Relative	0.6	0.6	0.6	1	1
Flash Point, F	NA	NA	-306		125

REFERENCE CHART #2

Recommended Service Intervals

	Conversion Date	1k	5k	10k	15k	20k	25k	30k	35k	40k	45k	50k	55k	60k	65k	70k	75k	80k	85k	90k	95k	100k
CARBURETION SECTION																						
Adjust idle mixture [a]	X	X					X					X					X					X
Adjust wide open throttle mixture [a]	X	X					X					X					X					X
Check air/gas valve diaphragm				X			X					X					X					X
Replace air/gas valve assy [c]												X										X
Check idle diaphragm CA425				X			X					X					X					X
Replace CA425 idle diaphragm if needed											X									X		
Check for vacuum leaks on complete intake system including adapters				X			X					X					X					X
Check gas orifice for wear							X					X					X					X
Service open air cleaner:																						
• Normal conditions						X				X				X				X				X
• Dirty condition				X		X		X		X		X		X		X		X		X		X
REGULATOR SECTION																						
Check FCV for proper OHM reading [e]	X						X					X					X					X
Replace FCV												X										X
Inspect secondary diaphragm [d]				X			X					X					X					X
Test secondary pressures [b]				X			X					X					X					X
Test primary pressures [b]				X			X					X					X					X
Rebuild regulator												X										X
LOCKOFF SECTION																						
Replace filter							X					X					X					X
GENERAL MAINTENANCE																						
Check all vacuum lines and fittings (Replace as needed)	X						X					X					X					X
Check all fuel fittings and hoses (Replace as needed)	X						X					X					X					X

[a] See air/fuel ratio adjustment procedures.
[b] See ITK-I test procedures.
[c] Side draft CA425 - Inspect each 10K miles for wear.
[d] If oil appears on diaphragm, disassemble and clean regulator of all oil and contaminants.
[e] No less than 22 OHM.

(Courtesy IMPCO Technologies, Inc.)

A Comparison Of New Purchase Requirements For Light-Duty Vehicle Fleets

YEAR	CAAA (% CFVs for Clean Fuel Fleet Program)	EPACT Federal (% AFVs)	EPACT State (% AFVs)	EPACT Fuel Provider (% AFVs)	EPACT Muni/Priv (early rule) (% AFVs)	EPACT Muni/Priv (late rule) (% AFVs)
1994		7500 AFVs				
1995		11250 AFVs				
1996		15000 AFVs				
1997		25%	10%	30%		
1998		33%	15%	50%		
1999	30%	50%	25%	70%		
2000	50%	75%	50%	90%	10%	
2001		75%	75%	90%	10%	
2002		75%	75%	90%	20%	20%
2003		75%	75%	90%	30%	40%
2004		75%	75%	90%	40%	60%
2005		75%	75%	90%	50%	70%
2006		75%	75%	90%	70%	70%
2007		75%	75%	90%	70%	70%

These numbers reflect increases due to Excecutive Order 12844.
CFV = Clean Fuel Vehicle
AFV = Alternative Fuel Vehicle
Based on EPACT final rules released in March 1996

(Courtesy James Madison University)

REFERENCE CHART #4

Alternative Fuels Comparison

CRITERIA	GASOLINE	CNG	LPG	METHANOL	ETHANOL	ELECTRICITY
Lower Heating Value (Btu/gal)	115,400	19,760	82,450	56,560	75,670	Not Applicable
Ignition Temp.	600°F	1,200°F	1,000°F	725°F	795°F	Not Applicable
State of Fuel	Liquid fuel may pool when leaked	Gaseous fuel which will disperse when leaked	Liquid fuel during storage, gaseous fuel enters engine	Liquid fuel may pool when leaked	Liquid fuel may pool when leaked	Electromagnetic with liquid contained in batteries
Octane Rating	87 to 93	120 to 130	104	100	111	Not Applicable
Toxicity	Toxic with a fatal dose of 12 oz.	Practically nontoxic	Practically nontoxic	Extremely toxic with a fatal dose of 2 to 8 oz.	Low toxicity	Batteries may contain toxic fluids
Carbon monoxide (CO) emissions (compared to gasoline)	Used as a base to compare other fuels	95% less	About the same	28% less	25% less	No tailpipe emissions but 97% less from electric generation source
Nitrogen oxide (NOx) emissions (compared to gasoline)	Used as a base to compare other fuels	34% less	59% less	32% less	35% less	No tailpipe emissions but 85% less from electric generation source
Reactive hydrocarbons (HC) emissions (compared to gasoline)	Used as a base to compare other fuels	45% less	43% less	28% less	30% less	No tailpipe emissions but 85% less from electric generation sources
Conversion Status	Not Applicable	Dedicated or Bi-fuel	Dedicated or Bi-fuel	Dedicated or Bi-fuel	Dedicated or Bi-fuel	Dedicated
Conversion Costs	Not Applicable	$2,500 to $3,000	$2,500 to $3,000	$1,500 to $3,000	$2,000 to $3,000	$4,000 to $5,000

REFERENCE CHART #4 *(cont.)*

Alternative Fuels Comparison *(cont.)*

CRITERIA	GASOLINE	CNG	LPG	METHANOL	ETHANOL	ELECTRICITY
Projected OEM cost over gasoline vehicle	Used as a base to compare other fuels	$0 to $2,000 more	$300 to $1,000 more	$400 to $1,000 more	$1,000 to $2,000 more	$1,950 to $7,600 more
Fuel supply	Foreign dependence subject to supply and price control	Domestic supply not dependent on foreign resources	Domestic supply produced from natural gas processing	Domestic supply produced from coal, natural gas, and biomass	Domestic supply produced from coal, natural gas, and biomass	Domestic supply produced from natural gas, hydro, wind, and geothermal
Power of converted vehicle compared to gasoline vehicle	Used as a base to compare other fuels	5% to 10% loss	2.5% to 5% loss	4% to 10% gain	7% to 10% gain	Can out-power gasoline but reduces vehicle range
Cold weather starting ability	Fair	Excellent	Good	Not good	Not good	Not good
Onboard fuel storage	Stored in steel tanks	Steel, aluminum, or composite cylinders which pose rate problems	Steel cylinders weigh more than gasoline tanks. Lighter fuel compensates for this problem	Tanks similar to gasoline tank but much larger for equivalent range	Tanks similar to gasoline tank but much larger for equivalent range	Stored in onboard batteries for a range of approximately 120 mi.
Fuel economy compared to 1 gal. of gasoline	Used as a base to compare other fuels	1.25 to 1	1.25 to 1	1.7 to 1	1.4 to 1	6 to 1
Fuel cost compared to 1 gal. of gasoline	Used as a base to compare other fuels	30 to 60% less	50% less to 50% more	30% to 60% less	30% to 100% more	30% to 75% more
Fueling station costs	Used as a base to compare other fuels	Significantly more than gasoline stations due to compressor costs	About the same as gasoline station			

(Courtesy Highlands University, Department of Technology Education)

Index